51.50

Graphicßks

51.50

Graphicßks

GRAPHIS CORPORATE IDENTITY 1

VISUAL CORPORATE IDENTITIES

VISUELLE FIRMENERSCHEINUNGSBILDER

L'IDENTITÉ VISUELLE DES ENTREPRISES

EDITED BY/HERAUSGEGEBEN VON/RÉALISÉ PAR

B. MARTIN PEDERSEN

PUBLISHER AND CREATIVE DIRECTOR: B. MARTIN PEDERSEN

ASSISTANT EDITORS: ANNETTE CRANDALL, HEINKE JENSSEN

DESIGNERS: MARTIN BYLAND, UDI NADIV

PHOTOGRAPHER: WALTER ZUBER

GRAPHIS PRESS CORP., ZURICH (SWITZERLAND)

GRAPHIS PUBLICATIONS

GRAPHIS, International bi-monthly journal of graphic art and photography

GRAPHIS DESIGN, The international annual on design and illustration

GRAPHIS PHOTO, The international annual of photography

GRAPHIS POSTER, The international annual of poster art

GRAPHIS PACKAGING, An international survey of packaging design

GRAPHIS DIAGRAM, The graphic visualization of abstract, technical and statistical facts and functions

GRAPHIS COVERS, An anthology of all GRAPHIS covers from 1944–86 with artists' short biographies
   and indexes of all GRAPHIS issues

GRAPHIS ANNUAL REPORTS, An international compilation of the best designed annual reports

GRAPHIS CORPORATE IDENTITY 1, An international compilation of the best in Corporate Identity design

POSTERS MADE POSSIBLE BY A GRANT FROM MOBIL, A collection of 250 international posters commissioned by Mobil
   and selected by the Poster Society

GRAPHIS-PUBLIKATIONEN

GRAPHIS, Die internationale Zweimonatszeitschrift für Graphik und Photographie

GRAPHIS DESIGN, Das internationale Jahrbuch über Design und Illustration

GRAPHIS PHOTO, Das internationale Jahrbuch der Photographie

GRAPHIS POSTER, Das internationale Jahrbuch der Plakatkunst

GRAPHIS PACKUNGEN, Ein internationaler Überblick der Packungsgestaltung

GRAPHIS DIAGRAM, Die graphische Darstellung abstrakter, technischer und statistischer Daten und Fakten

GRAPHIS COVERS, Eine Sammlung aller GRAPHIS-Umschläge von 1944–86 mit Informationen über die Künstler
   und Inhaltsübersichten aller Ausgaben der Zeitschrift GRAPHIS

GRAPHIS ANNUAL REPORTS, Ein internationaler Überblick über die Gestaltung von Jahresberichten

GRAPHIS CORPORATE IDENTITY 1, Eine internationale Auswahl des besten Corporate Identity Design

POSTERS MADE POSSIBLE BY A GRANT FROM MOBIL, Eine Sammlung von 250 internationalen Plakaten, von Mobil
   in Auftrag gegeben und von der Poster Society ausgewählt

PUBLICATIONS GRAPHIS

GRAPHIS, La revue bimestrielle internationale d'arts graphiques et de la photographie

GRAPHIS DESIGN, Le répertoire international de la communication visuelle

GRAPHIS PHOTO, Le répertoire international de la photographie

GRAPHIS POSTER, Le répertoire international de l'art de l'affiche

GRAPHIS EMBALLAGES, Le répertoire international des formes de l'emballage

GRAPHIS DIAGRAM, La représentation graphique de faits et données abstraits, techniques et statistiques

GRAPHIS COVERS, Recueil de toutes les couvertures de GRAPHIS de 1944–86 avec des notices biographiques
   des artistes et le sommaire de tous les numéros du magazine GRAPHIS.

GRAPHIS ANNUAL REPORTS, Panorama international du design de rapports annuels d'entreprises

GRAPHIS CORPORATE IDENTITY 1, Panorama international du meilleur design de l'identité corporate

POSTERS MADE POSSIBLE BY A GRANT FROM MOBIL, Une collection de 250 affiches internationales commandées par Mobil
   et choisies par la Poster Society

CONTENTS / INHALT / SOMMAIRE

REMARKS

■ We extend our heartfelt thanks to contributors throug- hout the world who have made it possible for us to publish a wide and international spectrum of the best work in this field.

■ Entry instructions may be requested at:
Graphis Press Corp., Dufourstrasse 107
8008 Zurich, Switzerland

ANMERKUNGEN

■ Unser herzlicher Dank gilt den Einsendern aus aller Welt, die es uns durch ihre Beiträge möglich gemacht haben, ein breites, internationales Spektrum der besten Arbeiten zu veröffentlichen.

■ Teilnahmebedingungen:
Graphis Verlag AG, Dufourstrasse 107,
8008 Zurich, Schweiz

ANNOTATIONS

■ Toute notre reconnaissance va aux designers du monde entier dont les envois nous ont permis de cons- tituer un vaste panorama international des meilleurs travaux.

■ Modalités d'envoi de travaux:
Editions Graphis SA, Dufourstrasse 107,
8008 Zurich, Suisse

As I recall, it was the great blues singer Bessie Smith who I first heard sing "it ain't what you do, it's the way that you do it." Old Bessie was way ahead of her time. And so it took a while for that point of view to become widely accepted.

These days I often feel that many people behave as if they really believe style is more important than substance. Of course, it has always been easy to recognize and appreciate style. Especially when we are surrounded by so many self-appointed mavens anxious to share their values. (Have you ever wondered how a person who has the gall (chutzpah) to refer to himself as Mr. Blackwell gets the right to lecture us on bad taste?) The ability to recognize meaning, quality and substance, on the other hand, requires some preparation.

Of course no one sets out to be superficial. It just sort of happens. For those of us who counsel companies, when it does happen, it is particularly dangerous. When today's fashion replaces good thinking, our clients will fail, and eventually, so will we.

My friend, the late Bill Bernbach once said, more or less: "the best way to kill a poor product is with good advertising." What he meant, of course, is that folks generally resent promises not kept. The burden of keeping promises applies at least as much to companies as it does to products. Indeed a product can fail and the company that made it can still persevere, but if a company becomes known as dishonest, heaven help it.

Let's acknowledge then that at least theoretically, a company's substance has ultimately greater impact on public attitudes than its style. I am not saying that style doesn't count, just that it doesn't count as much.

That should be said; first, because it's true, and second, because it establishes a perspective from which we can more easily separate fact from fancy. And when it comes to Corporate Identity, which is nominally the subject of this piece, the fact is that, though a Corporate Identity program will not turn a sow's ear into a silk purse, it can be terrifically useful in letting people know what you are up to.

In theory, a professionally conceived and executed Corporate Identity program expresses both what a company is and what it aspires to be. It is a promise as well as a commitment. But we know that promises, though well-intentioned, are sometimes hard to keep.

One of the reasons managers are sometimes uneasy about Corporate Identity is that it is often hard to know if a Corporate Identity program is worth what it costs. For one thing, the subject is harder than most to research. But even more significantly, only part of the program meets the eye.

The visible part of the program, usually the trademark itself, is accessible to all, and outsiders, to a certain extent, can judge its effectiveness. The strategy that informed the design however, is usually not available to people outside the company.

In many cases therefore, only a handful of people know whether or not a Corporate Identity program is genuinely successful. In these situations the judgments which are made by outsiders are very likely to be superficial, based on style or what people feel is fashionable these days rather than the underlying substance. As a result, successes occur in daylight, failures frequently in the dark. After all, who can blame a designer or a client for not wanting to publicize an error?

Notwithstanding misconceptions, the potential benefits of Corporate Identity are sufficient to keep many of us working more or less full-time. For most companies, opportunities to expose their Corporate Identity are vast. Every public contact represents an impression. From letterheads to signage, from advertising to packaging, to how the phone is answered - all are media; all have the capacity to affect how a company is perceived.

The effective utilization of this "owned" medium, especially when compared to the cost of conventional media, represents a substantial bargain. And I for one am grateful that human nature makes it hard for most of us to resist a real bargain.

Companies which are relatively invisible or misunderstood simply have a tougher time competing. Whether it is to sell products or securities or to attract people.

Finally, here are a few thoughts I try to remember. Good work is hard to do. My clients expect me to tell them the truth. Values are not negotiable. There's nothing I'd rather be doing. I expect to be in business for a long time.

. . . .

SAUL BASS is one of the United States' most respected designers, and he has designed special sequences for major feature films including Psycho, Spartacus, West Side Story, and The Shining. He received Academy Award nominations for his work on Notes of the Popular Arts and The Solar Film. His firm, Bass/Yaeger Associates, has produced Corporate Identity programs for many major companies. Mr. Bass is a resident of Los Angeles. PORTRAIT BY GEORGE ARAKAKI

GEDANKEN ÜBER STIL, SUBSTANZ, CORPORATE IDENTITY UND ANDERE DINGE

Wenn ich mich recht entsinne, war es die grosse Blues-Sängerin Bessie Smith, die ich zum ersten Mal die Worte «es ist nicht was du machst, es ist die Art, wie du es machst» singen hörte. Die gute Bessie war ihrer Zeit voraus.

Heutzutage habe ich oft das Gefühl, dass viele Leute sich so verhalten, als glaubten sie wirklich, Stil sei wichtiger als Substanz. Es ist immer leicht gewesen, Stil zu erkennen und zu schätzen, aber die Fähigkeit, Aussage, Qualität und Substanz zu erkennen, verlangt einige Vorbereitung. Natürlich hat niemand von vornherein die Absicht, etwas Oberflächliches zu machen. Es passiert einfach irgendwie. Für all jene von uns, die Firmen beraten, ist es besonders schlimm, wenn dies geschieht. Wenn der gegenwärtige Trend an die Stelle von seriöser Arbeit tritt, wird unser Kunde keinen Erfolg haben und wir letztlich auch nicht.

Der verstorbene Bill Bernbach sagte einmal in etwa folgendes: «Die beste Art, ein minderwertiges Produkt zu ruinieren, ist, gute Werbung dafür zu machen.» Er meinte damit, dass die Leute es übelnehmen, wenn Versprechen nicht gehalten werden.

Die Verpflichtung, Versprechen zu halten, gilt für Firmen mindestens so sehr wie für Produkte. Tatsächlich kann ein Produkt ein Misserfolg sein, während der Hersteller sich weiterhin behaupten kann, aber wenn eine Firma das Vertrauen verliert, dann helfe ihr Gott. Das Verhalten einer Firma ist mindestens theoretisch von grösserer Bedeutung für ihr Bild in der Öffentlichkeit als ihr Stil. Ich sage nicht, dass Stil nicht zählt, nur dass er nicht so viel ausmacht.

Das muss einmal gesagt werden; erstens, weil es wahr ist und zweitens, weil wir mit dieser Einstellung Tatsachen und Einbildung leichter unterscheiden können. Was nun Corporate Identity angeht, so sei gesagt, dass ein C.I.-Programm zwar aus einem Ackergaul kein Rennpferd machen kann, aber es kann ungeheuer nützlich sein, um den Leuten zu sagen, was die Firmenziele sind. Theoretisch drückt ein fachmännisch geplantes und ausgeführtes C.I.-Programm aus, was eine Firma ist und was sie sein möchte. Es ist Versprechen und Verpflichtung zugleich. Aber wir wissen, dass Versprechen, wenn auch in bester Absicht gegeben, schwer zu halten sind.

Einer der Gründe für die Zweifel, die manche Geschäftsleitung hinsichtlich der Notwendigkeit eines Erscheinungsbildes hegt, ist die Frage, ob das Programm seinen Preis wert ist. Zum einen ist der Erfolg relativ schwer messbar, zum anderen, und das ist noch wichtiger, wird nur ein Teil des Programms für das Auge sichtbar. Dieser Teil, gewöhnlich das Markenzeichen, ist allen zugänglich, und auch Aussenstehende können in gewissem Masse seine Wirksamkeit beurteilen. Die Strategie hinter dem Design ist Leuten ausserhalb der Firma jedoch normalerweise nicht bekannt.

In vielen Fällen weiss deshalb nur eine Handvoll Leute, ob ein C.I.-Programm tatsächlich erfolgreich ist oder nicht. Das Urteil von Aussenstehenden ist in den meisten Fällen oberflächlich, weil Stil und aktuelle Trends anstelle der zugrundeliegenden Substanz als Massstab gelten. Erfolge kommen immer ans Licht, Misserfolge kaum. Aber wer kann es einem Designer oder Auftraggeber verübeln, wenn er einen Irrtum nicht an die grosse Glocke hängt. Trotz Fehleinschätzungen reichen die potentiellen Vorteile von Corporate-Identity-Programmen aus, viele von uns mehr oder weniger voll zu beschäftigen.

Für viele Firmen gibt es zahlreiche Gelegenheiten, sich selbst darzustellen. Jeder Kontakt mit der Öffentlichkeit hinterlässt einen Eindruck. Ob es sich um Briefpapier, Beschilderung, Werbung, Verpackung oder um die Art, das Telephon zu beantworten, handelt, alles sind Mittel, die Einfluss darauf haben, welches Bild von einer Firma entsteht. Der wirkungsvolle Einsatz dieser eigenen «Medien» bedeutet besonders im Kostenvergleich mit den konventionellen Medien eine erhebliche Ersparnis.

Firmen, die vergleichsweise unsichtbar sind oder missverstanden werden, haben eine schlechtere Wettbewerbsposition, egal ob es darum geht, Produkte oder Wertpapiere zu verkaufen oder Leute anzuziehen.

Hier ein paar Gedanken, die ich nicht vergessen möchte: Gute Arbeit ist schwer. Meine Kunden erwarten, dass ich die Wahrheit sage. Über Werte lässt sich nicht verhandeln. Es gibt nichts, was ich lieber täte. Ich hoffe, noch lange im Geschäft zu bleiben.

. . . .

SAUL BASS ist einer der angesehensten Designer in den Vereinigten Staaten, und er hat für so bekannte Filme wie «Psycho», «Spartacus», «West Side Story» und «The Shining» spezielle Sequenzen gestaltet. Für seine Arbeit an «Notes of the Popular Arts» und «The Solar Film» wurde er für den Academy Award nominiert. Seine Firma, Bass/Yaeger Associates, hat C.I.-Programme für viele grosse Firmen gestaltet. Saul Bass lebt in Los Angeles.

PENSÉES SUR LE STYLE, LA SUBSTANCE ET LA PUBLICITÉ INSTITUTIONNELLE ET AUTRES SUJETS

Si mes souvenirs sont exacts, c'est la grande chanteuse de blues Bessie Smith que j'ai entendue chanter «c'est pas ce que vous faites, c'est comment vous le faites.» Old Bessie était bien en avance sur son temps. Il a donc fallu attendre pas mal de temps pour que son point de vue devienne monnaie courante.

Ces temps-ci, j'ai souvent l'impression que pas mal de gens font comme s'ils croyaient vraiment que le style compte plus que la substance. Il est vrai qu'il a de tout temps été facile d'identifier et d'apprécier un style donné. L'aptitude à reconnaître le sens, la qualité et la substance requiert par ailleurs quelque préparation. Bien sûr que personne n'a l'intention de se cantonner dans le superficiel. Ça arrive sans qu'on le veuille. Quand ça arrive, c'est particulièrement dangereux pour ceux d'entre nous qui conseillent des entreprises. Si la mode d'aujourd'hui se substitue à la justesse de pensée, nos clients courent à leur perte, et en fin de compte, c'en est fait aussi de nous.

Le regretté Bill Bernbach, a dit une fois: «Le meilleur moyen de tuer un produit sans envergure, c'est de lui appliquer une bonne publicité.» Ce qu'il voulait dire par-là, c'est bien entendu que les gens ne sont pas contents quand on ne tient pas ses promesses. La lourde tâche de tenir ses promesses incombe au moins autant aux entreprises qu'à leurs produits. En fait, un produit peut fort bien connaître l'échec sans que la société qui l'a mis en vente n'en pâtisse, mais gare si une société acquiert une réputation de malhonnêté! Retenons donc, au moins en théorie, que la substance d'une entreprise exerce en fin de compte un plus grande influence sur les attitudes du public que son style. Je ne veux pas dire que le style compte pour beurre, mais en réalité il ne compte pas autant qu'on le croit communément.

En théorie, un programme de publicité conçu et réalisé de manière professionnelle exprime aussi bien ce qu'une entreprise donnée est effectivement que ce qu'elle aspire à être. Il renferme donc une promesse aussi bien qu'un engagement. Nous savons néanmoins que les promesses même bien intentionnées sont parfois difficiles à tenir.

L'une des raisons pour lesquelles les dirigeants d'entreprises sont parfois mal à l'aise quand ils ont à examiner un programme d'identité corporate, c'est qu'il est souvent difficile de savoir s'il vaut la dépense. C'est que, d'une part, le sujet admet moins facilement les sondages et les enquêtes que d'autres. D'autre part seule une partie du programme est visualisable.

La partie visible du programme, généralement la marque déposée, est accessible à tous, de sorte que les personnes extérieures à l'entreprise sont dans une certaine mesure à même de juger de son efficacité. La stratégie qui commande le design est toute fois généralement inconnue hors de l'entreprise.

Dans de nombreux cas, seuls quelques individus triés sur le volet savent vraiment si un programme de publicité institutionnelle est efficace ou non. Dans cette situation, les jugements portés de l'extérieur ont bonne chance de rester superficiels puisqu'ils ne s'inspirent que du style ou de ce que l'on ressent comme répondant au goût du jour, au lieu de prendre en compte la substance sous-jacente. Le résultat en est que les succès se produisent à la lumière du jour, les échecs souvent dans l'obscurité. Après tout, qui blâmerait un designer ou un client de ne pas être désireux d'afficher une erreur?

La plupart des entreprises perçoivent une foule d'occasions où faire état de leur identité. Chaque contact public déclenche une impression dans l'esprit de l'observateur. Des en-têtes à la signalétique, des annonces aux emballages et à la façon dont on répond au téléphone – tous ces éléments ont valeur de médias -, tout contribue à l'impression que l'on reçoit de l'entreprise. L'utilisation efficiente de ces «médias» que l'entreprise possède en propre représente une bonne affaire surtout si on la compare au coût des médias conventionnels.

Les entreprises relativement invisibles ou mal comprises ont davantage de difficultés à s'imposer dans l'arène concurrentielle. Qu'il s'agisse de vendre des produits ou d'attirer des gens.

Pour finir, voici quelques pensées que j'essaie de me rappeler. Le bon travail est difficile à faire. Mes clients s'attendent à ce que je leur dise la vérité. Les valeurs ne se négocient pas. Il n'y a rien que je préfère à ce que je fais. J'espère travailler longtemps encore dans ma branche professionnelle.

· ·

SAUL BASS est l'un des designers les plus respectés des Etats-Unis. On lui doit des séquences pour des grands films tels que «Psycho», «Spartacus», «West Side Story», «The Shining». Nominé pour l'Academy Award pour ses travaux «Notes on the Popular Arts» et «The Solar Film», il a, à travers sa société Bass/Yaeger Associates, réalisé des programmes d'identité institutionelle pour un grand nombre d'entreprises de premier plan. M. Bass habite Los Angeles.

▼
ALC▲TEL

Thierry Roucher, Manager Advertising and Communications Services, Alcatel Paris, France
Alcatel was formed at the end of 1986 from the merger of the communications systems and associated activities of Compagnie Générale d'Electricité of France and ITT Corporation of the USA. The company has subsidiaries in 75 countries and major manufacturing facilities in 21. Alcatel is a leading communications systems supplier. The name Alcatel was chosen after exhaustive evaluation. Among the positive qualities associated with the name were its image of high technology and its accessibility. A carefully thought out approach to using the name as a corporate emblem enabled it to be flexible in its application to printed promotional matter, stationery, products, and advertising. It allows rigid guidelines to give strong, unified identity while respecting local companies' needs to remain national.

Thierry Roucher, Manager Advertising and Communications Services, Alcatel Paris, France
Alcatel entstand Ende 1986 durch die Fusion der Kommunikationssysteme und damit verbundener Bereiche der Compagnie Générale d'Electricité, Frankreich, und der ITT Corporation, USA. Die Firma hat Niederlassungen in 75 und Fabrikationsbetriebe in 21 Ländern. Damit gehört Alcatel zu den führenden Firmen der Branche. Der Name Alcatel wurde aufgrund eingehender Untersuchungen ausgewählt. Zu den mit diesem Namen verbundenen positiven Eigenschaften gehören das Image hochstehender Technologie und Zugänglichkeit. Ein sorgfältig überlegtes Konzept für die Verwendung des Namens im Firmenlogo ermöglicht Flexibilität in der Anwendung. Während strenge Richtlinien für ein starkes Gesamterscheinungsbild sorgen, bleibt genügend Spielraum für nationale Besonderheiten.

Thierry Rocher, directeur de la publicité et des communications, Alcatel Paris, France
Alcatel a résulté en 1986 de la fusion entre des systèmes de communication et les activités connexes de la Compagnie Générale d'Electricité en France et de l'ITT Corporation aux Etats-Unis. La nouvelle société entretient des filiales dans 75 pays, des unités de production importantes dans 21 pays du monde. Alcatel est l'un des leaders mondiaux en matière de systèmes de communication. Au nombre des qualités positives associées à cette raison sociale figurent l'image de haute technologie qui s'y reflète, ainsi que son accessibilité. L'usage de ce nom comme emblème institutionnel obéit à un ensemble de réflexions approfondies. Les instructions impératives quant à l'utilisation du logo assurent la nécessaire homogénéité de cette image expressive tout en respectant les besoins nationaux des sociétés affiliées.

Landor Associates, San Francisco, CA/USA
Landor's task was to create a new identity with flexible graphics to enable product or country names to be incorporated in either a primary or secondary fashion. During our analysis, it became clear that Alcatel, truly the first unified European company, could uniquely own the attribute "enduring quality". To differentiate Alcatel from its key competitors, we emphasized this aspect in the visual expression by utilizing a simple, classical typography elegantly spaced apart to appear as if engraved in granite. The pulsating triangles and the visual synergy created between them are representative of the Alcatel industry, Total Communications. The top orange triangle is suggestive of that spark of ingenuity and innovation that is putting Alcatel in the forefront today. The project time was extremely tight from the initial briefing in January to the acceptance in April.

Landor Associates, San Francisco, CA/USA
Landors Aufgabe bestand in der Schaffung einer neuen Identität durch den Einsatz flexibler graphischer Elemente, so dass Produkte- und Ländernamen als Hauptteil oder Zusatz integriert werden konnten. Bei unserer Analyse wurde klar, dass Alcatel, die erste wirklich vereinte europäische Firma, ein Inbegriff von «solider Qualität» werden konnte. Um Alcatel von der Hauptkonkurrenz abzusetzen, stellten wir diesen Aspekt in der visuellen Umsetzung heraus, indem wir einfache, klassische Typographie einsetzten, die so spationiert ist, als sei sie in Granit gemeisselt. Die Dreiecke und die zwischen ihnen entstehende Spannung stehen für Alcatels Industrie, totale Kommunikation. Das orangefarbene Dreieck suggeriert den Funken, der Einfallsreichtum und Innovation bedeutet und Alcatel zu einem führenden Unternehmen der Branche macht.

Landor Associates, San Francisco, CA/USA
Landor a été chargé de créer une nouvelle identité aux éléments graphiques assez flexibles pour que des noms de produits ou de pays puissent y être intégrés au premier ou au second plan. Au cours de notre analyse, nous nous sommes rendu compte que les termes de «qualité durable» revenaient de plein droit à Alcatel, la première société européenne unifiée. Afin de distinguer Alcatel de ses concurrents essentiels, nous avons souligné cet aspect en utilisant pour l'expression visuelle une typo simple de caractère classique aérée avec élégance pour donner l'impression d'être gravée dans le granite. Les triangles vibrants et la synergie visuelle qui se développe entre eux sont représentatifs de l'industrie même d'Alcatel, la communication globale. Le triangle orange du haut suggère l'étincelle d'ingéniosité et d'esprit novateur qui font d'Alcatel un leader de tout premier plan.

DESIGN FIRM:
LANDOR ASSOCIATES

ART DIRECTOR:
MARGARET YOUNGBLOOD

PROJECT DIRECTOR:
MARGARET YOUNGBLOOD

DESIGNER:
CREIGHTON DINSMORE

PHOTOGRAPHER:
DAMIAN CONRAD

CLIENT:
ALCATEL N.V.

■The Interim Graphic Standard Manual, business stationery, office material, crockery, and an example of a newspaper advertisement in which the rising sun becomes the Alcatel triangle – a component of the logo. It suggests the electrifying sparks of genius and innovation. These are attributes that make Alcatel a leader in the field of communications.

■Das Interim Graphic Standard Manual, Geschäftspapier, Büromaterial, Geschirr und Beispiel einer Zeitungsanzeige, in der die aufgehende Sonne zum Alcatel-Dreieck wird, das Bestandteil des Logos ist. Es suggeriert den zündenden Funken von Genialität und Innovation, Attribute, die Alcatel zu einem führenden Unternehmen der Kommunikationsbranche machen.

■Guide provisoire des normes graphiques, papier à lettres, matériel de bureau, vaisselle et exemple d'annonce de journal où le soleil levant se transforme en un triangle Alcatel tel qu'il figure dans le logo, incarnant l'étincelle du génie et de l'innovation de cette entreprise. Ce sont bien là les qualités qui ont fait d'Alcatel un leader dans le domaine des communications.

Susao Fukuda, Director Corporate Planning Office, Kansai Paint Co., Ltd., Osaka, Tokyo

Our company has been in existence since 1918 and is now counted among the ten largest paint manufacturers of the world. While 90% of sales come from paints and lacquers, Kansai has made efforts in recent years to strike out in new fields. In doing this the long tradition and "colors" image has proved to be an advantage. In addition, the result of an internal questionnaire brought to light that there was "too little challenge" and "not enough change". This led us to introduce a new Corporate Identity program, the aim of which is to convey the company's new future-oriented policy to employees – and also to demonstrate this philosophy to the public and to our customers.

Liza Hurtley, Minale Tattersfield & Partners Ltd., London, Great Britain

Since its foundation in 1918 Kansai Paint has always prided itself on quality, reliability, and pacesetting originality. Our brief for the company's new Corporate Identity was to project an image of Kansai not only as a paint company, but also as an all-round highly technical chemical company. In addition, the identity had to reflect safety and stability and the Kansai Paint slogan "to advance with people and technology" was to be shown in the styling of the symbol. The chosen name "Alesco" was decided on as the word "Alesco" means "to grow up" in Latin. Also, as the word "Ales" means "with wings" in Latin, it quite appropriately signifies the firm setting off into the international market with wings open to the future. The logo shows the "A" of Alesco as a chemical formula.

Susao Fukuda, Director Corporate Planning Office, Kansai Paint Co., Ltd., Osaka, Tokio

Unser Unternehmen existiert seit 1918 und gehört zu den zehn grössten Farbenherstellern der Welt. Während 90% des Umsatzes mit Farben und Lakken erreicht wurden, hat sich Kansai in den letzten Jahren bemüht, in neue Bereiche vorzustossen. Dabei erwiesen sich die lange Tradition und das «Farben»-Image nicht nur als Vorteil. Hinzu kamen die Ergebnisse interner Untersuchungen, denen zufolge die allgemeine Arbeitsmoral unter «zu wenig Herausforderung» und «wenig Abwechslung» litt. Dies veranlasste uns zur Einführung eines neuen Corporate-Identity-Programms, dessen Ziel es ist, den Mitarbeitern die zukunftsorientierte neue Firmenpolitik zu vermitteln.

Liza Hurtley, Minale Tattersfield & Partners Ltd., London, Grossbritannien

Kansais Leitmotiv war immer Qualität, Zuverlässigkeit und beispielhafte Originalität. Wir wurden beauftragt, ein neues Corporate-Identity-Design zu schaffen, das verdeutlichen würde, dass Kansai nicht nur Farben herstellt, sondern auch eine Chemiefirma ist. Ferner sollte es Sicherheit und Stabilität ausstrahlen und Kansais Motto «Fortschritt mit Menschen und Technologie» zum Ausdruck bringen. «Alesco» bedeutet im Lateinischen «heranwachsen», man kann das Wort aber auch in «Ales» und «co» zerlegen, was auf Lateinisch «mit Flügeln» heisst, ein passender Name für eine Firma, die mit weitgeöffneten Flügeln der Zukunft entgegenfliegt und den internationalen Markt erobern möchte. Unsere Lösung ist ein Logo, in dem das «A» von Alesco wie eine chemische Formel dargestellt ist.

Susao Fukuda, directeur du Corporate Planning Office, Kansai Paint Co., Ltd., Osaka, Tokyo

Notre entreprise, qui existe depuis 1918, compte aujourd'hui parmi les dix plus grands fabricants de peintures du monde. Les peintures et vernis représentant 90% du chiffre d'affaires, Kansai s'est intéressé à d'autres secteurs d'activité ces dernières années. Ce faisant, la longue tradition et l'image du fabricant de «couleurs» ont pesé d'un poids parfois excessif. En outre, des enquêtes menées à l'intérieur de l'entreprise ont révélé que le climat de travail souffrait d'un «manque de défis à relever» et d'une certaine «monotonie». La création d'un nouveau programme d'identification a pour but de faire connaître la nouvelle politique d'entreprise tournée vers l'avenir.

Liza Hurtley, Minale Tattersfield & Partners Ltd., Londres, Grande-Bretagne

La fondation de Kansai Paint remonte à 1918. La production a toujours obéi aux impératifs de la qualité, de la fiabilité et de l'originalité faisant époque. Nous avons été chargé d'élaborer une nouvelle image d'entreprise élargissant la vocation de Kansai, au départ spécialisé dans les peintures, au domaine entier de la chimie de haute technologie. Il fallait qu'il s'en dégage une forte impression de sécurité et de stabilité, ainsi qu'une interprétation de la devise de Kansai Paint, «progrès par les hommes et la technologie.» Nous avons déterminé le nom d'Alesco en raison de sa signification: «grandir» en vieux latin, mais aussi «ales» = «ailé» en latin, interprétation justifiée par l'essor que prend la société dans son élan vers le futur. Notre solution pour le logo retient le «A» d'Alesco sous forme de symbole chimique.

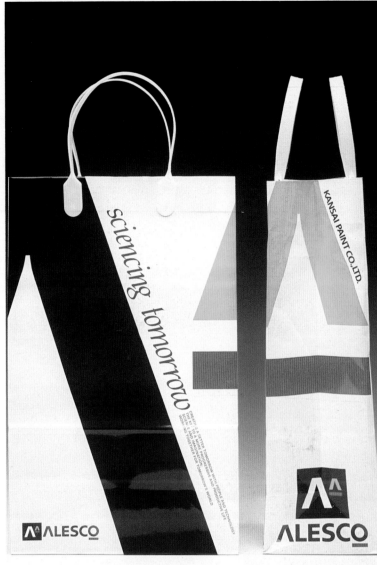

DESIGN FIRM:
MINALE, TATTERSFIELD AND PARTNERS LTD.

ART DIRECTOR:
MARCELLO MINALE/ BRIAN TATTERSFIELD

DESIGNER:
DAVID TURNER/ MARCELLO MINALE

CLIENT:
KANSAI PAINT CO. LTD.

■ The future-oriented logotype for Alesco, the chemical division of Kansai Paint, is directly associated with the literal concept of the word, which can mean either "rising" or "with wings". The stylized A and its variation are used together with the logo or standing alone, as can clearly be seen by the instructions for application on packaging, signs, and vehicles, or in the example of printed matter and carrier bags.

■ Der Schriftzug für Alesco, die chemische Abteilung von Kansai Paint, entspricht der Bedeutung des Wortes, das entweder «heranwachsen» oder auch «mit Flügeln» heissen kann. Das stilisierte A und dessen Variante werden zusammen mit dem Schriftzug oder allein angewendet, wie hier anhand der Anwendungsvorschriften für Verpakkungen, Schilder und Fahrzeuge oder auch am Beispiel der Drucksachen und der Tragtaschen deutlich wird.

■ Le caractère orienté vers l'avenir choisi pour Alesco, le département chimique de Kansai Paint, est conforme à la signification du mot, qui veut dire «grandir», mais aussi «doté d'ailes». L'A stylisé et sa variante sont soit utilisés de pair avec le sigle, soit seuls, comme on le voit par les prescriptions relatives à leur utilisation pour les emballages, les enseignes et les véhicules, mais aussi pour les imprimés et les cabas.

REMAKING

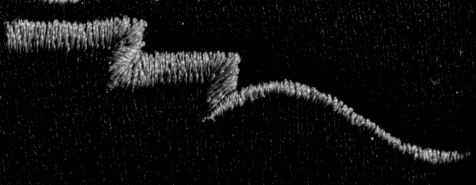

Sylvester Damianos, First Vice President, American Institute of Architects, Pittsburgh, PA/USA
The American Institute of Architects, founded 133 years ago to promote design excellence, education, fellowship, and the profession in general, is committed to improving the quality of life. Recognizing that we must prepare for societal needs of the next century, the AIA launched VISION 2000; "Remaking Cities" was the first major program initiated. The identity program had to attract the attention of a variety of people to join us in this venture – futurists, politicians, planners, educators, businessmen, social scientists, etc. The response was immediate and overwhelming, and the graphics package certainly played an important part in "selling" the conference. The intelligent design developed an image of the highest quality and communicated the essence of the conference to each of the participants.

Sylvester Damianos, First Vice President, American Institute of Architects, Pittsburgh, PA/USA
Das AIA - gegründet, um hervorragendes Design, Ausbildung, Kollegialität und den Beruf als solchen zu fördern - hat sich zum Ziel gesetzt, die Lebensqualität zu verbessern. Im Bewusstsein, dass etwas für die gesellschaftlichen Bedürfnisse des nächsten Jahrhunderts getan werden muss, hat das Institut VISION 2000 ins Leben gerufen; «Remaking Cities» war die erste Konferenz, die in diesem Zusammenhang entstand. Das Identitätsprogramm musste die verschiedensten Gruppen von Menschen ansprechen. Das Echo war überwältigend, wobei die graphische Darstellung sicher eine wichtige Rolle gespielt hatte, die Konferenz zu «verkaufen». Das durchdachte Design liess ein Image von höchster Qualität entstehen und verdeutlichte jedem Teilnehmer den Sinn der Konferenz.

Sylvester Damianos, 1er vice-président, American Institute of Architects, Pittburgh, PA/USA
L'AIA fondé il y a 133 ans afin de promouvoir la bienfacture optimale, la formation, la recherche et les intérêts généraux de la profession s'engage surtout pour l'amélioration de la qualité de vie. A cet égard, nous devons nous préparer aux besoins de la société au siècle à venir. C'est pourquoi l'AIA a lancé le programme VISION 2000, avec pour premier volet «Reaménager nos villes». Le programme de publicité institutionnelle correspondant devait inciter une partie notable du public à seconder nos efforts dans ce sens, notamment des futurologues, des hommes politiques, des urbanistes, des sociologues, etc. L'emballage du graphisme a indubitablement joué un rôle important dans la publicité pour cette conférence. Le design intelligent a résulté en une image nec plus ultra qui a fait saisir l'essence même du programme à tous.

G. Reed Agnew, Agnew Moyer Smith Inc., Pittsburgh, PA/USA
The basic design idea was to develop a mark that represented the basic components of a modern city – environment, commercial buildings, and neighborhoods. These are represented with curvilinear and geometric shapes and by the forms of the letter. The type is integrated with the other elements so that it forms a part of the city. The double-stroke letters in the word "Cities" are reminiscent of neon and the broken, incomplete forms evoke the idea of city lights. Bright, lively colors reinforce the forms – sky (blue), city lights (yellow), neighborhoods (red), earth (green) and provide a strong palette of colors that could be used either individually or in combinations. The conference captivated the minds of delegates and the public. And, by the end, the mark had become a symbol for the rebirth of our cities.

G. Reed Agnew, Agnew Moyer Smith Inc., Pittsburgh, PA/USA
Die Grundidee, von der wir ausgingen, war ein Zeichen, das die Hauptelemente einer modernen Stadt enthält - Umfeld, Bürogebäude und Wohnquartiere. Wir verwendeten runde und geometrische Formen in Kombination mit Buchstaben. Die Typographie ist so eng mit den andern Elementen verbunden, dass sie Teil der Stadt wurde. Die in Doppellinien ausgeführten Buchstaben des Wortes «Cities» implizieren Neonbeleuchtung, die unterbrochenen, unvollständigen Formen die Lichter einer Stadt. Lebhafte Farben unterstützen die Formen - Himmel (blau), Stadtlichter (gelb), Wohnquartiere (rot), Erde (grün). Diese Farben wurden einzeln oder in Kombination angewendet. Die Konferenz beschäftigte die Teilnehmer so sehr, dass das Zeichen schliesslich zum Symbol für eine Wiedergeburt unserer Städte wurde.

G. Reed Agnew, Agnew Moyer Smith Inc., Pittsburgh, PA/USA
L'idée de base de la conception recherchée était de développer un emblème qui concentrerait la quintessence d'une ville moderne - l'environnement, les immeubles à usage commercial, les quartiers résidentiels. Ces éléments sont représentés au moyen de formes curvilinéaires et géometriques, ainsi que par la forme des caractères. La typo est intégrée aux éléments linéaires de manière à devenir partie intégrante de la cité. Les lettres à traits doubles dans le mot «Cities» évoquent les tubes néon, les formes brisées incomplètes, les lumières de ville. Des couleurs vives, éclatantes servent à renforcer les formes - le ciel (bleu), les lumières de la ville (jaune), les quartiers (rouge), le sol (vert). La conférence a captivé les délégués et la nouvelle image institutionnelle est devenue un symbole du renouveau de nos villes.

DESIGN FIRM:
AGNEW MOYER SMITH INC.

ART DIRECTOR:
AGNEW MOYER SMITH INC.

DESIGNER:
AGNEW MOYER SMITH INC.

CLIENT:
*AMERICAN INSTITUTE OF
ARCHITECTS/
THE MARKETING PLACE*

■ The symbol for this British-American Conference on the future of cities appears in polychrome (blue, yellow, red, and green) or in one only of these colors. It is effective over wide areas in the conference rooms as well as on letter-heads, conference literature, brochures, and – even in the smallest space – on admission cards to various events. One particular version has the stamped-out silhouettes in the four basic colors, used as single pages in a brochure about the conference.

■ Das Signet dieser britisch-amerikanischen Konferenz über die Zukunft der Städte erscheint mehrfarbig in Blau, Gelb, Rot und Grün oder in einer dieser Farben. Es kommt auf grossen Flächen in den Konferenzräumen ebenso zur Geltung wie auf Briefbogen, Konferenzunterlagen, Prospekten und - auf kleinstem Raum - auf Eintrittskarten zu Veranstaltungen. Eine besondere Variante sind die ausgestanzten Silhouetten, als einzelne Seiten in einer Broschüre über die Konferenz verwendet.

■ L'emblème de cette conférence anglo-américaine sur l'avenir architectural des villes est exécuté en bleu, jaune, rouge et vert ou bien dans une seule de ces couleurs. Son impact est indiscutable sur les murs d'une salle de conférences, mais aussi sur des surfaces réduites - en-têtes, documentation, prospectus - et même sur les billets d'entrée aux manifestations. Les silhouettes découpées constituent une variante intéressante pour certaines pages de la brochure de la conférence.

Apple Computer, Inc.

Apple Creative Services, Cupertino, CA/USA
The meaning of the Apple logo. "One of the deep mysteries is our logo - the symbol of lust and knowledge, bitten into, all crossed with the colors of the rainbow in the wrong order. You couldn't dream of a more appropriate logo: lust, knowledge, hope, and anarchy," says Jean-Louis Gassée, President, Apple Products Division.
To understand the Apple logo - the essence of our Corporate Identity - is to understand Apple.
In many ways, our logo has become synonymous with the "computer revolution" - a revolution started a decade ago by a couple of hackers in a backyard garage in Silicon Valley. The dream: to create a computer for the rest of us.
The logo stands for the individual, for we believe that the individual is at the heart of everything we do - both the individual outside Apple and the employee inside the company.
From the very beginning, the logo has given our customers and employees something to rally around. On every continent, it can be seen on our products, packaging, signage, advertising, and collateral. In an industry that changes with the rising and setting of the sun, it has come to symbolize the values and mission of our company.
As we enter the 1990s and the century beyond, the Apple logo will not only function as the mark of the first computer revolution, but will, we hope, be associated as well with an even more dramatic behavioral revolution - a revolution made possible, in part, by Apple computers.

Apple Creative Services, Cupertino, CA/USA
Die Bedeutung des Apple-Logos. «Eines der tiefen Geheimnisse ist unser Logo - das Symbol von Lust und Wissen, ein angebissener Apfel, in den Farben des Regenbogens, in verkehrter Reihenfolge. Man kann sich kein geeigneteres Logo erträumen: Lust, Wissen, Hoffnung und Anarchie», sagt Jean-Louis Gassée, Präsident, Apple Products Division.
Das Apple-Logo - Basis unserer Corporate Identity - zu verstehen heisst, Apple verstehen.
In vieler Hinsicht ist unser Logo gleichbedeutend mit der «Computer-Revolution» geworden - einer Revolution, die vor einem Jahrzehnt von ein paar Hackern begonnen wurde. Der Traum: einen Computer für den Rest der Welt zu schaffen.
Das Logo steht für den Einzelnen, denn wir glauben, dass das Individuum das Herz aller Dinge ist, - das gilt für den Einzelnen ausserhalb von Apple ebenso wie für den Angestellten in der Firma.
Von Anfang an hat das Logo unseren Kunden und Mitarbeitern etwas gegeben. Auf jedem Kontinent ist es auf unseren Produkten, unserer Verpackung, Schildern, Werbung und ähnlichem zu sehen. Und in einer Industrie, die sich von Tag zu Tag verändert, ist es ein Symbol für die Werte und das Anliegen unserer Firma geworden.
Während wir uns dem nächsten Jahrhundert nähern, wird das Apple-Logo nicht nur ein Zeichen der ersten Computer-Revolution sein, sondern, wie wir hoffen, mit einer Revolution der Verhaltensweisen verbunden sein, die zum Teil dank der Apple-Computer möglich wurde.

Apple Creative Services, Cupertino, CA/USA
La signification du logo Apple. «L'un des grands mystères, c'est notre logo - symbole de plaisir et de savoir, croqué en partie, dans les couleurs de l'arc-en-ciel, mais pas dans l'ordre qui convient. On ne saurait imaginer un logo plus adéquat: plaisir, savoir, espoir et anarchie,» affirme Jean-Louis Gassée, président de l'Apple Products Division.
Comprendre le logo Apple - l'essence de notre identité corporate -, c'est comprendre Apple.
A beaucoup d'égards, notre logo est devenu synonyme de «révolution de l'ordinateur» - une révolution commencée par deux francs-tireurs de l'informatique dans un garage de Silicon Valley. Leur rêve: créer un ordinateur pour nous autres.
Le logo incarne l'individualisme, car nous croyons que l'individualisme est au cœur de tout ce que nous faisons - aussi bien pour l'individu extérieur à Apple que pour l'employé à l'intérieur.
D'emblée, ce logo a fourni un point de ralliement à nos clients et à nos collaborateurs. On le voit sur chaque continent, sur nos produits, dans notre signalisation, notre publicité et tout le reste. Au sein d'une industrie qui change avec le lever et le coucher du soleil, il en est venu à symboliser les valeurs et la mission de notre société.
Alors que nous abordons le siècle à venir, le logo Apple ne fonctionnera pas seulement comme signe de la première révolution de l'ordinateur, mais sera associé également à une révolution comportementale autrement dramatique rendue possible en partie par les ordinateurs Apple.

No. Neen. Nej. 否や Nao.

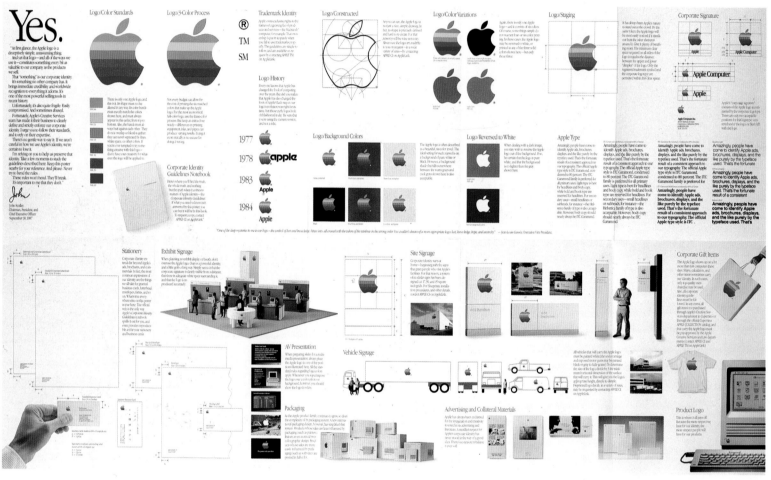

■Front and back of a folder, which takes the place of a comprehensive design standard manual, and is mailed to smaller distributors. It gives information on the application of the logo and shows examples of how it ought *not* to be used. *(Opposite)* A further instrument to help distributors keep to the standard is a folder ("Essentials") containing color and paper samples as well as instructions for the use of logotype and logo.

■Vorder- und Rückseite eines Faltprospektes, der anstelle eines umfangreichen Design Standard Manuals an kleinere Verteiler geschickt wird und über die Anwendung des Logos Auskunft gibt, sowie anhand von Beispielen zeigt, wie man es *nicht* machen soll. *(Gegenüber)* Ein weiteres Instrument für die Einhaltung des Standards ist ein Umschlag («Essentials») mit Farb- und Papiermustern sowie Instruktionen für Schriftzug und Logo.

■Recto et verso d'un dépliant remis aux petits distributeurs en lieu et place d'un gros manuel de design standardisé; on y explique les applications du logo, avec des contre-exemples à l'appui. *(Ci-contre)* Autre instrument propre à assurer le maintien des standards de design, cette enveloppe renfermant des règles essentielles ainsi que des échantillons de couleur et de papier et des instructions précises quant au sigle et au logo.

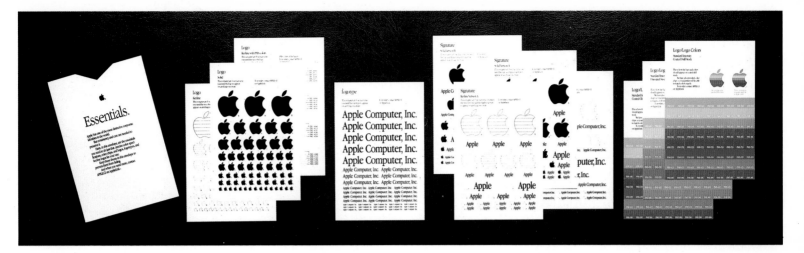

DESIGN FIRM:
APPLE CREATIVE SERVICES

CREATIVE DIRECTOR:
PAUL PRUNEAU

ART DIRECTORS:
DEVIN IVESTER/
TIM BRENNAN/ROB GEMMELL

DESIGNERS:
ANDREA KELLEY/
JILL SAVINI

PHOTOGRAPHERS:
PAUL MATSUDA/
WIL MOSGROVE

CLIENT:
APPLE COMPUTER, INC.

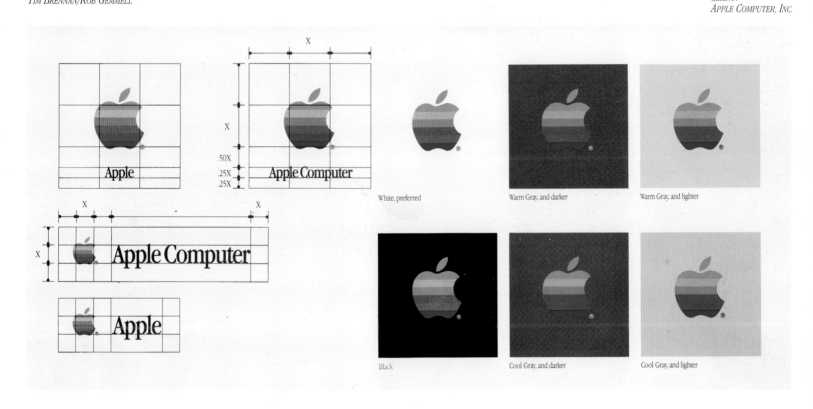

White, preferred

Warm Gray, and darker

Warm Gray, and lighter

Black

Cool Gray, and darker

Cool Gray, and lighter

"There should be a quick, easy way for us to get the information we need to run our business—and to get that information to the people who can use it."

"So where do we go from here?"

"We should be producing a newsletter for our clients, but we don't have the time or money to do a high-quality job."

"So where do we go from here?"

Apple Business Forum

Desktop Communications Seminar
Sharing Information Among Different Computers

Apple Business Forum

Desktop Publishing Seminar
Creating High-Impact Business Publications

Macintosh Small Business Accounting

"So, how's business?"

Unless you have a nice, clean, clear, simple way to get answers.

You're in business to succeed. And one way or another, that success is going to be measured in dollars.

So if the simple question "How's business?" makes you wonder how your business measures up, maybe you should take a long, hard look at your current accounting system.

Whether you handle your accounts manually or use an outside service, you just might find that when you're looking at your books, you're looking backward—to last month's financial report.

Which gives you last month's answers to these important questions.

Who owes you money? How much? And for how long?

Which customers are adding to your bottom line? And who's a credit risk?

How much time should your salespeople spend on each customer based on his or her purchase history?

How much inventory are you carrying, and how often does it turn?

Can you afford to buy new equipment? Or hire more help?

Hard questions. Today's questions. And last month's answers just aren't good enough.

If you're tired of looking backward with your accounting system, we'd like you to take a look forward—with ours.

Macintosh.

When you look to the Apple® Macintosh® personal computer for answers, you aren't alone.

Because every minute of every business day, there are thousands of people

From standard reports, envelope, labels, and multipart forms to full size financial statements and spreadsheets, the ImageWriter LQ printer's 15-inch-wide carriage can handle the biggest of jobs.

doing exactly what you're doing. They're balancing their books, managing their cash, mailing their invoices, paying their bills, and getting their answers.

But unlike you, they're already doing it on a Macintosh—a computer so simple to learn and use that all that accounting work won't seem like much work at all.

For a couple of reasons.

First, because Macintosh was designed to understand a very sophisticated language you're already familiar with—English. Using the now-famous Macintosh mouse, it's simple to make a

Macintosh program do what you want. You just point to a command on the screen, and press the mouse button.

And second, because all Macintosh programs work in much the same way, with easy-to-use pull-down menus, icons, and the mouse. Which makes learning new Macintosh programs even simpler than learning your first.

There's a lot you can do for your business besides managing your books. Because there's a lot of different Macintosh software that can handle a lot of different jobs. Word processing programs—like Microsoft Word or FullWrite Professional—for proposals or form letters. Desktop publishing programs like Aldus PageMaker or Quark XPress for ads, flyers, and signs for your business. Programs like Microsoft PowerPoint, MORE from Living Videotext, or Cricket Presents… for outlines and presentations.

There are database programs like FileMaker Plus and Reflex to keep track of your customers and mailing lists, as well as to generate templates for business forms and applications. And financial analysis programs like Microsoft Excel to help you with budgeting, forecasting, and the hard job of staying on the good side of your banker.

There's also a family of different-sized Macintosh computers, one of which is probably just right for all the things you'd like to do with all that software.

There's even a family of high-capacity Apple hard disks to let you store all your software with your Macintosh files—in one convenient place.

Accounting software.

At Apple, we build very useful computers that can help you run your accounting system very smoothly.

And there are a lot of software companies that build the very useful accounting software that our computers run. This software ranges from simple bookkeeping

Macintosh SE

to sophisticated programs that can produce in-depth financial reports about the daily profitability of your business.

We'd like you to consider two of these sophisticated programs—Insight, from Layered Inc., and The Great Plains Accounting Series from Great Plains Software.

Like all Macintosh software, both take advantage of pull-down menus and on-screen help to make the task of getting answers a lot less difficult.

And both can meet the basic accounting needs of your business—general ledger, accounts payable, and accounts receivable.

Insight instantly produces easy-to-understand graphic representations of your financial status. It's best for companies with smaller transaction volumes but greater need for financial analysis, because it features built-in expert reports that explain what your numbers mean and suggest various avenues of action.

The Great Plains Accounting Series adds to the basics a very fast, advanced group of accounting modules to process high volumes of transactions for payroll, order entry, inventory, and purchasing.

Great Plains even has a special Network Manager version that's especially useful if you have an AppleTalk® network connecting your Macintosh systems. It allows several people simultaneous access to accounting information when it's stored on an AppleTalk® file server.

No matter which accounting software you choose, you'll find that once you get a Macintosh, you'll get a better picture of how your business is doing and where it's going.

And then you just might find a little more time to work on an answer to that other simple question people ask.

The one that really matters. The one your mother asks.

"So how come we never see you?"

DESIGN FIRM:
APPLE CREATIVE SERVICES

CREATIVE DIRECTOR:
PAUL PRUNEAU

ART DIRECTORS:
ELLEN ROMANO/
LIZ SUTTON/
ROB SMILEY

DESIGNER:
ELLEN ROMANO

PHOTOGRAPHERS:
STUART SCHWARTZ/
MARK TUSCHMANN/
PAUL MATSUDA

CLIENT:
APPLE COMPUTER, INC.

■ *(Opposite above)* Posters, in which Apple gives details about the special aids that enable the disabled to write, to calculate or to speak – all with the help of the computer. *(Opposite below)* Front and double spread of a folder for *Macintosh* Accounting Software intended for the small business. *(This page above)* Folder and double spreads from a brochure about *Macintosh* Computers, presenting information in the form of reports.

■ *(Gegenüber oben)* Plakate, mit Informationen über spezielle Hilfsmittel, die behinderten Menschen die Möglichkeit geben, mit Hilfe des Computers zu schreiben, zu rechnen oder zu sprechen. *(Gegenüber unten)* Vorderseite und Doppelseite eines Faltprospekts für *Macintosh*-Buchhaltungs-Software. *(Oben)* Umschlag und Doppelseiten aus einer Broschüre über *Macintosh*-Computer mit technischen Informationen in Bericht-Form.

■ *(Ci-contre, en haut)* Affiches présentant les moyens particuliers mis à la disposition des handicapés pour écrire, calculer ou parler avec l'aide de l'ordinateur. *(Ci-contre, en bas)* Recto et verso d'un dépliant de présentation pour les logiciels de comptabilité du *Macintosh* pour les petites entreprises. *(En haut)* Couverture et doubles pages d'une brochure consacrée à l'ordinateur *Macintosh*, avec des informations techniques.

The Apple Collection

Nineteen Hundred Eighty-Eight
Two Dollars

DESIGN FIRM:
APPLE CREATIVE SERVICES

CREATIVE DIRECTOR:
PAUL PRUNEAU

ART DIRECTORS:
LIZ SUTTON/
THOM MARCHIONNA/
CAROL GOLDEN

PHOTOGRAPHERS:
DIANE PADYS/
PAUL MATSUDA/
TOM LANDECKER

CLIENT:
APPLE COMPUTER, INC.

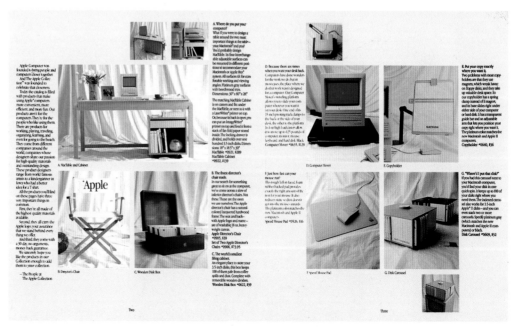

■ *(On preceding spread and bottom left)* Complete sales kit for Apple dealers developed for the introduction of the *Apple IIGS* personal computer. The kit contains product, pricing, positioning and promotional communications. *(Bottom right)* Point of purchase display for Apple dealers presenting applications and information about the benefits of the Apple Leasing and Apple Business Credit Card programs. *(Opposite page)* Cover and double spreads from an order catalog for various articles distributed by Apple.

■ *(Vorangehende Doppelseite und unten links)* Verkaufsunterlagen für Apple-Händler zur Einführung des *Apple IIGS* Personal Computers. Die Mappe enthält Informationen über das Produkt, den Preis, die Positionierung sowie Promotionsmaterial. *(Unten rechts)* Ausstellungsmaterial für Apple-Händler zur Information der Kunden über die Vorteile des Apple-Leasing-Programms und der Apple-Kreditkarte. *(Gegenüber)* Umschlag und Doppelseiten eines Katalogs für verschiedene von Apple vertriebene Artikel.

■ *(Double page précédente et ci-dessous à gauche)* Kit de vente créé pour le lancement de l'ordinateur personnel *Apple IIGS*. Le kit renferme des informations sur la mise en place sur le lieu de vente et la promotion du PC. *(Ci-dessous, à droite)* Présentoir P.L.V. pour revendeurs Apple mettant en évidence les applications et informations concernant les programmes Apple Leasing et Apple Business Credit Card. *(Ci-contre)* Couverture et doubles pages d'un catalogue pour divers articles vendus par Apple.

Art Center

David A. Brown, President, Art Center College of Design, Pasadena, CA/USA

Founded in Los Angeles in 1930, Art Center has grown into one of the world's leading colleges of industrial design, graphic design, illustration, photography, film, and fine art. In 1985, the Art Center (Europe) was established in Switzerland. The new identification program was introduced in 1986 to signal a management change, to sharpen its visual identity, and to coincide with a much more outgoing communications program. The new program reflects the Art Center's philosophy of professionalism and practicality in design education. The visual identity is built around a "wordmark" that is the most often used name of the school combined with classic modernist typography and the primary colors of red, yellow, and blue - plus black and gray - symbolizing the importance of the basics in an Art Center education.

David A. Brown, Präsident, Art Center College of Design, Pasadena, CA/USA

Das Art Center - 1930 in Los Angeles gegründet - wurde zu einer der weltweit führenden Schulen für Industrie-Design, Graphik-Design, Illustration, Photographie, Film und Kunst. Das Art Center (Europe) wurde 1985 in der Schweiz eröffnet. Das 1986 eingeführte neue Identifikationsprogramm sollte einen Direktionswechsel anzeigen, die visuelle Identität unterstreichen und einem offeneren Kommunikationsprogramm gerecht werden. Es reflektiert die Grundhaltung des Art Centers, seine Professionalität und praxisbezogene Ausbildung durch die Kombination eines frischen Identitätszeichens, der Kurzform des Namens in klassischer, modernistischer Typographie und der Primärfarben Rot, Gelb und Blau, die - ergänzt durch Schwarz und Grau - symbolisch für die Wichtigkeit der Grundausbildung sind.

David A. Brown, président, Art Center College of Design, Pasadena, CA/USA

Fondé à Los Angeles en 1930, l'Art Center est devenu l'un des grands collèges du monde enseignant l'estétique industrielle, le design graphique, l'illustration, la photo, le cinéma et les beaux-arts. En 1985, la branche européenne de l'Art Center était installée en Suisse. Le nouveau programme de publicité institutionnelle signale un changement au niveau de la direction, une identité visuelle affinée et un programme de communications plus ouvert sur le monde. Il reflète la philosophie de l'établissement qui met l'accent sur le professionnalisme et le caractère pratique des études. L'identité visuelle percutant se construit autour d'une marque typo - le nom simplifié du collège - en caractères classiques et modernistes à la fois, avec les couleurs primaires, soit le rouge, le jaune et le bleu, plus du noir et du gris.

Kit Hinrichs, Pentagram Design Inc., San Francisco, CA/USA

As the strength of the school has always been its ability to encourage individual creativity, it was important not to reflect graphically a specific "school of design". We established a set of criteria: 1. The typography should be classic, not trendy. 2. The logo must work with, and not compete with, a broad range of communications. 3. The color palette should represent the basic foundation of designs, not a "contemporary" color scheme. 4. The primary "signature" of the school would be simply "Art Center", not the stiff "Art Center College of Design". The program itself is purposely quite restrained, but we've countered that with the use of strong primary colors. Our concept for the various publications was *not* to have a rigid structured sameness but to rather create a specific vocabulary of visual elements.

Kit Hinrichs, Pentagram Design Inc., San Francisco, CA/USA

Da die Stärke dieser Schule immer in der Förderung individueller Kreativität lag, war es wichtig, dass wir uns graphisch nicht auf eine spezifische Design-Richtung festlegten. Wir stellten folgende Kriterien auf: 1. Die Typographie sollte klassisch, nicht modisch sein. 2. Das Logo sollte für ein breites Spektrum von Kommunikationsmitteln passen und nicht mit deren Gestaltung konkurrieren. 3. Die Farbpalette sollte eine Basis für das Design bieten, es sollte kein «zeitgenössisches» Farbschema sein. 4. Die Schule sollte einfach als «Art Center» auftreten, nicht so steif als «Art Center College of Design». Das Design-Programm ist zurückhaltend, fast förmlich, aber es wird durch Primärfarben aufgelockert. Statt eines starren Einheitsbildes entwickelten wir ein bestimmtes visuelles Vokabular für die Publikationen.

Kit Hinrichs, Pentagram Design Inc., San Francisco, CA/USA

Ce qui a toujours fait l'intérêt de cette école, c'est qu'on y encourage grandement la créativité individuelle. Il fallait donc éviter de faire miroiter l'image d'une école de design spécifique. Nous avons donc fixé les critères suivants: 1. une typo classique, pas au goût du jour; 2. un logo s'adaptant à une vaste gamme de communications; 3. une palette de coloris servant de base au design et ne représentant pas un schéma chromatique contemporain; 4. la limitation de la «signature» de l'école aux mots «Art Center». Le programme de design est assez restrictif, quasi formaliste, mais les intenses couleurs primaires apportent la correction nécessaire. Notre conception pour les diverses publications n'est *pas* celle d'une homogénéité rigidement imposée, mais consiste à mettre en œuvre un vocabulaire d'éléments visuels spécifiques.

■The primary colors blue, red, and yellow are used throughout, either individually or in combination, as design elements – e. g. for business stationery *previous page)* and brochures. The brochure "Why Design?" deals with aesthetics, economy, communications, and function, etc.; "Why Art Center?" stresses the importance of superior design training as a prerequisite for maintaining and improving the quality of life. Shown are double spreads from these brochures that are presented in a slipcase.

■Die Grundfarben Blau, Rot und Gelb werden – z. B. für Geschäftspapiere *(vorangehende Seite)* und Broschüren – einzeln oder als Kombination überall als Gestaltungselement eingesetzt. Die Broschüre «Warum Design» befasst sich mit den Impulsen (Schönheit, Wirtschaftlichkeit, Kommunikation, Funktion etc.); «Warum Art Center» behandelt die Bedeutung erstklassiger Design-Ausbildung als Voraussetzung für Lebensqualität. Hier einige Doppelseiten aus diesen in einer Kassette zusammengefassten Broschüren.

■Les couleurs primaires, soit le bleu, le rouge et le jaune, sont employées séparément ou en combinaison, sur des en-têtes *(page précédente)* commerciaux et des brochures. La brochure «Pourquoi le design?» traite des aspects essentiels (beauté, rentabilité, communication, fonction, etc.), celle intitulée «Pourquoi l'Art Center?» de l'importance qui revient à une formation de design de haut niveau pour préserver et améliorer la qualité de vie. On voit ici quelques pages doubles de ces brochures réunies sous cassette.

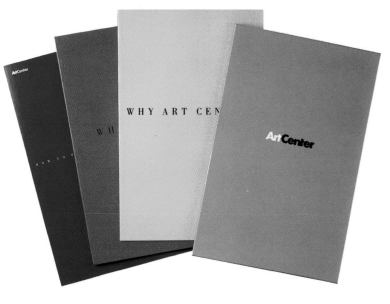

ECONOMY

George Bernard Shaw overstated the case when he said, "Love of economy is the root of all virtue." But, as usual, he made his point. It is a point not lost on designers, who know they can offer manufacturers and consumers excellence without breaking the bank.

The role of design in helping clients and consumers hang onto their money seldom is recognized by the general public.

Designers find the least expensive materials to do a job well, and work with engineers to discover the most economical methods of assembling those materials, thereby minimizing production costs.

Designers advise manufacturers about personnel matters related to factory working environments that affect worker productivity, thereby minimizing labor costs.

Designers offer expert advice on packaging, distribution and merchandising, thereby minimizing marketing costs.

Design's relationship to saving money is obvious in products like disposable razors and good looking, inexpensive wristwatches. It is less obvious, but no less important, in big ticket items like factory machinery and automobiles.

The designer's role in cutting production, labor, and marketing costs results in more prosperous clients and a buying public that can get more value for less money.

In short, economies effected by designers make people richer, more successful, and happier. The designer's role reflects Samuel Johnson's comment that "without frugality, none of us can be rich."

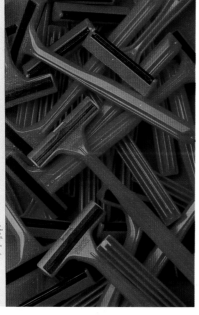

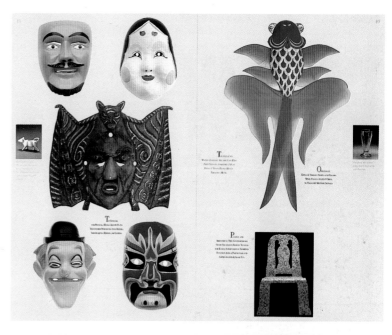

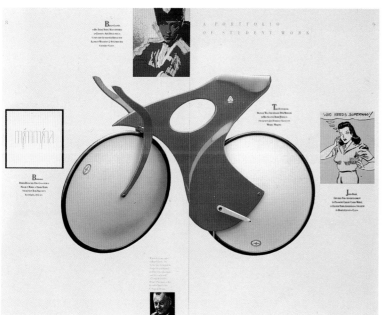

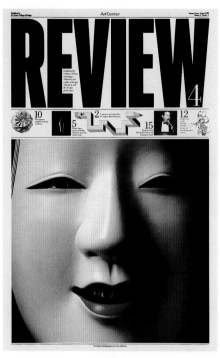

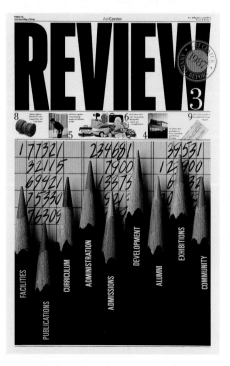

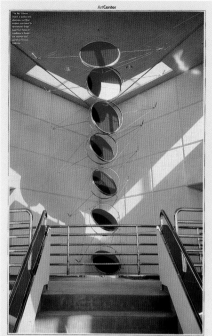

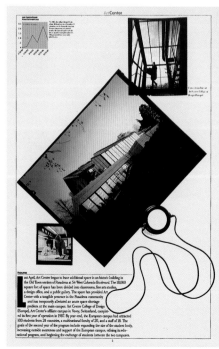

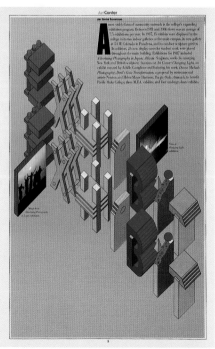

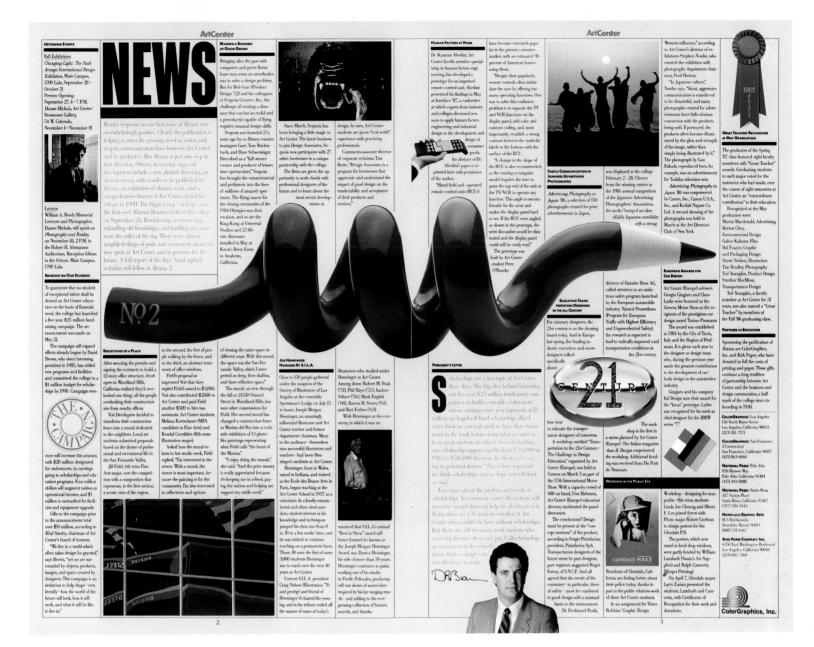

DESIGN FIRM:
PENTAGRAM DESIGN

ART DIRECTOR:
KIT HINRICHS/NEIL SHAKERY

DESIGNERS:
KIT HINRICHS/
NEIL SHAKERY/
LENORE BARTZ/
TERRI DRISCOLL/
KAREN BOONE

PHOTOGRAPHERS:
JIM BLAKELEY/
STEVEN A. HELLER/
HENRIK KAM

CLIENT:
ART CENTER COLLEGE
OF DESIGN, PASADENA

■ The *Art Center Review* is a 12-16 page publication giving information on the activities of the college and its present and former students. David Brown, the director, wanted moreover to create a forum for debating essential and topical design questions. One of the recurring motifs in each issue it the pencil – interpreted by the center's students and famous alumni.

■ *Art Center Review* ist eine 12 bis 16 Seiten starke Publikation über die Aktivitäten der Schule, ihre gegenwärtigen und ehemaligen Studenten. Darüber hinaus wollte David Brown, der Direktor, ein Forum für die Diskussion wichtiger aktueller Design-Fragen schaffen. Ein in jeder Ausgabe wiederkehrendes Element ist der Bleistift, von Studenten und auch von Absolventen interpretiert.

■ L'*Art Center Review* est une publication de 12 à 16 pages consacrée aux activités de l'école, à ses étudiants et aux anciens élèves. Le directeur, David Brown, a voulu faire de ce house organ un lieu d'échanges et de débats sur d'importantes questions d'actualité liées au design. On retrouve dans chaque numéro le thème du crayon, interprété par des étudiants ou d'anciens élèves parvenus à la gloire.

BMW AG, Munich, Germany

In 1977 BMW decided to regard the identity of the corporation from a different point of view and to develop it along a new path. New dimensions of corporate activities always necessitate such a re-orientation. New products and product segments call for a correspondingly autonomous identitiy. The perfected procedure that was introduced gave BMW a clear and unmistakable profile that is determined by special products and a distinctive environment. The commercial success is evidence of the soundness of the direction taken.

BMW AG, München, Deutschland

Die Firma BMW entschliesst sich 1977, die Identität des Unternehmens unter einem anderen Blickwinkel zu sehen und in eine neue Richtung zu entwickeln. Neue Dimensionen des unternehmerischen Handelns erfordern eine Umorientierung. Neue Produkte und Produktsegmente bedürfen einer eigenständigen Darstellung. Der damals eingeleitete und in der Folge perfektionierte Prozess hat BMW zu einem unverwechselbaren, klaren Profil gebracht, das durch besondere Produkte und ein prägnantes Umfeld bestimmt wird.

BMW SA, Munich, Allemagne

C'est en 1977 que BMW a pris la décision de reconsidérer son image d'entreprise et de lui donner une nouvelle orientation. Les dimensions nouvelles de la politique du groupe imposaient ce lifting. De nouveaux produits et segments de produits nécessitaient une présentation spécifique. Le processus amorcé à l'époque et perfectionné par la suite a procuré à BMW un profil clair et net, à nul autre pareil, caractérisé par des produits spéciaux et un environnement distinctif. Le succès économique a démontré la justesse de l'orientation choisie.

Zintzmeyer & Lux, Zurich, Switzerland

The fascination and success of the BMW brand is not a matter of pure chance, but is the result of a consistent strategy directed towards the requirements of discerning customers. The rule that there is a plausible connection between appearance and "inner values" of every product is not limited to BMW automobiles. This rule has proved to be a valuable instrument in the overall image to hold on to customers longterm. We have been working on this project with our partners at BMW now for twelve years. Zintzmeyer & Lux act as consultants in this procedure, supporting BMW in the planning and realization of their identity program, as well as assisting in the development of future visions of their Corporate Identity.

Zintzmeyer & Lux, Zürich, Schweiz

Die Faszination und der Erfolg der Marke BMW sind nicht Zufall, sondern Resultat einer konsequent auf die Bedürfnisse anspruchsvoller Kunden ausgerichteten Strategie. Die Gesetzmässigkeit, dass zwischen Auftritt und «innerem Wert» jedes Produktes ein Zusammenhang besteht, beschränkt sich nicht auf BMW Automobile, sondern hat sich als Instrument zur langfristigen Kundensicherung auch im Gesamtauftritt bewährt. An diesem Projekt arbeiten wir zusammen mit unseren Partnern von BMW seit nunmehr zwölf Jahren. Zintzmeyer & Lux versteht sich in diesem Prozess als Berater, der BMW in der Planung und Umsetzung sowie in der Entwicklung zukünftiger Visionen ihrer Identity-Programme unterstützt.

Zintzmeyer & Lux, Zurich, Suisse

La fascination et le succès que rencontre la marque BMW ne sont pas le fruit du hasard, mais le résultat d'une stratégie orientée de manière conséquente vers les besoins d'une clientèle exigeante. La régularité avec laquelle la manifestation publique de l'identité de BMW et la valeur intrinsèque de chacun de ses produits entrent dans une relation réciproque harmonieuse n'apparaît pas seulement dans le secteur automobile, mais teinte tous ses rapports avec une clientèle fidèle à long terme. Nous travaillons depuis douze ans à ce projet avec nos partenaires de BMW. Au sein de ce processus, Zintzmeyer & Lux assument le rôle de conseiller au stade du planning et de la mise en œuvre des programmes de publicité institutionnelle.

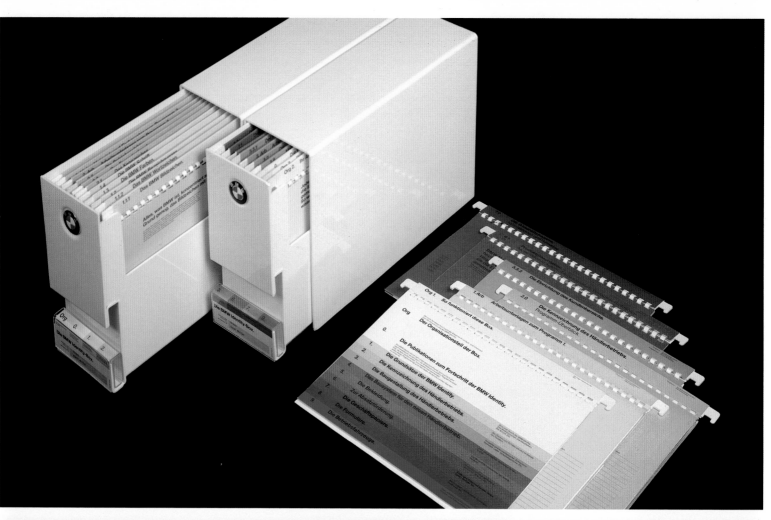

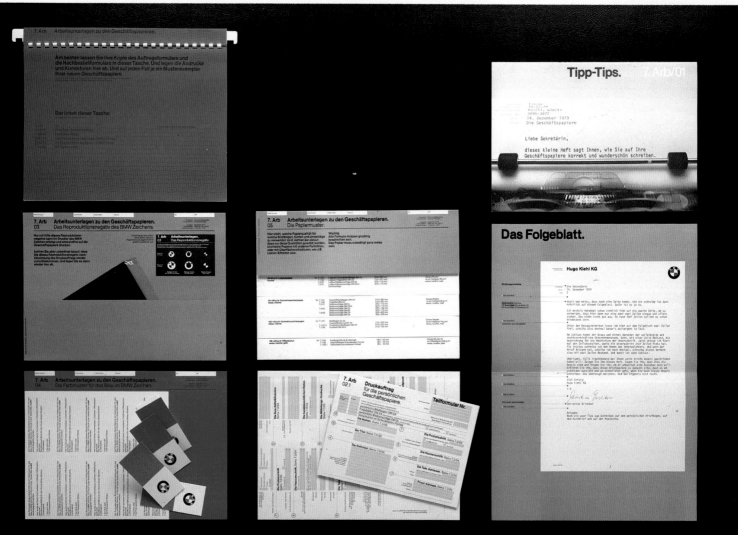

■The identity boxes are only one of the working instruments – even if an important one – for the realization of BMW's corporate design program. The development of partial programs is based on the modular principle, which is in itself reewable, so that the working tools are always up to date. These include technical literature reagarding manufacture, application principles, as well as information about adaption and instructions on introduction and usage for all thos directly involved.

■Die Identity-Boxen sind nur ein, wenn auch ein wesentliches Arbeitsinstrument zur Realisierung des Corporate-Design-Programms bei BMW. Der Aufbau der Teilprogramme entspricht einem modularen Prinzip, das in sich erneuerungsfähig ist, so dass die Arbeitsmittel immer auf dem aktuellen Stand sind. Diese beinhalten technische Unterlagen wie Herstellung, Einsatzprinzipien und Angaben zum Unterhalt wie auch Anleitungen zur Einführung und Anwendungsbeispiele für die direkt Betroffenen.

■Les boîtes documentaires ne sont qu'un instrument de travail parmi d'autres pour la mise en œuvre du programme de publicité institutionnelle élaboré chez BMW. Les programmes sectoriels sont structurés de façon modulaire, ce qui favorise leur mise à jour permanente. La documentation y relative comprend des descriptifs techniques concernant la fabrication, le mode d'utilisation et l'entretien, ainsi que des instructions pour l'introduction et des exemples d'application pour les services concernés.

DESIGN FIRM:
ZINTZMEYER & LUX

ART DIRECTOR:
ZINTZMEYER & LUX

DESIGNER:
ZINTZMEYER & LUX

CLIENT:
BMW BAYERISCHE MOTOREN WERKE AG

BMW in Fahrt.

Rahmenrichtlinien für den weltweiten Auftritt von BMW Betriebsfahrzeugen.

BMW on the move. 9.1 01

General guidelines for the appearance of BMW company vehicles worldwide.

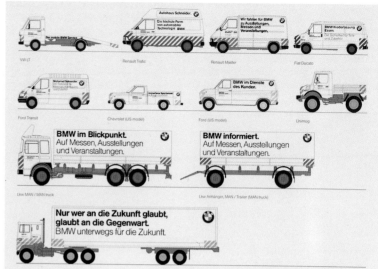

DESIGN FIRM:
ZINTZMEYER & LUX

ART DIRECTOR:
ZINTZMEYER & LUX

DESIGNER:
ZINTZMEYER & LUX

CLIENT:
BMW BAYERISCHE MOTOREN WERKE AG

Aus diesen Farben können Sie wählen...

Die Farbe der Streifen kann aus den sieben Gestaltungsfarben individuell ausgewählt werden. Diese Farbauswahl bietet somit z.B. Händlern die Möglichkeit, nach eigenem Geschmack „ihre" Farbe für Mobiliar, Regalsysteme und jetzt für die Betriebsfahrzeuge auszuwählen. Es kann eine Farbe für alle Betriebsfahrzeuge, oder aus der vorgegebenen Farbpalette für jedes Fahrzeug eine andere Farbe ausgesucht werden. Auch Radkappen setzen Farbakzente. Sie werden immer im gleichen Farbton wie die Streifen gespritzt. Um eine präzise Definition der Farbtöne zu ermöglichen, sind diese auf der Farbkarte (siehe 9.2/03 in den Arbeitsunterlagen) zusammengefaßt. Dazu ein wichtiger Hinweis: Da die beiden Farbreihen (Scotchcal und RAL) leicht voneinander abweichen, sollten sie nicht vermischt werden. Sonst könnte es passieren, daß z.B. Streifen und Radkappen farblich voneinander abweichen.

Choose from these colours...

The stripes can be in any one of seven recommended colours, to suit your preferences and the nature of the vehicle to which they are applied. Dealers can for example use a "house colour" for their vehicles as well as for furniture, shelf systems and other items of equipment. Either a single colour can be adopted for all company vehicles, or else each vehicle or group of vehicles can be in a different colour from the recommended range. The wheels or hub caps provide an additional colour accent: they are always painted in the same colour as the stripes. For precise definitions of the colours, please refer to the summary on the colour card (9.2/03 in the working documentation). But remember: Scotchcal and RAL colours differ slightly in some cases and should therefore not be used together, or else stripes and hub caps, for example, may not match accurately.

14

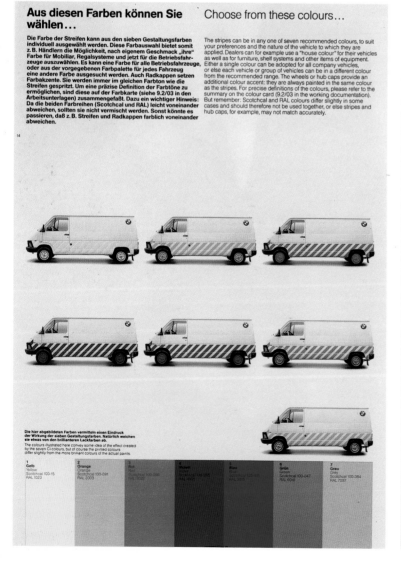

Die hier abgebildeten Farben vermitteln einen Eindruck der Wirkung der sieben Gestaltungsfarben. Natürlich weichen sie etwas von den brillanteren Lackfarben ab.
The colours illustrated here convey some idea of the effect created by the seven CI colours, but of course the printed colours differ slightly from the more brilliant colours of the actual paints.

1 Gelb Yellow Scotchcal 100-15 RAL 1023	2 Orange Orange Scotchcal 100-091 RAL 2003	3 Rot Red	4 Violett	5 Blau	6 Grün Green Scotchcal 100-047 RAL 6018	7 Grau Grey Scotchcal 100-384 RAL 7037

...und so präsentiert sich das neu gestaltete Fahrzeug.

Die Gestaltungsprinzipien 1 bis 6 ergeben zusammen das Bild des typischen BMW Betriebsfahrzeugs. Das Zusammenspiel funktioniert so, daß aus jeder Position die wesentlichen Merkmale, insbesondere die verbale Aussage, stets prägnant und plakativ zu erkennen sind.
Die Seitenansicht gibt den Blick frei auf die Schlagzeile und den Absender. Das Fahrzeugdach ist eine nicht alltägliche und effektive Werbefläche. Insbesondere in Städten wird das so gekennzeichnete BMW Fahrzeug auch von höheren Gebäuden aus erkannt. Darum trägt das Dach, wenn immer möglich, die Schlagzeile und das BMW Bildzeichen.

And this is how the finished vehicle should look!

Design principles 1 to 6, if applied together, yield the typical appearance which we feel a BMW company vehicle should have. Viewed from any angle, the main elements of the design, and in particular the verbal statements, are always clearly identifiable and striking in their effect.
The side view exposes the headline and the company name.
The vehicle's roof is a highly unusual advertising surface, but one that catches the onlooker's eye, particularly when viewed from upper-floor windows in cities. For this reason, the roof of the vehicle should carry the punchline and BMW badge wherever possible.

20

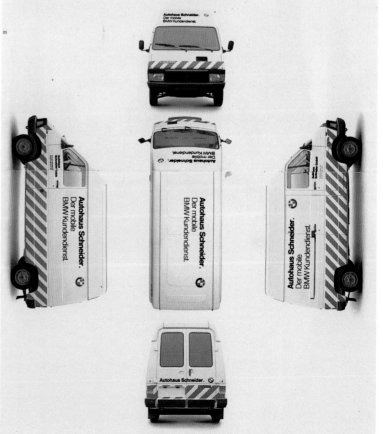

■ The quality of a corporate identity program is measured chiefly by its realization; a few figures on the design program for the company's own fleet of vehicles show how complex such a matter can be. There are 7,600 vehicles for about 4,000 dealers and subsidiaries in 14 countries and as many languages – and this for the most varied types of vehicles. In total a potential advertising space of 110,000 m2 is used, whose effects are felt both externally and internally.

■ Die Qualität eines C.-I.-Programms misst sich vorrangig an seiner Realisierung – ein paar Zahlen zum Design-Programm für die betriebseigenen Fahrzeugflotten lassen erahnen, wie komplex ein solcher Sachverhalt sein kann: 7'600 Fahrzeuge für rund 4'000 Händlerbetriebe und Niederlassungen in 14 Ländern und ebenso viele Sprachen und das für die verschiedensten Fahrzeugtypen! Insgesamt wird dadurch eine potentielle Werbefläche von 110'000 m2 genutzt, die ihre Wirkung auch nach innen entfaltet.

■ La qualité d'un programme de publicité corporate s'évalue avant tout en termes de réalisation. Voici quelques chiffres qui feront saisir la complexité de la tâche des designers face aux besoins du parc de véhicules de l'entreprise: 7'600 véhicules pour 4'000 agents commerciaux et filiales dans 14 pays et autant de langues, et cela pour les types de véhicules les plus divers! La surface publicitaire correspondante peut être estimée à 110'000 m2; son action s'exerce aussi bien à l'extérieur qu'à l'intérieur.

Design Basics.
Das Gestaltungsprogramm für den 5er Auftritt.
Design programme for the introduction of the new 5 Series.

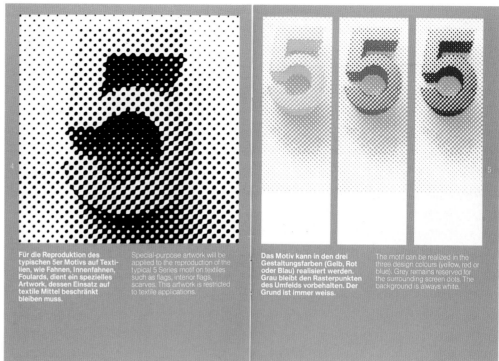

Für die Reproduktion des typischen 5er Motivs auf Textilien, wie Fahnen, Innenfahnen, Foulards, dient ein spezielles Artwork, dessen Einsatz auf textile Mittel beschränkt bleiben muss.

Special-purpose artwork will be applied to the reproduction of the typical 5 Series motif on textiles such as flags, interior flags, scarves. This artwork is restricted to textile applications.

Das Motiv kann in den drei Gestaltungsfarben (Gelb, Rot oder Blau) realisiert werden. Grau bleibt den Rasterpunkten des Umfelds vorbehalten. Der Grund ist immer weiss.

The motif can be realized in the three design colours (yellow, red or blue). Grey remains reserved for the surrounding screen dots. The background is always white.

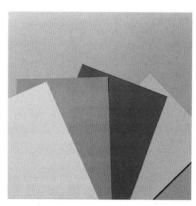

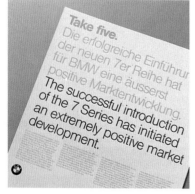

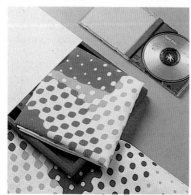

DESIGN FIRM:
ZINTZMEYER & LUX

ART DIRECTOR:
ZINTZMEYER & LUX

DESIGNER:
ZINTZMEYER & LUX

CLIENT:
*BMW BAYERISCHE MOTOREN
WERKE AG*

■The development of a new automobile takes about seven years. Correspondingly the same amount of time is taken for the promotional framework that is needed for its introduction. For the worldwide premiere of the new "5 series", literature was drawn up to allow dealers specific translations. The guidelines embrace the basic elements for the design and show exemplary ways to achieve presentations that become memorable events.

■Die Entwicklung eines neuen Automobils dauert etwa sieben Jahre; entsprechend wichtig ist der Rahmen, der zur Einführung gesetzt wird. Für die weltweite Premiere des neuen 5er wurden Unterlagen erarbeitet, die als Arbeitshilfen den Händlern spezifische, kreative Umsetzungen erlaubten. Die Richtlinien umfassen die Basiselemente für die Gestaltung und zeigen Anwendungsbeispiele, die zu ereignisbetonten Präsentationen verhelfen.

■Il est important de prévoir un cadre adéquat pour le lancement d'une voiture. La première mondiale de la nouvelle Cinq a nécessité la production d'une documentation destinée aux revendeurs, avec une marge d'adaptabilité créatrice de cet instrument de travail aux besoins du commerce local. Ces instructions présentent les éléments de base du design et proposent des exemples d'application garantissant une présentation de toute beauté.

3.3.2
05
Die Einrichtung des Kundenbereichs.
Das Mobiliar.

Programm: Die Baugestaltung des Handlerbetriebs.
Der Kundenbereich
Ausgabe: Dezember 1983
Herausgeber: BMW AG, Abt. VM-23
Bestellnummer: 3.3.2/05 - 6012

Gute Arbeit setzt einen guten Arbeitsplatz voraus. Wo immer mehr Arbeit von immer weniger Mitarbeitern erledigt werden soll, wird das besonders gelten. BMW hat deshalb für den administrativen Bereich mit der Verwaltung, der Kundendienst-Annahme, dem Teileverkauf und der Kasse ein Einrichtungssystem ausgewählt, das konsequent alle geforderten arbeitsphysiologischen Bedingungen erfüllt.

Nach den folgenden sechs Gesichtspunkten bestimmen Sie die Einrichtung Ihres BMW Kundenbereichs:

1. Die Flexibilität. Arbeitsbereiche, Arbeitsflächen und Ablageraum müssen den Bedürfnissen im Betrieb immer angepasst sein. Darum können Sie vorgreifen oder vorkleinern, wie Sie es gerade brauchen. Sowohl im Einzel- als auch im Grossraumbüro muss daher das Einrichtungssystem flexibel und ausbaubar sein.

2. Die Variabilität. Nutzen bringt nur, was an verschiedenen Orten oder in neuer Kombination oder für einen anderen Zweck gebraucht werden kann. Eine Ablage in Ordnern kann durch ein Hängeregistratur ersetzt, oder die wiederum durch ein Microfiche System. Solche Umwandlungen des Mobiliars und auch seine neue Anordnung. Die Einrichtungssysteme bieten darum heute den hohen Grad an Variabilität, den Sie in Ihrem Betrieb brauchen. Alle anderen sind unwirtschaftlich.

3. Die Funktionalität. Funktionalität ist hier in ihrer umfassenden Bedeutung gemeint. So soll die Einrichtung heutigen arbeitsphysiologischen und ergonomischen Anforderungen gerecht werden. D.h. sie soll den Bedürfnissen des Menschen nach einem gesunden, störungsfreien und angenehmen Arbeiten entsprechen. Die Einrichtung muss sich aber auch den vielfältigen und unterschiedlichen organisatorischen und räumlichen Bedingungen eines Kfz-Betriebs anpassen lassen. Und ihre einzelnen Elemente sollen sowohl in Einzel-, wie auch in Grossraumbüros verwendbar sein.

4. Der Stil. Im BMW Kundenbereich sind Qualitätsprodukte ausgestellt. Wirkt ihre Umgebung billig, dann bleibt eine verkaufsfördernde Einstimmung Ihrer Kunden aus. Eine zeitlose Gestaltung des gesamten Mobiliars, die sorgfältige Abstimmung aller Einzelheiten zu einem funktionellen, harmonischen, technisch-sachlich anmutenden und zeitgemässen System ist notwendig. Erst dann hat Ihr Kundenbereich die Anmutung und Attraktivität, die der BMW Fahrer von seinem BMW kennt.

5. Die Materialqualität. Im BMW Kundenbereich kommen, gehen, stehen und sitzen viele Menschen. Jeden Tag. Woche für Woche, jahrelang. Und immer soll alles wie neu aussehen und sauber sein. Darum kommt nur ein Einrichtungssystem aus Materialien in Frage, die dauerhaft, strapazierfähig und pflegeleicht sind.

6. Die Farben. Farben bringen in den Kundenbereich Freundlichkeit und entspannte Atmosphäre. Sie sind eine sympathische Verkaufshilfe und lassen die Arbeit angenehm erscheinen. Der ideale Träger für Farben ist das Einrichtungssystem aus Farben, zwischen denen Sie entscheiden können. Denn farbig und nicht kunterbunt.

Alle diese Kriterien finden Sie in unserem vorgestellten Einrichtungssystem erfüllt.

Kundendienstannahme

Die Arbeitstische: Sie sind vor allem nach physiologischen und funktionellen Gesichtspunkten ausgewählt. Der Farbton des Tischflächen ist für das Arbeiten besonders angenehm.

Die Arbeitsstühle: Die Information dazu steht auf der Ausserseite dieser Karte. Der Farbton des Stoffüberzugs gehört zu der Farbreihe, für die Sie sich entscheiden haben. Auf der Karte **3. Arb/02 Das Farbsystem im Kundenbereich** lesen Sie alles über die zur Auswahl stehenden Farbreihen Rot, Gelb, Braun und Grün.

Die Schreibmaschinen-Tische. Sie stehen auf Rollen. Die Tischhöhe von ca. 65 cm lässt genügend Kniefreiheit.

Die Thekenstühle. Sie ermöglichen ein ergonomisch richtiges Sitzen. Auch beim Heraufsitzen an die hohen Theke. Der Farbton des Stoffüberzugs gehört zu der Farbreihe, für die Sie sich entscheiden haben. Alle Informationen dazu finden Sie auf der Karte **3. Arb/02 Das Farbsystem im Kundenbereich.**

Die Rollkorpusse. Die Rollkorpusse lassen sich auf Doppelrollen unter die Arbeitstische schieben. Die Farbe der Oberfläche haben Sie mit der Wahl einer Farbreihe entschieden. Alle Informationen in Farbe Reihen Sie über die zur Auswahl stehenden Farbreihen Rot, Gelb, Braun und Grün.

Die Büroregale: Die Regaltiefe beträgt 35 oder 50 cm. Die Höhe ist je nach Bedarf und Einsatz variabel. Die Ausfachungen können vielseitig benutzt werden: als Schublade, als Hängeregistratur, als verschliessbares Fach etc. Die Farbe der Oberfläche ist wie die der Rollkorpusse. Welche Farbwahl Sie haben, steht auf der Karte **3. Arb/02 Das Farbsystem im Kundenbereich.**

3.2
04
Die Umgebungsgestaltung.
Die Beleuchtung.

Programm: Die Baugestaltung des Handlerbetriebs.
Die Umgebungsgestaltung
Ausgabe: August 1981
Herausgeber: BMW AG, Abt. VM-32
Bestellnummer: 3.2/04 - 859

Es gibt Bereiche auf dem Betriebsgelände, die eine möglichst gleichmässige Ausleuchtung verlangen, z.B. der Platz, auf dem die gebrauchten Automobile stehen. Viel Licht hält hier u.a. dunkle Gestalten ab.

Eine andere Funktion hat das Licht im Gehbereich. Hier darf es ruhig etwas stimmungsvoll sein. Und dann brauchen wir auch noch eine geeignete Beleuchtung.

um Pylon, Fahnen, Betriebsschilder usw. gut sicht- und lesbar zu machen. Lassen Sie sich in jedem Fall von einem Lichtplaner beraten. Er sorgt für eine optimale Ausleuchtung Ihres Betriebsgeländes.

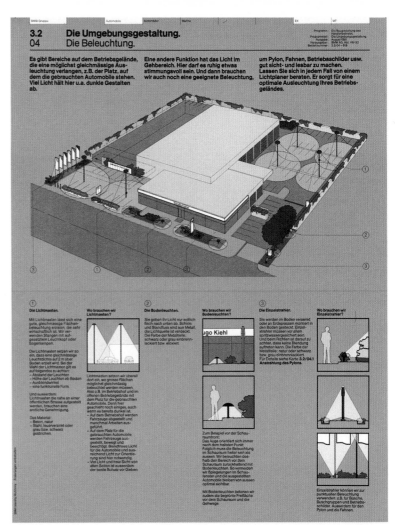

① Die Lichtmasten.
Mit Lichtmasten lässt sich eine gute, gleichmässige Flächenbeleuchtung erzielen, die sehr wirtschaftlich ist. Wir verwenden Stangen mit aufgesetztem Leuchtkopf oder Bogenlampen.

Die Lichtmasten setzen wir so ein, dass eine gleichmässige Leuchtdichte ab 2 m über Boden erzielt wird. Bei der Wahl der Lichtmasten gilt es auf folgendes zu achten:
– Abstand der Leuchten
– Höhe der Leuchten ab Boden
– Ausblendwinkel
– eine funktionelle Form.

Und ausserdem: Lichtmasten die nahe an einer öffentlichen Strasse aufgestellt werden, brauchen eine amtliche Genehmigung.

Das Material:
– Beton, natur
– Stahl, feuerverzinkt oder grau bzw. schwarz gestrichen.

Wo brauchen wir Lichtmasten?
Lichtmasten setzen wir überall dort ein, wo grosse Flächen möglichst gleichmässig beleuchtet werden müssen. Also z.B. im Betriebshof und im offenen Betriebsgelände mit dem Platz für die gebrauchten Automobile. Denn hier geschieht noch einiges, auch wenn es bereits dunkel ist.
– Auf den Betriebshof werden Fahrzeuge abgestellt und manchmal Arbeiten ausgeführt.
– Auf dem Platz für die gebrauchten Automobile werden Fahrzeuge ausgestellt, bewegt und besichtigt. Blendfreies Licht für die Automobile und ausreichend Licht zur Orientierung sind hier notwendig.
– Viel Licht und freie Sicht von allen Seiten ist ausserdem der beste Schutz vor Dieben.

② Die Bodenleuchten.
Sie geben ihr Licht nur seitlich flach nach unten ab. Schirm und Blendfuss sind aus Metall, die Lichtquelle ist verdeckt. Die Farbe der Metallteile: schwarz oder grau einbrennlackiert bzw. eloxiert.

Wo brauchen wir Bodenleuchten?
Mit Bodenleuchten betonen wir zudem die begrünte Freifläche vor dem Schauraum und die Gehwege.

③ Die Einzelstrahler.
Sie werden im Boden versenkt oder in Gebäudenischen montiert. Einzelstrahler müssen vor allem spritzwassergeschützt sein. Und beim Richten ist darauf zu achten, dass keine Blendung auftreten kann. Die Farbe der Metallteile: natur oder schwarz bzw. grau einbrennlackiert. Für Details siehe Karte **3.2/04.1 Anstrahlung des Pylons.**

Zum Beispiel vor der Schauraumfront:
Das Auge orientiert sich immer nach dem hellsten Punkt. Folglich muss die Beleuchtung im Schauraum heller sein als aussen. Wir beleuchten deshalb den Bereich vor dem Schauraum zurückhaltend mit Bodenleuchten. So vermeiden wir Spiegelungen im Schaufenster und die ausgestellten Automobile bleiben von aussen optimal sichtbar.

Wo brauchen wir Einzelstrahler?
Einzelstrahler können wir zur punktuellen Beleuchtung verwenden, z.B. für Büsche, Buschgruppen und Betriebsschilder. Ausserdem für den Pylon und die Fahnen.

DESIGN FIRM:
ZINTZMEYER & LUX

ART DIRECTOR:
ZINTZMEYER & LUX

DESIGNER:
ZINTZMEYER & LUX

CLIENT:
BMW BAYERISCHE MOTOREN WERKE AG

■ "Corporate design is the final result of thinking and doing". Design programs – as active policies presenting the essential core elements of a company – help to give it or the marque a visual image. This is shown by the examples of BMW's building design. Exterior identification, as well as the customers' area of a dealer-ship, the interior of the BMW Gallery in New York, or the BMW Pavillon in Munich, all bring to the fore the inherent substance of the marque in a concise manner.

■ «Corporate Design ist der Schlusspunkt von Denken und Handeln»; dass Gestaltungsprogramme als prozesshafte Richtlinien den wesentlichen Kernelementen eines Unternehmens oder einer Marke zum visuellen Auftritt verhelfen, zeigen die Beispiele zur Baugestaltung bei BMW: Aussenkennzeichnung oder auch Kundenbereich eines Händlerbetriebs, Interieur der BMW Gallery New York wie auch der BMW Pavillon in München – alle tragen auf prägnante Art die innere Substanz der Marke nach aussen.

■ «Le design institutionnel est l'aboutissement de la réflexion et de l'action»: le fait que les programmes de design contribuent largement à la mise en valeur visuelle de l'entreprise et de la marque est amplement démontré par ces exemples de l'architecture BMW; décoration extérieure d'une agence, décoration des zones de réception de la clientèle, intérieur de la BMW Gallery de New York et du pavillon BMW de Munich - tous ces éléments transposent la quintessence de la marque en la rendant visible.

Paul Wielgus, Marketing Controller, Boddingtons' Breweries Ltd., Manchester, U.K.

Boddingtons' Breweries Ltd. was established in 1778 in Manchester. The company not only brews, wholesales and distributes beers, wines, and spirits throughout its 500 outlets, but also operates a chain of restaurants in its heartland of the North West of England, as well as a recently acquired chain in the South East. The brief for a new Corporate Identity was given for the core business of pub retailing and the core brand *Boddingtons Bitter*. The designers were asked to sensitively upgrade the livery for pubs and liquid brands image. The key graphic components – the dominant milestone shape, the barrel, and the bees (symbol of Manchester as the "hive of industry") – were sensitively and effectively treated. Subsequent research with trade and consumers strongly confirmed the effectiveness of the new identity.

Paul Wielgus, Marketing Controller, Boddingtons' Breweries Ltd., Manchester, U.K.

Boddingtons' Breweries Ltd., 1778 in Manchester gegründet, ist heute nicht nur Brauerei, Grosshändler und Verteiler von Bier, Wein und Spirituosen mit 500 Läden, sondern die Firma ist ausserdem Besitzerin von Restaurantketten im Nordwesten und neuerdings auch im Südosten Englands. Bei der Neugestaltung des Erscheinungsbildes der Biermarke *Boddingtons Bitter*, insbesondere in Bezug auf die Flaschenausstattung und das Promotionsmaterial für Lokale, ging es um eine Belebung und Aufwertung des Designs im Hinblick auf die starke Marktposition des Biers. Die neue Gestaltung überzeugt durch die sensible Handhabung der Hauptelemente: der prägnanten Form und des Fass-Bienen-Motivs (Symbol der Stadt Manchester als «Bienenstock der Industrie»), was das Ergebnis einer Umfrage bestätigte.

Paul Wielgus, coordonnateur du marketing, Boddingtons' Breweries Ltd., Manchester, U.K.

Boddingtons' Breweries a été fondé à Manchester en 1778. L'entreprise ne se contente pas de la fabrication, de la vente de gros et de la distribution de bière, de vins et de spiritueux à travers ses 500 points de vente; elle contrôle également une chaîne de restaurants dans le Nord-Ouest de l'Angleterre, ainsi qu'une seconde chaîne récemment acquise dans le Sud-Est. Le lifting de l'image institutionnelle visait l'activité principale du groupe, la vente au détail dans les pubs, et la marque vedette, la *Boddingtons Bitter*. Les designers ont été invités à améliorer avec doigté la décoration des pubs et l'image de marque des boissons. C'est ainsi que les éléments-clefs de la forme dominante de la borne milliaire, du tonneau et des abeilles (évoquant la «ruche industrielle» de Manchester) ont été traités de manière sensible et efficace.

Steve Gibbons/Malcolm Swatridge, The Partners Design Consultants Ltd., London, U.K.

Boddingtons had an identity that was designed in the early seventies and didn't accurately reflect the quality and traditional brewing methods of their beers. Our brief was to upgrade their image, but in an evolutionary rather than a revolutionary way. Although their old identity was looking dated, there were idiosyncratic visual elements that were strongly associated with the Brewery. It was important they didn't think that a change to the identity meant a change in the brewing process and hence in the product. The new identity was applied to the exterior signing of pubs, to packaging, point of sale, promotional material, and to the vehicle fleet. The aim has been to apply the identity consistently bearing in mind the different materials that are used on each application, and the need to retain some flexibility on the pub exteriors.

Steve Gibbons/Malcolm Swatridge, The Partners Design Consultants Ltd., London, U.K.

Das Erscheinungsbild von Boddingtons stammte aus den siebziger Jahren und entsprach nicht ganz der Qualität und den traditionellen Braumethoden. Wir bekamen den Auftrag, dieses Erscheinungsbild weiterzuentwickeln und nicht völlig neu zu gestalten, denn einige der visuellen Elemente waren für die Kunden stark mit Boddingtons verbunden. Es war ausserdem wichtig, dass diese Änderung des Erscheinungsbildes nicht mit einer Änderung des Brauprozesses und damit der Qualität in Verbindung gebracht würde. Das neue Symbol wurde für die Aussenbeschilderung von Lokalen verwendet, für Flaschengestaltung, Verpackungen, Ladendisplays, Promotionsmaterial und Firmenautos. Beim neuen Design mussten auch die verschiedenen Materialien für die Ausführung berücksichtigt werden.

Steve Gibbons/Malcolm Swatridge, The Partners Design Consultants Ltd., Londres, U.K.

L'identité d'entreprise de Boddingtons datait du début des années 1970. Notre tâche consistait à assurer le lifting de cette image de manière évolutive, non révolutionnaire. Malgré le caractère jugé suranné de l'image existante, celle-ci comportait néanmoins des éléments visuels typiques de l'identité de la brasserie dans l'esprit de ses clients. Il était essentiel de s'assurer que le changement d'image ne ferait pas conclure à un changement intervenu dans les méthodes de fabrication, et affectant donc le produit même. La nouvelle identité a été appliquée aux enseignes des pubs, aux emballages, à la P.L.V., au matériel promotionnel, à la décoration des véhicules. La cohérence du programme n'excluait pas son interprétation en fonction des matériaux constituant le support.

Design Firm:
The Partners (Design Consultants) Limited

Art Directors:
Malcolm Swatridge/ Stephen Gibbons

Designers:
Karen Morgan/ Peter Carrow/ Colin Goddhew/ Greg Quinton

Client:
Boddingtons' Breweries Limited

■The rectangular label that distinguishes *Oldhams* beer, and a label shaped like a milestone for beer from Boddingtons Brewery (proprietors of Oldhams); shown here to mark beer pumps and for display purposes. In both cases the emphasis is on tradition.

■Das rechteckige Etikett der *Oldhams*-Biere und das in Form eines Meilensteins gestaltete Etikett für Biere der Boddingtons-Brauerei (Besitzerin von Oldhams) als Kennzeichnung von Zapfsäulen und Displays. Beiden gemeinsam ist die Betonung von Tradition.

■L'étiquette rectangulaire des bières *Oldhams* et l'étiquette sous forme de borne milliaire créée pour les bières de la brasserie Boddingtons (propriétaire d'Oldhams) servent à caractériser des robinets et à agrémenter une présentation de marchandise. Toutes deux soulignent la tradition du brasseur.

DESIGN FIRM:
THE PARTNERS (DESIGN
CONSULTANTS) LIMITED

ART DIRECTORS:
MALCOLM SWATRIDGE/
STEPHEN GIBBONS

DESIGNERS:
KAREN MORGAN/
PETER CARROW/
COLIN GODDHEW/
GREG QUINTON

CLIENT:
BODDINGTONS' BREWERIES
LIMITED

■ Disposable bottles, cans, and glass bottles with versions of the label for *Boddingtons* beer. The labels must also be suitable for advertising and promotional articles such as ashtrays, showcards, etc. For certain applications, ceramic, goldleaf, and enamelling are used in order to underscore the quality and tradition of this beer.

■ Einwegflaschen, Dosen und Glasflaschen mit Varianten des Etiketts für *Boddingtons*-Bier, das auch für Aussenwerbung und Promotionsartikel wie Aschenbecher, Aufsteller etc. geeignet sein musste. Für einige Bereiche wurden Keramik, Blattgold und Emaillierungen eingesetzt, um Qualität und Tradition des Bieres zu unterstreichen.

■ Verres perdus, boîtes et bouteilles de verre garnis de diverses variantes de l'étiquette des bières *Boddingtons*, qui s'adapte également à la publicité extérieure et aux articles-cadeaux, aux cendriers, aux présentoirs, etc. L'emploi de la céramique, de l'or en feuilles et de l'émail accentuent encore la tradition de qualité de ces bières.

James F. Fletcher, Secretary/Treasurer, Aussies, Inc. - Bonza Tucker, San Francisco, CA/USA
Bonza Tucker (Australian slang for "good food") is a joint venture of Red Rooster, an Australian chicken franchiser, and Round Table Pizza, California's largest pizza franchiser. It is the first restaurant to introduce Australian-style fast food chicken to America. The primary design criterion was to differentiate the product - stuffed chicken roasted on a rotisserie – from American-style fried chicken. Our preliminary consumer research also showed that roast chicken was perceived as lighter, less greasy, healthier than fried chicken. We wanted the graphics to communicate a "clean" contemporary feeling and a distinctively Australian attitude: irreverent, unconventional, and uncorporate. The design was approved virtually without discussion and without change.

Nicolas Sidjakov, Sidjakov Berman Gomez & Partners, San Francisco, CA/USA
The illustration of an outback character riding an oversized chicken was created to give Bonza Tucker a highly unique and memorable image, differentiating the facility from other U.S. take-out restaurants, particularly from other eateries serving chicken. We felt this unusual visual would give Bonza Tucker a strong individual personality and would have tremendous recall value. The character was designed to appear brash yet friendly. The white stars along with the red and blue colors were extracted from the Australian flag to further support a genuine Australian theme. The typeface chosen was Copperplate Gothic to add a nostalgic feeling. Application of the retail identity includes signage, tabletops, carry-out packaging, aprons, menus, and various promotional materials.

James F. Fletcher, Secretary/Treasurer, Aussies, Inc. - Bonza Tucker, San Francisco, CA/USA
Bonza Tucker (australischer Jargon für «gutes Essen») ist ein Gemeinschaftsunternehmen einer australischen Hähnchen-Kette und dem grössten Pizzahersteller Kaliforniens. Bei der Ausarbeitung des Designs war es wichtig, das Produkt - gefüllte Hühner vom Grill - von der amerikanischen Machart - fritiertes Huhn - zu unterscheiden. Umfragen ergaben, dass das Huhn vom Grill als leichter, weniger fett und gesünder als das fritierte Huhn empfunden wurde. Deshalb sollte das neue Design das Gefühl von «sauber» und zeitgemäss vermitteln und typisch «australisch» sein: unangepasst, unkonventionell und originell. Das neue Design wurde sowohl von Amerikanern als auch von Australiern praktisch ohne Diskussion und ohne Änderungen akzeptiert.

Nicolas Sidjakov, Sidjakov Berman Gomez & Partners, San Francisco, CA/USA
Die Darstellung eines australischen Hinterwäldlertypen, der ein überdimensioniertes Hähnchen reitet, sollte Bonza Tucker ein einzigartiges, einprägsames Erscheinungsbild geben. Wir fanden, dass diese ungewöhnliche Illustration Bonza Tucker eine starke Individualität verleihen und gleichzeitig einen grossen Erinnerungswert haben würde. Der Typ sollte frech, aber freundlich wirken. Die weissen Sterne mit dem Rot und dem Blau sind eine Anspielung auf die australische Flagge und damit auf die Herkunft der Hähnchen. Als Typographie wählten wir Kupferstich-Gothik, um ein Gefühl von Nostalgie zu vermitteln. Das Logo wurde für die Beschilderung, Tischplatten, Verpackungen, Schürzen, Speisekarten und verschiedenes Promotionsmaterial verwendet.

James F. Fletcher, Secrétaire/Trésorier, Aussies, Inc. - Bonza Tucker, San Francisco, CA/USA
Bonza Tucker (en argot australien, «bonne bouffe») est une entreprise cogérée par une chaîne australienne d'élevage de poulets et le plus gros producteur de pizzas californien. L'idée essentielle du design était de distinguer clairement le produit - des poulets farcis grillés - des poulets frits à l'américaine. Nos enquêtes auprès des consommateurs ont montré que le poulet grillé est apprécié en tant que produit plus léger, moins graisseux et plus sain que le poulet frit. La présentation graphique se devait donc de communiquer une sensation de «propreté» assortie aux goûts contemporains caractère spécifiquement australien mariant l'irrévérence, le non-conformisme et la liberté d'esprit. Le nouveau design était accepté sans discussion et sans aucun changement.

Nicolas Sidjakov, Sidjakov Berman Gomez & Partners, San Francisco, CA/USA
L'image d'un type du fin fond des bois chevauchant un poulet géant est destinée à ancrer dans les esprits une représentation mémorable et exceptionnelle de Bonza Tucker et de distinguer ce restaurant de tous les autres prêts-à-manger. Nous estimons que cette illustration insolite confère à Bonza Tucker une forte individualité et favorise grandement le rappel de la marque. Le personnage évoque un fort en gueule bourru, mais amical. Les étoiles blanches, ainsi que le rouge et le bleu, sont empruntés au drapeau australien et soulignent l'origine des poulets. Pour la typo, une écriture gothique moulée renforce l'aspect nostalgique. Le nouveau logo a servi pour la signalisation, les dessous de tables, les emballages à l'emporter, les tabliers, les menus et divers matériels promotionnels.

DESIGN FIRM:
*Sidjakov Berman Gomez
& Partners*
ART DIRECTORS:
*Nicolas Sidjakov/
Jerry Berman*
DESIGNER:
Ben Wheeler
CLIENT:
Aussies Enterprises

■ This logo is to promote a chain of chicken restaurants in the US whose origins are in Australia. The logo had to be unique and catchy and radiate cleanliness – as well as signifying the Australian descent and the difference with American chickens. Shown is the application in large format as table decoration *(previous double spread)* and restaurant decoration, and in various smaller sizes on promotional items, textiles, and also the menu.

■ Das für die Einführung einer Hähnchenkette australischen Ursprungs in den USA entwickelte Logo sollte einmalig und einprägsam sein und gleichzeitig Sauberkeit ausstrahlen sowie auf den Unterschied zu amerikanischen Hähnchen hinweisen. Hier die Anwendung im Grossformat als Tisch *(vorangehende Doppelseite)* und Restaurantdekoration und in verschiedenen kleineren Grössen auf Promotionsartikeln, Textilien und der Speisekarte.

■ Le logo développé pour l'implantation aux Etats-Unis d'une chaîne de restaurants de poulet grillé d'origine australienne devait être à la fois mémorable et exceptionnel, donner une impression de propreté et faire comprendre la différence le séparant de son équivalent américain. On en voit ici l'application au grand format d'une décoration de table *(page double précédente)* et au petit format: articles-cadeaux, textiles, menus.

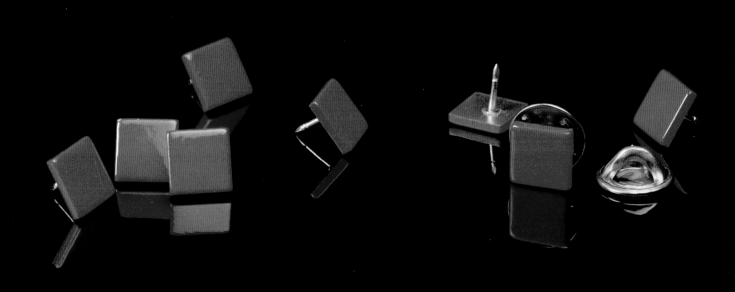

Stephen Brickel, Executive Vice President, Brickel Associates, New York, USA

Brickel Associates was founded in 1959. The main line of business is manufacturing and distributing high-quality, well-designed furniture and textiles. The main objective was to develop a recognizable graphic language that would become associated with our company and should reinforce our concern for good design and high-quality communication with the rest of the world. As our relationship with designer Ward Bennett had become so identifiable with our company, we decided to officially make it our public identity. We also wanted to avoid a rather uncomfortable combination of our corporate name, the designer's name, the product name and often other qualifying aspects. The red square has been so well received that it can be used without type and is still always recognizable as our identity.

Michael P. Donovan, Donovan and Green, New York, NY/USA

We set out to give Brickel a strong and consistent identity and look that paralleled Ward Bennett's clean and classic product designs. The image needed to be bold, strong, minimal. While consistency was necessary to build a recognizable identity over time, energy and diversity were also required for marketing purposes. The system needed to be highly flexible so that it could change in the advertising yet remain clearly recognizable. Our basic solution was to put the cumbersome name in a red square tilted at a precise eight-degree angle. With time, the red square became synonymous with Brickel and the type could even be dropped occasionally - without loss of identity. In our eight years' association with Brickel the company doubled in size and projected an even stronger image in the marketplace than its size might suggest.

Stephen Brickel, Executive Vice President, Brickel Associates, New York, USA

Unsere Firma wurde 1959 gegründet. Der Hauptgeschäftszweig ist die Herstellung und der Verkauf von hochwertigen Designer-Möbeln und Textilien für Büros. Unser Hauptziel war es, ein graphisches Erscheinungsbild für unsere Firma zu finden, das unserem Bemühen um gutes Design und entsprechend anspruchsvolle Kommunikation mit der Aussenwelt gerecht werden würde. Da der Name des Designers Ward Bennett zu einem Begriff für unsere Firma geworden war, entschlossen wir uns, ihn offiziell zu unserer Identität zu machen. Ausserdem wollten wir komplizierte Kombinationen aus Firmennamen, Namen des Designers, Produktnamen und weiterer Kennzeichnungen vermeiden. Das rote Quadrat ist inzwischen so gut eingeführt, dass es auch ohne jeglichen Zusatz als unser Zeichen erkannt wird.

Michael P. Donovan, Donovan and Green, New York, NY/USA

Wir wollten Brickel eine starke, konstante Identität geben, ein Erscheinungsbild, das dem klaren, klassischen Produktdesign von Ward Bennett entsprach. Es musste ausdrucksvoll, stark, schlicht sein. Einerseits sollte es ein Erscheinungsbild sein, das auf lange Dauer Gültigkeit haben würde, andererseits musste es dynamisch sein und Spielraum für Marketing-Zwecke lassen. Es sollte sehr flexibel sein, in der Werbung vielseitig anwendbar und trotzdem klar erkennbar bleiben. Die Grundidee basiert auf einem roten Quadrat, das in einem exakten Neigungswinkel von 8° plaziert wird. Dorthinein setzten wir den etwas schwerfälligen Namen, auf den aber mit der Zeit in manchen Fällen verzichtet werden konnte, da sich das rote Quadrat als Synonym für Brickel durchsetzte und sofort erkennbar war.

Stephen Brickel, vice-président exécutif, Brickel Associates, New York, NY/USA

Brickel Associates a été fondé en 1959. Les activités principales de la société consistent à fabriquer et à distribuer des ameublements et textiles de haut niveau tant par la conception que par la qualité de la réalisation. Nous avons voulu mettre au point un langage graphique aisément identifiable évoquant notre société et étayant notre souci permanent d'un design de qualité et d'une communication optimale avec l'extérieur. Nos rapports avec le designer Ward Bennett étant patents aux yeux du public, c'est lui que nous avons choisi pour notre image institutionnelle. Par ailleurs, il fallait éviter les combinaisons compliquées associant la raison sociale, le nom du designer, celui du produit et d'autres caractéristiques. Le carré rouge a été si bien accueilli que même employé sans texte sa valeur d'identification reste intacte pour le public.

Michael P. Donovan, Donovan and Green, New York, NY/USA

Nous entendions donner à Brickel une identité ferme et cohérente, une image assortie à la clarté et au classicisme des créations produits de Ward Bennett. Le design recherché devait être expressif et marier vigueur et dépouillement. Il s'agissait d'envisager le long terme tout en veillant à créer une image dynamique et variée ouverte aux besoins du marketing. L'idée de base a consisté à inscrire la raison sociale complexe dans un carré rouge incliné d'exactement 8°. Par la suite, ce carré rouge est devenu synonyme de Brickel, de sorte que nous avons par moments pu nous passer du texte, sans porter atteinte à l'identification. Durant les huit années de notre collaboration avec Brickel, la société a doublé son chiffre d'affaires tout en projetant sur le marché une image bien plus importante que ne le laisserait supposer sa taille.

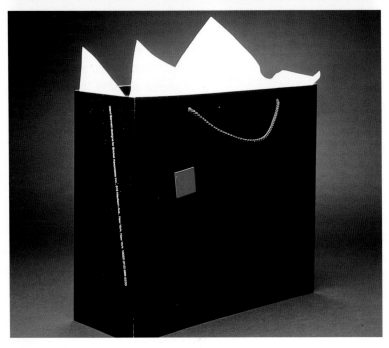

DESIGN FIRM:
DONOVAN AND GREEN

ART DIRECTORS:
MICHAEL DONOVAN/
NANCYE GREEN

DESIGNERS:
MICHAEL DONOVAN/
NANCYE GREEN/
JANE ZASH

CLIENT:
BRICKEL ASSOCIATES

■ The red square that became the trademark of Brickel Associates, in different forms of application for notepaper, brochures, catalogs, promotional items, and as a stickpin. The variations of the square include the use of colors other than red, the adaptation of the shape for illustrations or as overall format type area. The design is relevant to the simple, classic style of the furniture, textiles, and objects that Ward Bennett designs for this company.

■ Das rote Quadrat, das zum Markenzeichen von Brickel Associates wurde, in spielerischer Anwendung für Briefpapier, Prospekte, Kataloge, Promotionsartikel und als Anstecknadel – in allen möglichen Varianten, auch in anderen Farben, als Bildausschnitt oder als Format und Satzspiegel. Es entspricht dem schlichten, klassischen Stil der Möbel, Textilien und Gegenstände, die der Designer Ward Bennett für die Firma entwirft.

■ Le carré rouge qui sert désormais d'image de marque à Brickel Associates est utilisé de façon plaisante pour les en-têtes, les prospectus, les catalogues, les articles promo et les badges, dans une série de variantes, dans diverses autres couleurs, comme détail, format ou surface d'impression. Il s'harmonise avec le style sobre et classique des meubles, textiles et objets que l'esthéticien Ward Bennett crée pour cette entreprise.

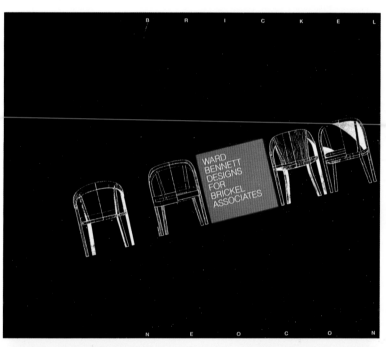

Christof Bonn, Business Manager, Bonn Tatje Fackiner, Cölbe, Germany

The company BTF numbers among the leading West German electrical wholesalers. The firm emanated from the merger of two companies which took place on January 1, 1988. This occasion gave a good opportunity for redesigning the corporate identity, whereby the special requirements of a wholesale business (no advertising and no packaging of its own) had to be taken into consideration. The point of departure was the design of a logo and the formulation of our company's subtitle. From the beginning we were guided by the maxim of didactic reduction of information (the "less is more" principle). The design team combined the electrical symbol of a closed and opened contact with the logo design. This made a direct reference to our trade and proved to leave some room for variations in design tasks.

Christof Bonn, Geschäftsführer, Bonn Tatje Fackiner, Cölbe, Deutschland

Die Firma BTF zählt zu den führenden bundesdeutschen Elektrogrosshandelsunternehmen. Sie ging am 1. Januar 1988 aus der Fusion zweier Unternehmen hervor. Dies war ein wesentlicher Anlass für die Neugestaltung des Erscheinungsbildes, wobei den speziellen Erfordernissen eines Grosshandelsbetriebes (keine Werbung, keine eigene Verpackung) Rechnung getragen werden musste. Ausgangspunkt war die Gestaltung eines Logos und Formulierung unseres Firmenuntertitels. Von Anfang an liessen wir uns von der Maxime der didaktischen Informationsreduktion («weniger ist mehr») leiten. Das Design-Team verband mit der Logogestaltung das elektrische Schaltzeichen eines Öffners bzw. Schliessers, was einen Bezug zu unserer Branche herstellt und sich bei Gestaltungsaufgaben als sehr variabel erweist.

Christof Bonn, Administrateur-délégué, Bonn Tatje Fackiner, Cölbe, RFA

La société BTF est l'un des principaux grossistes de produits électriques en RFA, né le 1er janvier 1988 de la fusion entre deux sociétés spécialisées. C'est là le facteur no 1 expliquant le lifting de l'image institutionnelle qui a dû tenir compte de la spécificité du commerce de gros: pas de publicité, pas d'emballages propres à l'entreprise. Le point de départ a été la mise au point d'un logo et l'adjonction d'un sous-tire à la raison sociale. D'emblée, nous avons adopté la maxime réductionniste de l'information didactique limitée - «moins, c'est plus». L'équipe de design a choisi pour le logo le symbole d'un contact électrique de repos et de travail, qui caractérise la branche et offre au designer une grande souplesse d'adaptation. Ce logo a renforcé la cohésion du personnel dans son ensemble et les liens entre le siège et les filiales.

Gerd Baumann, Baumann & Baumann, Schwäbisch Gmünd, Germany

The firm BTF is a wholesaler and service company active in the electric and electronics industry. With the goal of breaking new ground in customer care and service, we were commissioned to develop a suitable visual communications profile. The company is known by the three names: Bonn Tatje Fackiner, the three initials BTF as well as three open switch contacts in linear presentation as a symbol for electronics. The opened switch contacts do not form a rigid sign. The two elements of the sign always stand in visual tension with each other, form poles on the design surface between above and below, between right and left. The color climate is determined mainly by white, some pale gray, and splashes of green, orange, and blue. This minimum of color generates a bright, fresh atmosphere that is in no way rigid and static.

Gerd Baumann, Baumann & Baumann, Schwäbisch Gmünd, Deutschland

Mit dem unternehmerischen Ziel, neue Wege in der Kundenbetreuung und im -service zu beschreiten, wurden wir beauftragt, ein adäquates visuelles Kommunikationsprofil zu entwickeln. Das Unternehmen wird gekennzeichnet durch die drei Namen Bonn Tatje Fackiner, die drei Anfangsbuchstaben BTF sowie drei offene Schaltkontakte in linearer Darstellung als Symbol für Elektrik/Elektronik. Die geöffneten Schaltkontakte gehen keine feste Zeichenverbindung ein. Die beiden Elemente des Zeichens stehen immer in einem visuellen Spannungsverhältnis zueinander und bilden Pole auf der Gestaltungsfläche. Das Farbklima wird bestimmt durch vorwiegend Weiss, etwas Hellgrau, punktuell Grün, Orange und Blau. Diese minimale Farbigkeit erzeugt eine helle, frische Atmosphäre, die nicht starr und statisch ist.

Gerd Baumann, Baumann & Baumann, Schwäbisch Gmünd, RFA

Pour mettre en évidence une approche nouvelle du service à la clientèle, il fallait développer un profil de communication visuelle approprié. Nous avons résolu la tâche en associant les trois noms clefs de l'entreprise, Bonn Tatje Fackiner, les initiales BTF et trois contacts de commutation ouverts en représentation linéaire pour symboliser l'électricité et l'électronique. Les contacts ouverts ne forment pas un signe rigide. Les deux éléments du signe sont associés dans un champ de tension visuel, constituant sur la surface conceptuelle des pôles d'orientation. L'ambiance chromatique se nourrit surtout du blanc, du gris clair, d'un vert ponctuel, de l'orange et du bleu. Ces coloris minimalisés créent une impression de clarté et de fraîcheur qui défait les attributs habituels de la technicité, la rigidité et l'immobilisme.

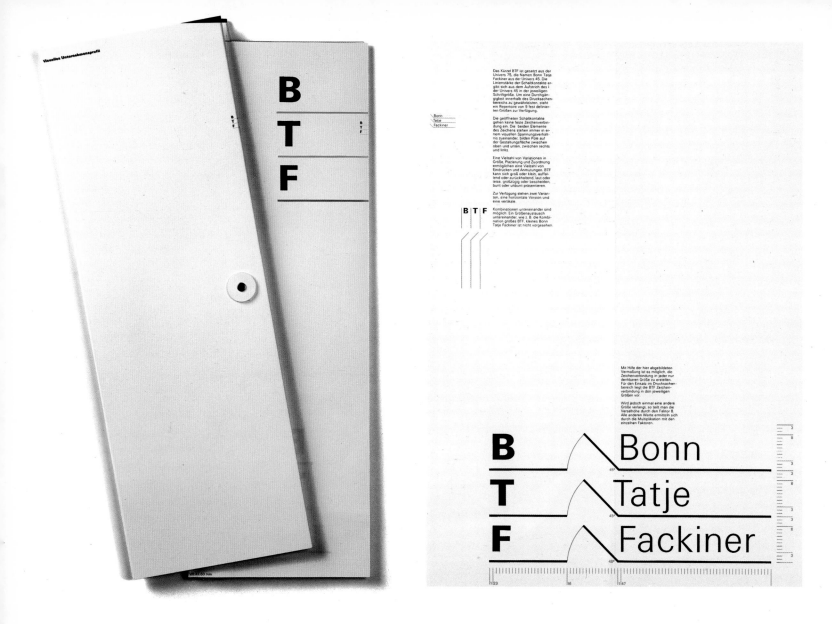

Das Kürzel BTF ist gesetzt aus der Univers 75, die Namen Bonn Tatje Fackiner aus der Univers 45. Die Linienstärke der Schaltkontakte ergibt sich aus dem Aufstrich des i der Univers 45 in der jeweiligen Schriftgröße. Um eine Durchgängigkeit innerhalb des Drucksachenbereichs zu gewährleisten, steht ein Repertoire von 9 fest definierten Größen zur Verfügung.

Die geöffneten Schaltkontakte gehen keine feste Zeichenverbindung ein. Die beiden Elemente des Zeichens stehen immer in einem visuellen Spannungsverhältnis zueinander, bilden Pole auf der Gestaltungsfläche zwischen oben und unten, zwischen rechts und links.

Eine Vielzahl von Variationen in Größe, Plazierung und Zuordnung ermöglichen eine Vielzahl von Eindrücken und Anmutungen. BTF kann sich groß oder klein, auffallend oder zurückhaltend, laut oder leise, großzügig oder bescheiden, bunt oder unbunt präsentieren.

Zur Verfügung stehen zwei Varianten, eine horizontale Version und eine vertikale.

Kombinationen untereinander sind möglich. Ein Größenaustausch untereinander, wie z.B. die Kombination großes BTF, kleines Bonn Tatje Fackiner ist nicht vorgesehen.

Mit Hilfe der hier abgebildeten Vermaßung ist es möglich, die Zeichenverbindung in jeder nur denkbaren Größe zu erstellen. Für den Einsatz im Drucksachenbereich liegt die BTF Zeichenverbindung in den jeweiligen Größen vor.

Wird jedoch einmal eine andere Größe verlangt, so teilt man die Versalhöhe durch den Faktor 8. Alle anderen Werte ermitteln sich durch die Multiplikation mit den einzelnen Faktoren.

■ The narrow, tall format of this manual is rather unusual - the loose sheets relate to the company's different activities. The pages taken from the manual show the versatile use of the logo: on business stationery and for signboards. The example of the use on vehicles also comes from the manual. The symbol for a closed and opened contact used in the logo refers to the electricity industry.

■ Ungewöhnlich für ein Manual ist das schmale, hohe Format und die losen Blätter. Die dem Manual entnommenen Seiten zeigen diverse Anwendungsbereiche des Logos: auf Geschäftspapieren und für Hinweisschilder. und die Verwendung auf Fahrzeugen. Das elektrische Schaltzeichen eines Öffners bzw. Schliessers im Logo stellt den Bezug zur Elektrobranche dar.

■ Ce qui est insolite pour un manuel, c'est son format oblong en hauteur, ainsi que les feuillets mobiles. Les pages tirées du manuel font état de diverses possibilités d'application du logo: sur les imprimés commerciaux, sur des panneaux de signalisation et l'utilisation sur véhicules. Le symbole d'ouverture/fermeture de circuit ancre le logo dans la référence à l'industrie électrique.

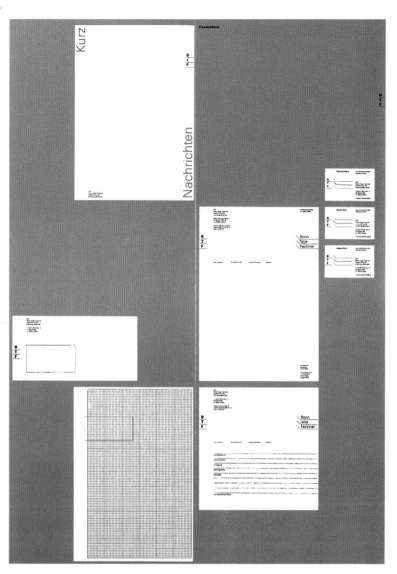

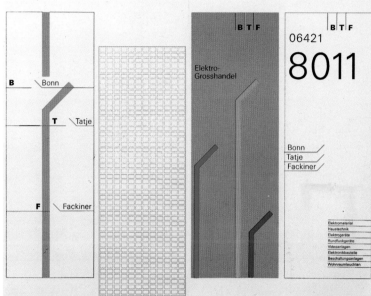

DESIGN FIRM:
BAUMANN & BAUMANN

ART DIRECTORS:
BARBARA & GERD BAUMANN

DESIGNERS:
BARBARA & GERD BAUMANN

PHOTOGRAPHER:
PETER VOGT

CLIENT:
BTF BONN TATJE FACKINER

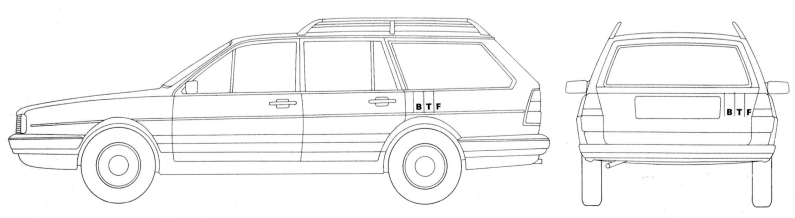

Dieter Skerutsch, freelance copywriter for Canton Elektronik GmbH, Weilrod, Germany

Canton was founded in 1973. Unlike some firms, whose Corporate Identity stems from a landmark event in the company's history, our Corporate Identity was regarded as an integral part of our business policy right from the start. The company's products all have to do with music. Our loudspeakers, for example, are built to reproduce music as naturally as possible, without pretentious special effects; their form and function should be in harmony with the ambiance of their surroundings. From this idea comes our Corporate Identity: if the consumer can be made to feel the philosophical underpinnings of our products, then his or her perception of their more profound qualities – neutrality, fidelity, and purity of tone – will be strengthened. Canton's success story has proven us right.

Dieter Skerutsch, freier Texter für Canton Elektronik GmbH, Weilrod, Deutschland

Die Firma Canton wurde 1973 gegründet. Corporate Identity zu pflegen und zu zeigen, war für Canton von der ersten Stunde an selbstverständlicher Teil der Unternehmensphilosophie. Die Produkte der Firma sind für Musikliebhaber gemacht. Lautsprecherboxen sollen die Musik natürlich, ohne Vertuschungen und ohne Effekte wiedergeben. Sie sollen keine Objekte für Prätention, sondern in Form und Funktion harmonierende Bestandteile eines gestalteten Ambiente sein. Wenn dieser Anspruch in allen Auftritten des Unternehmens zum Ausdruck kommt, wird dadurch auch verstärkt die Wahrnehmung der Konsumenten für solche nicht an der Oberfläche liegenden Produktqualitäten wie Neutralität, Feinzeichnung und Verfärbungsfreiheit mobilisiert. Das hat die Erfolgsgeschichte von Canton bewiesen.

Dieter Skerutsch, rédacteur conseil de la Canton Elektronik GmbH, Weilrod, RFA

La société Canton a été fondée en 1973. L'attention vouée à la publicité d'entreprise n'est ni occasionnelle ni fortuite: dès le départ, l'image institutionnelle de Canton a été intégrée dans la philosophie de l'entreprise, dont les produits s'adressent aux amateurs de musique. Ces enceintes acoustiques visent à reproduire la musique aussi naturellement que possible, sans déformation ni effets d'aucune sorte. Il ne s'agit pas d'objets prétentieux, mais d'éléments d'ambiance dont la forme et la fonction se marient harmonieusement. Souligner cette exigence dans l'image publique de l'entreprise, c'est aussi affiner la perception du consommateur face à des qualités peu visibles du produit - sa neutralité, sa conception affinée, son absence de déformation. L'histoire des succès de Canton est instructive à cet égard.

Christof Gassner, Grafik Design, Frankfurt am Main, Germany

At the very center of Canton communications is music, because Canton products – highgrade HiFi loudspeakers – should help to convey music. This close association with music is already apparent in the logo: the letters of the Canton logotype lead from "piano" through "crescendo" to "forte fortissimo". The logo is the focal point of many Canton appearances. Its basic form is extended to a "theme with variations" that can be reworked again and again by the designer. The layout is magazine-like and lively. It includes many aspects of photography and illustration. This diversity is held together by a strictly uniform typography. Only one typeface – Futura – is ever used.

Christof Gassner, Grafik Design, Frankfurt am Main, Deutschland

Im Zentrum der Canton Kommunikation steht die Musik. Denn die Canton Produkte sollen der Vermittlung von Musik dienen. Musik assoziiert schon das Logo: die Lettern des Canton Schriftzuges führen «crescendo» von «piano» bis zu «forte fortissimo». Dieses Logo steht im Mittelpunkt vieler Canton Auftritte, seine Grundform wird dabei erweitert zum «Thema mit Variationen», das vom Designer immer wieder neu bearbeitet werden kann. Das Layout ist magazinhaft lebendig, bezieht viele Formen von Photographie und Illustration ein. Diese Vielfalt wird duch eine sehr einheitliche Typographie zusammengehalten. Nur eine Schrift, die Futura, kommt zur Anwendung.

Christof Gassner, Grafik Design, Francfort-sur-le-Main, RFA

Au centre de Canton Communication, on trouve la musique. C'est que les produits Canton servent les intérêts de l'écoute musicale. La musique est déjà associée au logo en ce que les lettres de Canton vont crescendo de piano jusqu'à forte fortissimo. Ce logo est la vedette de nombreuses manifestations publiques de Canton sous forme de variations sur la forme de base au sens d'un thème musical à variations que le designer peut reprendre à tout instant. La mise en pages, qui a la vivacité du magazine, fait appel à nombre de formes photographiques et illustratives dont la multiplicité est tenue en échec par un typo homogène. Un seul caractère, le Futura, est employé.

DESIGN FIRM:
CHRISTOF GASSNER

ART DIRECTOR:
CHRISTOF GASSNER

DESIGNER:
CHRISTOF GASSNER

PHOTOGRAPHER:
ULFERT BECKERT

COPYWRITER:
DIETER SKERUTSCH

CLIENT:
CANTON ELEKTRONIK

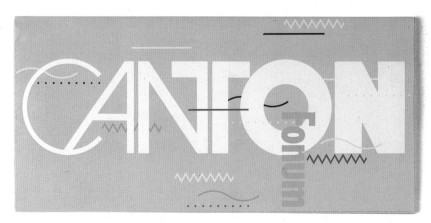

■The typographical logo designed in various type sizes is the focal point of all this company's information and advertising literature, as shown here in the series of brochures giving information on the technical aspects of sound reproduction. Remarkable is the lighthearted way of employing the typography.

■Das mit verschiedenen Schriftgraden gestaltete typographische Logo steht im Mittelpunkt sämtlichen Informations- und Werbematerials, wie bei der hier gezeigten Prospektreihe mit Informationen über die technischen Aspekte der Tonwiedergabe. Bemerkenswert ist der spielerische Umgang mit der Typographie.

■Le logo exécuté en différentes forces de corps est au centre de tout le matériel destiné à l'information et à la publicité, comme on le voit par cet exemple de prospectus dont la série complète dispense des renseignements sur les aspects techniques de la reproduction sonore. Ce qui est remarquable, c'est la légèreté d'emploi de la typo.

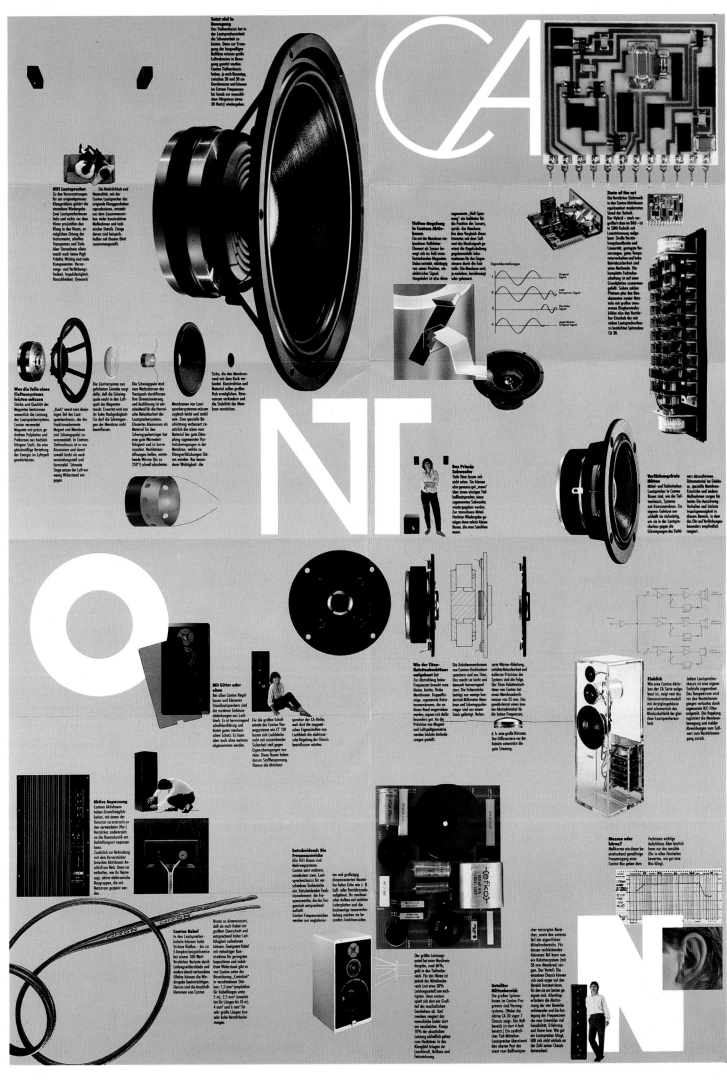

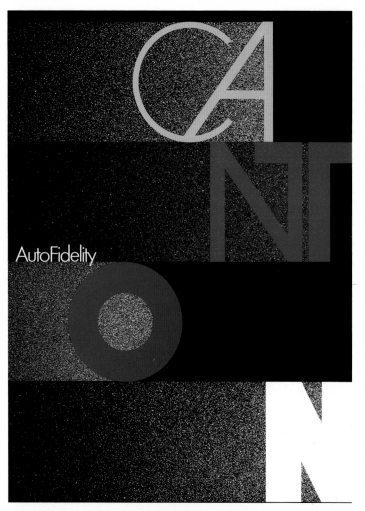

AutoFidelity

■ The many and varied ways the logo can be interpreted are evident, as shown here by its use on various objects including the products themselves; it also appeals to target groups with many different musical interests.

■ Das breite Spektrum der Interpretationsmöglichkeiten des Logos wird anhand seiner Anwendung auf verschiedenen Gegenständen, einschliesslich der Produkte selbst, und für verschiedene musikalische Zielgruppen deutlich.

■ Le large spectre des possibilités d'interprétation du logo ressort clairement de son application à divers objets, y compris les produits eux-mêmes, et à différents groupes ciblés du monde de la musique.

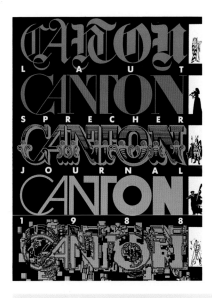

DESIGN FIRM:
CHRISTOF GASSNER

ART DIRECTOR:
CHRISTOF GASSNER

DESIGNER:
CHRISTOF GASSNER

PHOTOGRAPHER:
ULFERT BECKERT

COPYWRITER:
DIETER SKERUTSCH

CLIENT:
CANTON ELEKTRONIK.

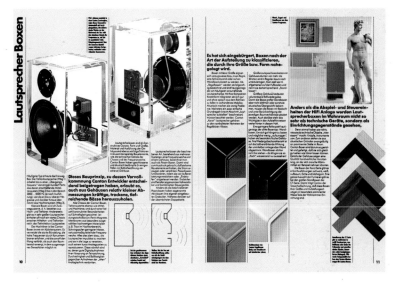

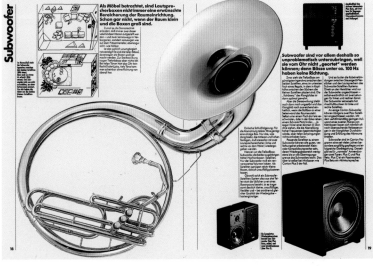

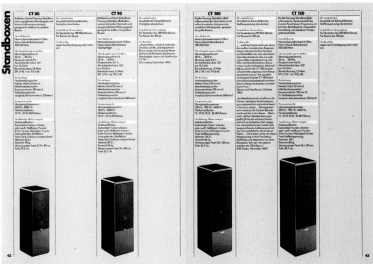

Patrick Shea, Director of Marketing Communications, Caremark Inc., Lincolnshire, IL/USA
Caremark Homecare was founded in 1979 as Home Healthcare of America. A new business at the time, Caremark introduced the idea of home infusion therapy to the health care industry. Our philosophy is to significantly improve a patient's quality of life by providing superior healthcare services in the home. The hand was chosen to symbolize the personal care, high quality and attention provided by Caremark. The various symbols that appear in the hand represent the divisions that provide the services, i.e. nursing, pharmacy, etc. Caremark has recently changed its identity to a wordmark. This change is a reflection of alterations to the corporate structure and the long term objectives of the corporation.

Patrick Shea, Director of Marketing Communications, Caremark Inc., Lincolnshire, IL/USA
Caremark Homecare wurde 1979 als Home Healthcare of America gegründet. Wir kamen mit einer zu jener Zeit neuen Art der medizinischen Versorgung auf den Markt: Der Pflege zu Hause. Unser Hauptanliegen ist es, durch einen erstklassigen medizinischen Hausdienst die Lebensqualität des Patienten zu verbessern. Die Hand ist das Symbol für die persönliche Fürsorge und Zuwendung durch Caremark. Die verschiedenen Symbole, die zusammen mit der Hand gezeigt werden, stehen für verschiedene Abteilungen z.B. Pflege, Medikamente etc. Vor kurzem hat Caremark das Symbol durch eine Wortmarke ersetzt. Dies steht im Zusammenhang mit Änderungen in der Firmenstruktur und langfristigen Zielsetzungen.

Patrick Shea, directeur des communications de marketing, Caremark Inc., Lincolnshire, IL/USA
Caremark Homecare a vu le jour en 1979 sous la raison sociale de Home Healthcare of America. Incarnant une idée neuve à l'époque, l'entreprise entendait couvrir les besoins des soins de santé à domicile. Caremark a pour philosophie d'aider le patient à améliorer sensiblement sa qualité de vie en lui fournissant à domicile des soins de santé de très grand niveau. La main a été choisie pour incarner la personnalisation des soins et la sollicitude vouée aux malades. Les divers symboles apparaissant dans cette main représentent les différents services. Caremark a récemment changé d'identité en adoptant une marque verbale. Ce changement reflète des modifications intervenues dans la structure de la société.

Robert Miles Runyan, Robert Miles Runyan & Associates, Playa Del Rey, CA/USA
Caremark presented challenges to the design team: The company needed an overall "umbrella" symbol and nomenclature that also could be adapted to a company-wide system that could differentiate its three, primary operating divisions – Data Systems, America's Pharmacy, and Home Health Care. The assignment was to create an identity system that underscored the company's primary product - services to the healthcare industry. It should be a system that immediately communicated a "caring attitude" towards its customers while at the same time communicate organization, diversity, and personal service. We designed a simple human hand symbol to communicate the caring attributes of the company with stylized symbols for each division, each reversed out of the hand concept.

Robert Miles Runyan, Robert Miles Runyan & Associates, Playa Del Rey, CA/USA
Die Arbeit für Caremark bedeutete eine Herausforderung für das Team: Die Firma benötigte ein allgemeingültiges Symbol und eine Nomenklatur, die firmenumfassend angewendet werden könnten und doch die drei Hauptbetriebe - Data Systems, America's Pharmacy und Heimpflege - voneinander unterscheiden würden. Es musste ein Erscheinungsbild gefunden werden, das die wichtigste Tätigkeit der Firma auf einen Nenner bringt: Dienstleistungen im Gesundheitswesen. Dem Kunden sollte auf Anhieb klar sein, dass es hier um «Pflege» geht. Gleichzeitig sollten Organisation, Vielfalt und persönlicher Service ersichtlich werden. Die Hand schien uns als Symbol geeignet, um den Aspekt der Pflege zu kennzeichnen. Stilisierte Symbole für die verschiedenen Abteilungen werden mit diesem Hand-Symbol kombiniert.

Robert Miles Runyan, Robert Miles Runyan & Associates, Playa Del Rey, CA/USA
La tâche à mener à bien pour le compte de Caremark a constitué un véritable défi pour l'équipe de design: l'entreprise avait besoin d'un symbole global et d'une nomenclature adaptable à tous les secteurs de l'entreprise et distinguant pourtant les trois divisions principales: Data Systems, Home Health Care ou les produits de santé pour la famille. L'image à créer devait fournir le dénominateur commun de ces activités, les services de santé. Il devait en ressortir pour le consommateur l'idée d'un souci réel pour son bien-être. En outre, l'accent serait mis sur l'organisation, la diversité et la personnalisation de ces services. Nous avons conçu un symbole simple fait d'une main pour exprimer la sollicitude pour la santé. Des symboles stylisés font référence aux diverses divisions à partir du symbole central de la main.

■The original logo – here in red with the cross – of this company active in health care, was modified to adapt to a company-wide system that could differentiate its three primary operating divisions. America's Pharmacy is symbolized by the yellow hand with the mortar, Home Health Care is symbolized by the blue hand with the house, and Data Systems by the green hand with the computer chip. These variants distinguish the notepaper, printed matter, and business stationery as well as the utensils and medicines, vehicles, buildings, etc.

■Das ursprüngliche Logo – hier in Rot mit dem Kreuz – dieses im Gesundheitswesen tätigen Unternehmens wurde für die verschiedenen Bereiche der Unternehmenstätigkeit abgewandelt. Der pharmazeutische Bereich wird durch die gelbe Hand mit dem Mörser symbolisiert, der Heimpflegedienst für Kranke durch die blaue Hand mit dem Haus, der Daten-Service durch die grüne Hand mit dem Computerchip. Diese Varianten kennzeichnen Briefpapier, Drucksachen und Geschäftspapiere ebenso wie Geschirr und Heilmittel, Fahrzeuge, Gebäude etc.

■Le logo original (que l'on voit ici en rouge, avec la croix) de cette entreprise active dans le domaine de la santé a subi différentes adaptations en fonction des secteurs d'activité. Le secteur pharmaceutique est symbolisé par la main jaune et le mortier, le service des soins à domicile par la main bleue et la maison, le service informatique par la main verte et la puce électronique. On retrouve ces variantes sur les en-têtes de lettres, les imprimés et les formulaires commerciaux aussi bien que sur la vaisselle, les médicaments, les véhicules, les bâtiments.

DESIGN FIRM:
ROBERT MILES RUNYAN
& ASSOCIATES

ART DIRECTOR:
JIM BERTÉ

DESIGNER:
VANIG TORIKIAN

CLIENT:
CAREMARK, INC.

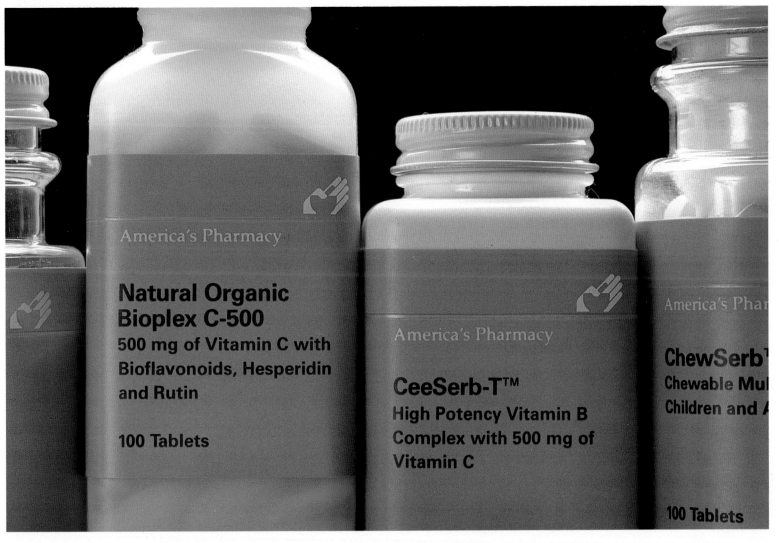

Natural Organic
Bioplex C-500
500 mg of Vitamin C with
Bioflavonoids, Hesperidin
and Rutin

100 Tablets

America's Pharmacy

CeeSerb-T™
High Potency Vitamin B
Complex with 500 mg of
Vitamin C

ChewSerb
Chewable Mul
Children and

100 Tablets

4.96
4.88
3.25

elf Snack

elf Libre Service

4.40 m

elf Snack

Automat 24/24

Philippe Renaudeau d'Arc, Service MCP, Société ELF France, Paris, France

Since the creation of its network in 1967, ELF has had to adapt to a shifting and competitive marketplace. In an attempt to satisfy the needs of the customer, who was no longer defined solely as a car-driving consumer, the company diversified its service offering. This led to a multiplicity of brands which diluted ELF's strong image. A re-vitalization was needed to communicate the strength of ELF Aquitaine to a younger and more dynamic French consumer. Research revealed that a functional, technological and consumer-driven approach to design was needed. By improving overall visibility to passing traffic, streamlining transactions and clearly organizing all signage, ELF could capture a greater marketshare.

Landor Associates Europe

The Landor solution to protect and enhance the ELF Brand Identity encompasses several key elements: The ELF "Flash", a new brand mark, is the endorsement of all services to communicate a commitment to the customer. In the retail environment, the food and automotive categories have been segmented, and a revised site layout now makes access and exit easier. These changes address the customer's needs by presenting him an image of efficiency and convenience. Also, new gasoline pumps, integrated into the island architecture, allow for automated debit card transactions and reinforce the concepts of technology and innovation. To reduce visual clutter and provide a level of dynamism, a carefully controlled and integrated promotional system was developed. In combination with crisp architecture, colors, materials, and lighting schemes, this reinforces ELF's position as an industry leader and a premier French company.

Philippe Renaudeau d'Arc, Service MCP, Société ELF France, Paris, France

Seit der Gründung des Tankstellennetzes 1967 musste ELF sich einem veränderten und härter umkämpften Markt anpassen. Um den Bedürfnissen des Kunden gerecht zu werden, die sich nicht mehr nur auf das Auto beziehen, hat ELF die Dienstleistungen ausgebaut. Eine Auffrischung war nötig, um einen starken Auftritt gegenüber dem jüngeren, dynamischeren französischen Publikum zu haben. Umfragen zeigten, dass ein funktionelles, technologisches, auf den Konsumenten ausgerichtetes Design gefragt ist. Durch allgemeine Verbesserung der Sichtbarkeit für den fahrenden Verkehr, eine Straffung der Abwicklung und klare Anordnung der Beschilderung konnte ELF einen grösseren Marktanteil erobern.

Landor Associates Europa

Landors Lösung zum Schutz und zur Stärkung der Markenidentität von ELF umfasst mehrere Schlüsselelemente: Der ELF-«Pfeil» steht für alle Dienstleistungen. Im Tankstellenareal wurde für leichte Zufahrt und Ausfahrt gesorgt. Diese Änderungen entsprechen den Bedürfnissen des Kunden und signalisieren Leistungsfähigkeit und Bequemlichkeit. Ausserdem wurden neue Tanksäulen für Kreditkarten-Service in die Anlage integriert, womit das Konzept von Technologie und Innovation gestärkt wird. Um Überflüssiges zu vermeiden und Dynamik auszustrahlen, wurde ein sorgsam kontrolliertes Promotionssystem entwickelt. Für die Mitarbeiter von ELF wurden neue Uniformen entworfen, die sie motivieren und gleichzeitig einen besseren Service signalisieren sollen. Zusammen mit frischer Architektur, Farben, Materialien und Beleuchtungssystemen wird ELF als französisches Unternehmen dargestellt und seine führende Stellung in der Industrie unterstrichen.

Philippe Renaudeau d'Arc, Service MCP, Société ELF France, Paris, France

Cherchant à satisfaire pleinement les besoins des consommateurs, qui vont désormais au-delà de ce qu'exige leur véhicule, ELF a diversifié ses services. Il en est résulté une multiplicité de marques qui ont quelque peu dilué l'image forte d'ELF. Un programme de revitalisation s'est imposé pour transmettre la puissance d'ELF Aquitaine à des consommateurs français plus jeunes, plus dynamiques. Les enquêtes ont démontré qu'il y fallait une approche du design à la fois fonctionnelle, technologique et orientée vers le consommateur. En améliorant la visibilité depuis la route, en rationalisant les transactions et en organisant clairement la signalisation, ELF a pu conquérir une part plus importante du marché.

Landor Associates Europe

La solution pour protéger et renforcer l'identité de la marque ELF comprend plusieurs éléments-clefs: le «flash» ELF, une nouvelle image de la marque, incarne l'engagement de tous les services au bénéfice du consommateur. Au sein de la vente au détail, les activités de restauration ont été séparées des activités centrées sur l'automobile, et l'aménagement rationalisé des sites en facilite l'accès et la sortie. Ces transformations signalent les avantages d'efficacité et de confort. Les nouvelles pompes à essence intégrées à l'architecture des îlots permettent la distribution à crédit et incarnent une technologie novatrice. Afin de réduire l'encombrement visuel et d'assurer un niveau visible de dynamisme, un système de promotion soigneusement étudié et intégré a été mis au point. En combinaison avec l'architecture, les couleurs, les matériaux et les systèmes d'éclairage de choc, cette conception du design renforce la position ELF en tant que leader industriel et première compagnie française.

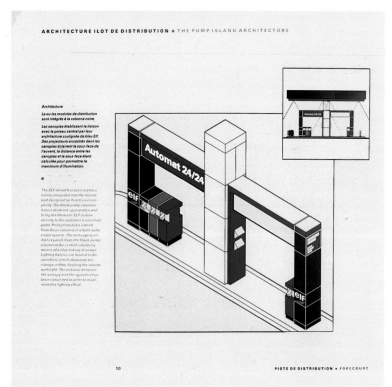

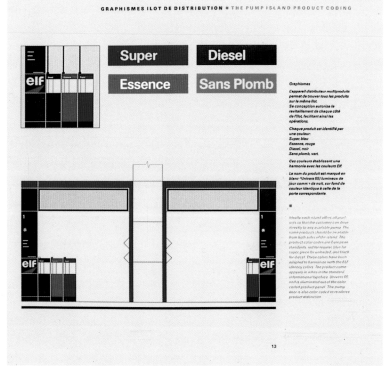

DESIGN FIRM:
Landor Associates

ART DIRECTORS:
*Claude Salzberger/
Jacqueline Palmer*

PROJECT DIRECTORS:
*Claude Salzberger/
Jacqueline Palmer*

DESIGNERS:
*Bobbi Long/
Dale Hoover/
Paul Siegel*

PHOTOGRAPHER:
Christian Délu

CLIENT:
Société ELF

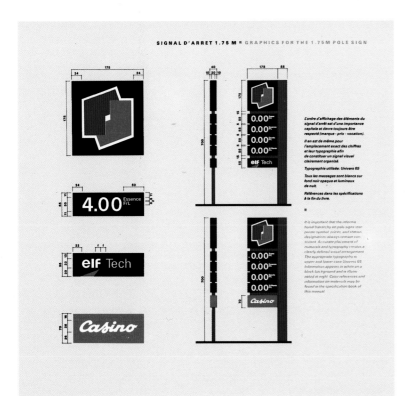

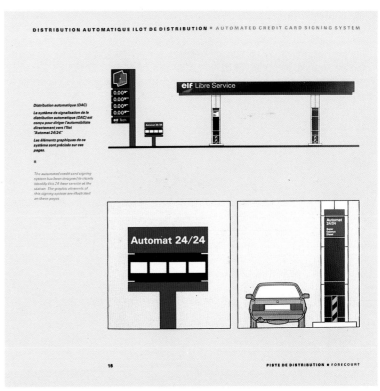

■Pages from the standard manual for the new Corporate Identity program – that extends right through to the design of the entire filling-station area. Not only the changing demands of filling-station customers, but also growing competition by service stations of department stores gave rise to this new C.I. program.

■Seiten aus dem Standard Manual für das neue Corporate-Identity-Programm, das sich auch auf die Gestaltung des gesamten Tankstellenareals bezieht. Nicht nur die Wandlung der Ansprüche der Tankstellenkunden, auch die wachsende Konkurrenz durch Service-Stationen von Kaufhäusern waren Anlass zu diesem neuen C.I. Programm.

■Pages tirées du guide standard des procédures d'application du nouveau programme d'identité institutionelle qui englobe également l'aménagement de toute la surface bâtie des stations-service. Les besoins nouveaux de la clientèle et la concurrence des centres commerciaux ont motivé l'élaboration de la nouvelle image.

■The red triangle can be varied in shape according to its use as a symbol for roads or as a direction arrow, as is shown clearly by the example of the carwash and garage. The concept and coloring of the buildings, facilities, and signboards are in keeping with the compact, clear style of the typography.

■Das in seiner Form variable rote Dreieck wird je nach Einsatz zum Symbol für die Strasse oder zu einem Hinweispfeil, wie hier z.B. anhand der Waschanlage und der Werkstattkennzeichnung deutlich wird. Die Konzeption und Farbgebung der Gebäude, Anlagen und Schilder entspricht dem kompakten, klaren Stil der Typographie.

■Le triangle rouge de forme variable qui caractérise le logo symbolise suivant l'emploi qu'on en fait la route ou une simple direction, par exemple pour le lavage des voitures et l'atelier de réparation. La conception et les couleurs des bâtiments, installations et panneaux correspondent au style clair et compact de la typo.

Bruce Lundvall, General Manager, East Coast, Capital Records, Inc., New York, NY/USA
Manhattan Records was formed in July 1984. We needed a name, a logo type, and a label that would convey the image of a new label based in New York City involved with quality artists and sophisticated music. The plan for the label is that it would grow to be more than a "boutique" company. The idea of the Mondrian design was adopted from his "Broadway Boogie Woogie" painting which stands as the most famous painting on the subject of New York City. Art Director Paula Scher cleared the adoption of the design with the Museum of Modern Art. The design had tremendous impact and radio stations, retailers, and the press commented most favorably on the label. It also was an attraction to recording artists who commented on the creative and definitive graphic approach of our label.

Bruce Lundvall, General Manager, East Coast, Capitol Records, Inc., New York, NY/USA
Manhattan Records wurde im Juli 1984 gegründet. Wir brauchten einen Namen, ein Logo und ein Label-Design passend zum Image einer neuen Plattenfirma mit Sitz in New York, die sich mit guten Musikern und anspruchsvoller Musik befasst. Geplant war ein Label, das über ein «Boutique-Label» hinauswachsen sollte. Die Design-Idee basiert auf Mondrians «Broadway Boogie Woogie», dem berühmtesten Bild zum Thema New York City. Art Direktorin Paula Scher holte die Erlaubnis für die Anpassung des Designs beim Museum of Modern Art ein. Der Erfolg des Designs war enorm; Radiostationen, der Einzelhandel und die Presse äusserten sich ausgesprochen positiv. Darüber hinaus gefiel es auch den Musikern, die sich von der kreativen und prägnanten graphischen Gestaltung begeistert zeigten.

Bruce Lundvall, directeur général pour la côte est, Capital Records, Inc., New York, NY/USA
Manhattan Records a été constitué en juillet 1984. Nous avions besoin d'une raison sociale, d'un logo et d'un label incarnant l'image d'une nouvelle marque new-yorkaise représentative d'une musique de grande qualité et d'artistes de premier plan. L'idée était de créer un label incorporant l'expansion future de la société par-delà sa conception «boutiques» originale. Le design s'inspire du «Broadway Boogie Woogie», la célèbre peinture de Mondrian. La directrice artistique, Paula Scher, procura l'autorisation du Musée d'art moderne pour l'adaptation au plan du design. Le label ainsi réalisé a eu un impact énorme, et les chaînes de radio, les détaillants et la presse l'ont commenté en des termes extrêmement favorables. Même les musiciens ont adopté d'emblée ce label pour son caractère créatif et définitif.

Paula Scher, Koppel & Scher, New York, NY/USA
Manhattan Records was founded in 1984 as Capitol Records' East Coast label. With regard to the music and the label name, a Corporate Identity design was requested that would reflect the spirit of New York City. The original design for the Manhattan Records' logo was based on Mondrian's famous painting "Broadway Boogie Woogie" which not only made reference to New York City, but to music as well. The Mondrian colors added distinction to the label and differentiated it from other record companies and the grid-like blocks with the Futura represented the structure of Manhattan. After the merger of EMI Records with Manhattan Records in 1987, the 4-color identity program was dropped for cost reasons. The colors were changed to a New York taxi cab yellow and black and Mondrian was lost.

Paula Scher, Koppel & Scher, New York, NY/USA
Manhattan Records wurde 1984 von Capitol Records als Ostküsten-Label gegründet. Der Musik und dem Namen Manhattan entsprechend, sollte das Corporate-Identity-Design den Geist der Stadt New York widerspiegeln. Das ursprüngliche Design basiert auf Mondrians Bild «Broadway Boogie Woogie», eine ideale Lösung, weil es sich nicht nur auf New York, sondern auch auf Musik bezieht. Mondrians Farben gaben dem Label einen speziellen Charakter, so dass es sich von anderen Firmen eindeutig unterschied; das Schema der Linien und die Futura implizieren das Strassennetz Manhattans. Nach der Übernahme dieser Schallplattenmarke durch EMI im Jahre 1987 wurde aus Kostengründen auf den Vierfarbendruck verzichtet. Mondrian ging verloren, übrig blieb ein gelb-schwarzer New-York-Taxi-Look.

Paula Scher, Koppel & Scher, New York, NY/USA
Manhattan Records a été fondé en 1984 pour porter les couleurs de Capital Records sur la côte Est des Etats-Unis. Tant au point de vue de la musique qu'à celui de la marque, l'image institutionnelle devait refléter le genius loci new-yorkais. Le projet de départ du logo s'inspirait de la célèbre peinture de Mondrian «Broadway Boogie Woogie», qui faisait référence à la ville de New York aussi bien qu'à la musique. Les couleurs de Mondrian conféraient au logo un cachet de distinction en le singularisant par rapport à d'autres producteurs de disques; le quadrillage des blocs et le Futura évoquaient la structure de Manhattan. Au lendemain de la fusion d'EMI Records avec Manhattan Records en 1987, les couleurs ont été remplacées par le jaune et noir caractéristique des taxis new-yorkais, et l'effet Mondrian s'est perdu.

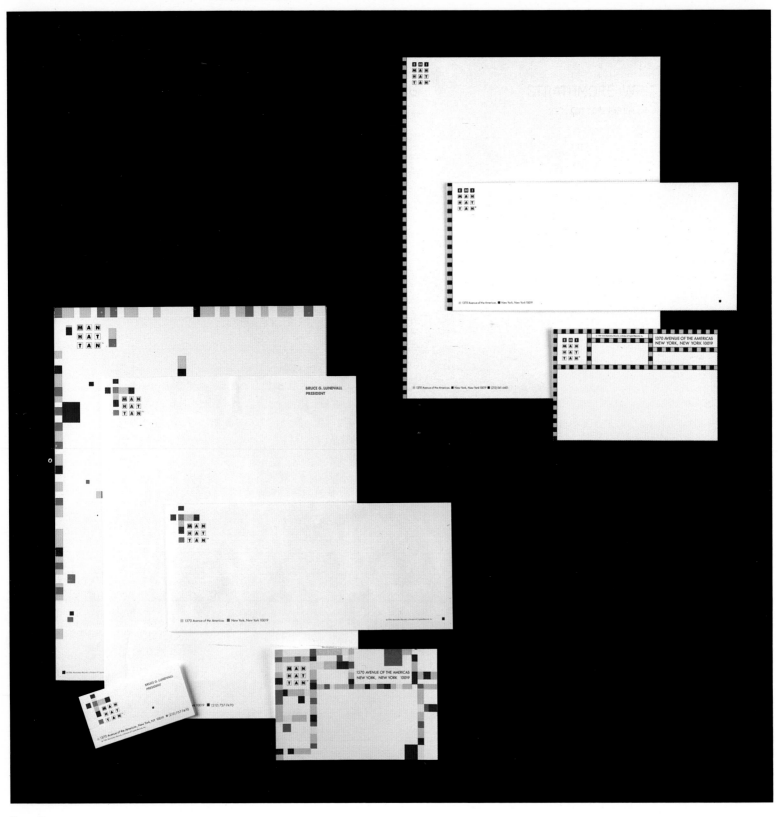

DESIGN FIRM:
KOPPEL & SCHER

ART DIRECTOR:
PAULA SCHER

DESIGNER:
PAULA SCHER

CLIENT:
EMI/MANHATTAN RECORDS

■ The logo for Manhattan Records was based on Piet Mondrian's picture "Broadway Boogie Woogie" and was originally translated in typical Mondrian colors. After the takeover by EMI the combination of black and yellow was adopted for reasons of economy, whereby the play on New York's road network was kept. However, Mondrian and the connection to music got lost on the way.

■ Das auf Piet Mondrians Bild »Broadway Boogie Woogie« basierende Logo für Manhattan Records wurde ursprünglich in den typischen Mondrian-Farben umgesetzt. Nach der Übernahme durch EMI ging man aus Kostengründen zu einer Schwarz-Gelb-Kombination über. Die Anspielung auf New Yorks Strassennetz blieb erhalten, Mondrian und der Bezug zur Musik jedoch gingen verloren.

■ Le logo de Manhattan Records inspiré du tableau de Mondrian, «Broadway Boogie Woogie», a d'abord été doté des couleurs originales du peintre. Après la reprise par EMI, ces couleurs coûteuses ont été remplacées par une combinaison de noir et de jaune. Résultat: la référence au réseau routier new-yorkais est intacte, mais Mondrian et le thème de la musique ont disparu de la scène.

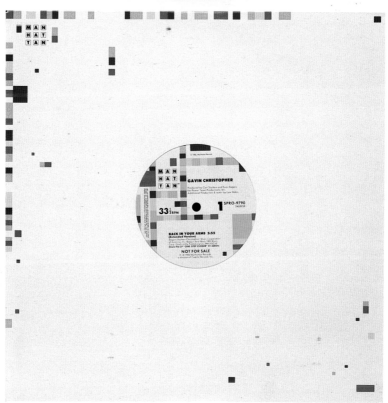

ESPRIT

Doug Tompkins, Owner and Creative Director, Esprit, San Francisco, CA/USA

Visual presentation of the product, or merchandise display as it is often called, ranks first among the other aspects of context such as image, advertising, packaging, graphics, etc. The way we view it, visual display is a form of customer service. Today, consumers generally don't have time to do a thorough, time-consuming search in the marketplace to locate exactly what they want. They need a stimulus, a suggestion, a direction. Good visual display performs this type of service. It sparks an idea. It reminds us of what we may need, and it creates needs by inducing a desirability for a product.

The visual display style that Esprit has developed over the years is one of simplicity in idea, but with craftsmanship in execution. We use the techniques of graphic design and architecture and apply it to merchandise display. Axis, datum, hierarchy, scale, perspective, and order are all the working components of our display techniques. We allow our visual display artists to spend only 5 cents on props, or in other words, nothing, to supplement display. We use only the product and parts and pieces of fixturing or store design such as chairs, boxes, tables to make a display. This seems limiting, but over time proves an advantage as it focuses attention on the product and creates an environment of creativity by the use of a limited palette; it also defines certain parameters to stay within, which results in a distinctive display style.

Doug Tompkins, Besitzer und Kreativdirektor, Esprit, San Francisco, CA/USA

Die visuelle Präsentation der Ware, also das Display, wie man häufig sagt, steht an erster Stelle vor Image, Werbung, Verpackung, Graphik etc. Wir finden, dass die visuelle Präsentation eine Art Dienst am Kunden ist. Heute haben die Verbraucher im allgemeinen keine Zeit, lange und ausgiebig nach dem Gewünschten zu suchen. Sie brauchen eine Stimulierung, eine Anregung, eine Richtung. Gute Warenpräsentation kommt dem entgegen. Sie inspiriert zu Ideen. Sie erinnert an das, was man brauchen könnte, und sie weckt Bedürfnisse, indem sie das angebotene Produkt attraktiv macht.

Der von Esprit über Jahre hinweg entwickelte Stil der Warenpräsentation basiert auf einem einfachen Prinzip und auf sorgfältiger Ausführung. Wir wenden Techniken des Graphik-Designs und der Architektur für das Display an. Achse, Basisdaten, Hierarchie, Massstab, Perspektive und Anordnung spielen eine Rolle. Für Requisiten erlauben wir unseren Dekorateuren nur Ausgaben bis zu 5 Cents, mit anderen Worten also überhaupt kein Zusatzmaterial. Wir setzen für das Display nur die Waren und Teile der Ladeneinrichtung ein: Stühle, Schachteln, Tische. Diese Methode hat sich bewährt, denn so wird die Aufmerksamkeit auf die Ware gelenkt, und gleichzeitig schafft diese sparsame Palette ein kreatives Ambiente. Ausserdem werden dadurch bestimmte Massstäbe gesetzt, die zu einem eigenen Dekorationsstil führen.

Doug Tompkins, propriétaire et directeur créatif, Esprit, San Francisco, CA/USA

La présentation visuelle du produit, soit la P.L.V., l'emporte sur les autres aspects connexes tels que l'image, la publicité, l'emballage, le graphisme, etc. La presentation visuelle à l'étalage est l'une des formes du service à la clientèle. Les consommateurs n'ont aujourd'hui guère le loisir d'effectuer une patiente recherche sur le marché pour situer avec précision ce dont ils ont besoin. Ce qu'il leur faut, c'est un encouragement, une suggestion, une orientation. Une bonne présentation visuelle procure précisément ces incitations. Elle nous rappelle nos besoins et en crée d'autres en suscitant un désir d'achat pour un produit déterminé.

Le style de présentation visuelle qu'Esprit a élaboré au fil des années se caractérise par des idées simples mises en œuvre de manière experte. Nous faisons appel aux techniques de design graphique et de l'architecture et les appliquons à la P.L.V. Les paramètres intégrés dans nos techniques d'exposition sont l'axe, la date, la hiérarchie, l'échelle, la perspective et l'ordre. Nous ne permettons à nos décorateurs aucune dépense en accessoires. Nous n'utilisons que le produit et des éléments ou parties des installations ou du design du magasin en question tels ques des chaises, des boîtes, des tables. L'avantage apparaît évident: la concentration accrue sur le produit et l'environnement créatif né de la palette limitée. En même temps, ce mode de faire rassemble l'image au lieu de la disperser, d'où un style de présentation distinctif.

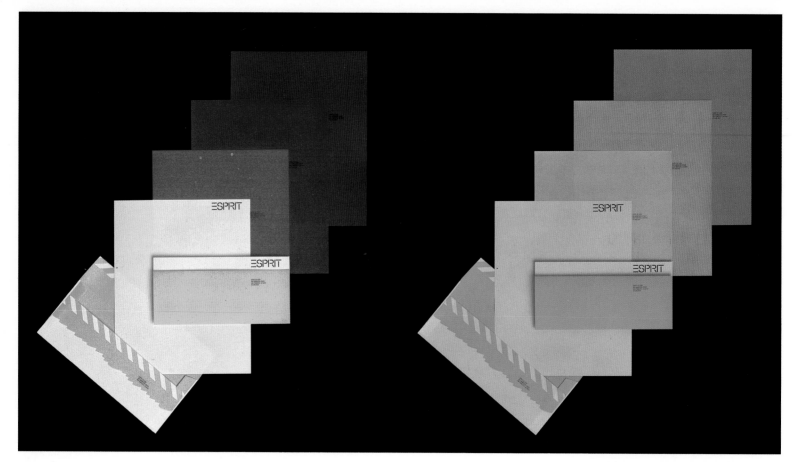

DESIGN FIRM:
ESPRIT GRAPHIC DESIGN

ART DIRECTOR:
TAMOTSU YAGI

DESIGNER:
TAMOTSU YAGI

PHOTOGRAPHERS:
SHARON RISEDORPH
(ARCHITECTURE)
ROBERTO CARRA (STILL LIFE)

CLIENT:
ESPRIT DE CORP.

■ *(Previous page)* Esprit shop in Georgetown. (*This page*) Versions of stationery from 1984 and 1985, and 1988. The original corporate stationery was printed in four bright colors. In 1985 the backs were printed in pastel. The letterheads fold from the bottom. Once folded the address is in place aligned with the logotype. The folding concept with color on the back is derivative of Origami. The beauty of this stationery lies in its simplicity, colored back and ingenious folding. The stationery for 1988 is distinguished by its dark colors and pattern.

■ *(Vorangehende Seite)* Esprit-Laden in Georgetown. *(Diese Seite)* Geschäftspapiervarianten von 1984, 1985 und 1988. Das hier anhand der Versionen für 1984 und 1985 gezeigte Faltkonzept mit der Adresse auf der farbigen Rückseite basiert auf einem Origami-Prinzip. Die leuchtenden Grundfarben wurden 1984 eingeführt, die Pastelltöne 1985, wobei diese auch für andere Projekte angewendet wurden. Einen Kontrast zu der farbenfrohen Mentalität des Unternehmens bildet das Briefpapier für 1988, das durch die dunklen Farben und das Muster geprägt ist.

■ *(Page précédente)* Boutique Esprit de Georgetown. *(Sur cette page)* Variantes des en-têtes commerciaux de 1984, 1985 et 1988. Le modèle pliant des versions de 1984 et de 1985 avec l'adresse au verso en couleur s'inspire de l'art de l'origami. Les couleurs primaires éclatantes datent de 1984, les tons pastel de 1985, avec à chaque fois une application conséquente pour les divers produits de l'époque. Contrastant significativement avec l'esprit haut en couleur de l'entreprise, l'en-tête de 1988 se caractérise par des coloris sombres et un dessin particulier.

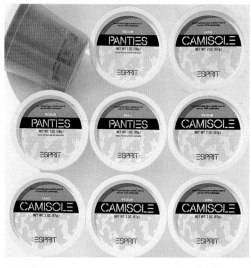 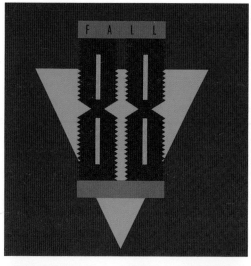 

 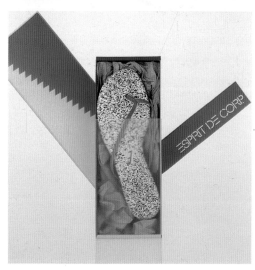 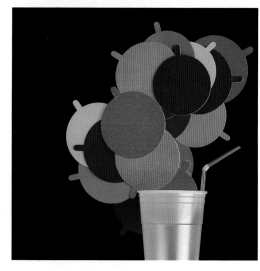

■ *(This page from left to right)* Packaging of panties and camisole – a typical design of the year digits for the catalog; carrier bags designed for the first shop in Los Angeles; shoebox in corrugated plastic with enlarged Zolatone printing; a version of the carrier bags, menus and special gift tokens for *Caffè Esprit*; the E graphic with primary geographic shapes that is used for various promotional material; mailing labels; special box for sandals that allows their pattern to be seen; range of plastic lids for *Caffè Esprit*; *(right page)* typical cash register receipts.

■ *(Diese Seite von links nach rechts)* Verpackung von Slips und Miederwaren, typische Gestaltung der Jahreszahl für Kataloge, für das erste Geschäft in Los Angeles entworfene Tragtaschen, Schuhkarton aus gewelltem Plastik, eine Variante der Tragtaschen, Menu-Karte und spezielle Gutscheine des *Caffè Esprit*, E-Graphik mit Kreis und Dreieck, die für verschiedenes Werbematerial und Versandetiketts verwendet wird, spezieller Karton für Sandalen, Sortiment von Plastikdeckeln für das *Caffè Esprit* und *(rechte Seite)* typische Kassenbons.

■ *(Sur cette page, de g. à dr.)* Emballages de slips et de corsets, style typique du millésime dans les catalogues, cabas conçus pour le premier magasin implanté à Los Angeles, carton à chaussures en plastique ondulé avec son grain ridé agrandi (1984-86), variante des cabas, menu, bons spéciaux du *Caffè Esprit*, E stylisé avec le cercle et le triangle utilisé pour divers matériels publicitaires et pour les étiquettes d'expédition, carton à sandales qui en révèle le dessin, assortiment de couvercles plastiques pour le *Caffè Esprit. (Page de droite)* Bons de caisse.

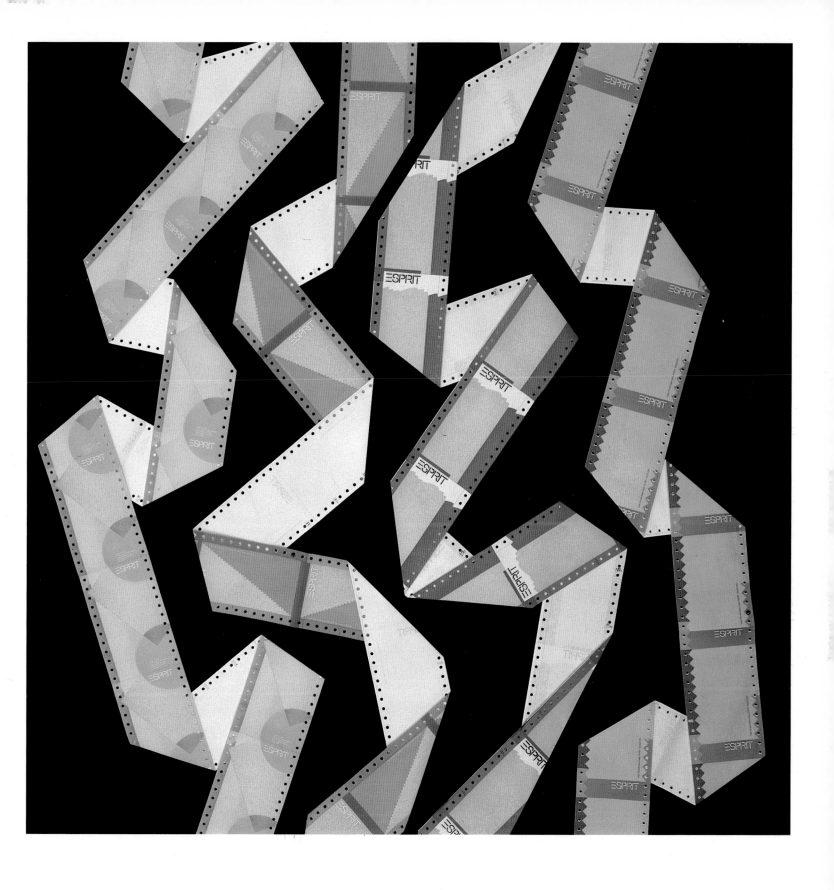

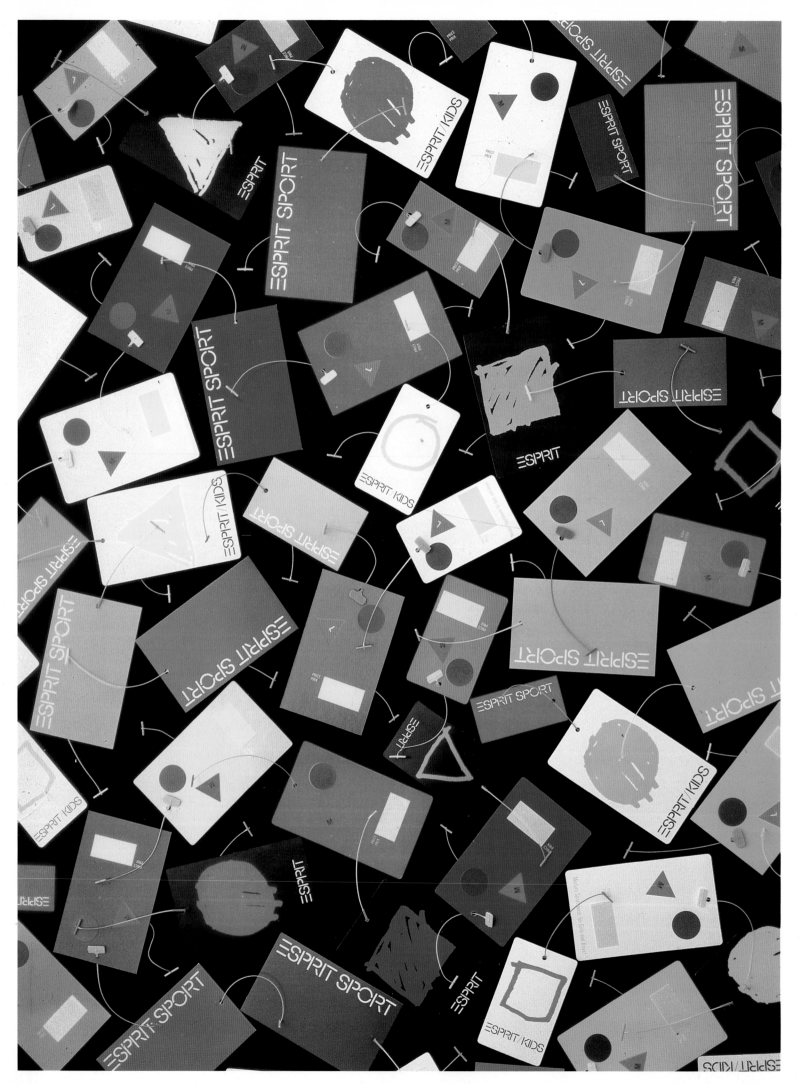

DESIGN FIRM:
ESPRIT GRAPHIC DESIGN

ART DIRECTOR:
TAMOTSU YAGI

DESIGNER:
TAMOTSU YAGI

PHOTOGRAPHER:
ROBERTO CARRA (STILL LIFE)

CLIENT:
ESPRIT DE CORP.

■ Hangtags in the typical Esprit color combinations – an important component of the Esprit look. Corrugated plastic, as shown here for shoe boxes, is one of Esprit's preferred packaging materials.

■ Anhänger in den typischen Esprit-Farbkombinationen, ein wichtiger Bestandteil des Esprit-Looks. Gewelltes Plastik, wie hier für Schuhschachteln verwendet, gehört zu den bevorzugten Packungsmaterialien von Esprit.

■ Etiquettes dans les combinaisons de couleurs typiques d'Esprit – une partie essentielle du look d'Esprit. Le plastique ondulé utilisé ici pour des boîtes à chaussures compte parmi les matériaux vedettes d'Esprit.

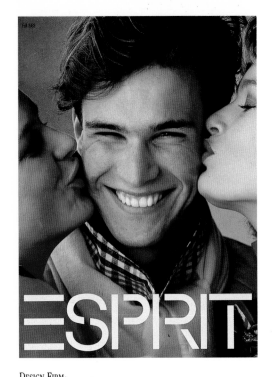

ESPRIT

ESPRIT

MADE IN ITALY

M   E   N

DESIGN FIRM:
Esprit Graphic Design

ART DIRECTOR:
Tamotsu Yagi

DESIGNER:
Tamotsu Yagi

PHOTOGRAPHERS:
Oliviero Toscani (Fashion)
Roberto Carra (Still Life)

CLIENT:
Esprit de Corp.

Getting serious or having fun?

ESPRIT TEENS · KIDS · MINI
FALL 1988

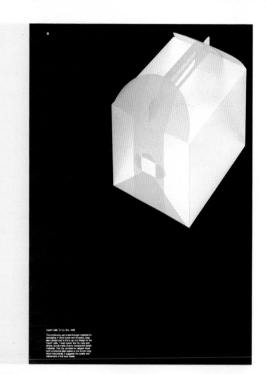

■ Examples showing the
design of catalog pages for
various fashion sectors
such as menswear, jeans,
teens' and children's wear.
The book *Esprit's Graphic
Work* contains information
on the transparent plastic
packaging material used
also for the café carrier
bags, on shoe advertising,
and on a poster mailing for
children.

■ Beispiele der Gestaltung
von Katalogseiten für verschiedene Bereiche wie
Männer-, Jeans- und Teen-
ager/Kinder-Mode. Im Buch
Esprit's Graphic Work wird
u.a. über Packungsmaterial
- durchsichtiges Plastik
auch für Tragkartons der
Cafés -, Schuhwerbung und
ein Plakat-Mailing für Kinder informiert.

■ Exemples de conception
de pages de catalogue pour
divers secteurs – modes
masculines, jeans, modes
pour teen-agers et enfants.
L'ouvrage *Esprit's Graphic
Work* renseigne entre
autres sur les matériaux
d'emballage (le plastique
transparent servant aussi
pour les cartons d'embal-
lage des cafés), la pub pour
les chaussures et une publicité directe sous forme
d'affiches destinées aux
enfants.

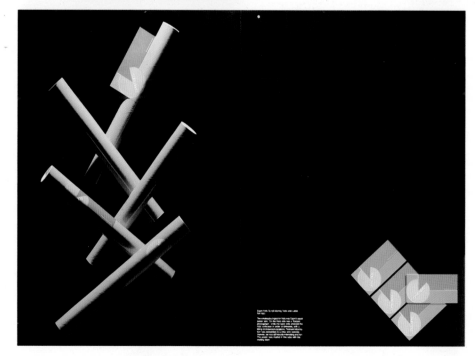

DESIGN FIRM:
ESPRIT GRAPHIC DESIGN

ART DIRECTOR:
TAMOTSU YAGI

DESIGNER:
TAMOTSU YAGI

PHOTOGRAPHERS:
SHARON RISEDORPH
(ARCHITECTURE)

CLIENT:
ESPRIT DE CORP.

■Architectural layout of the *Caffe Esprit* in San Francisco and the interior view of a shop in Dallas that is typical for the simple presentation of the merchandise. Only the interior decor and shop fittings are of significance and there are no decorative items of any kind.

■Architektur des *Caffe Esprit* in San Francisco und Innenansicht eines Ladens in Dallas, der typisch für die schlichte Warenpräsentation ist. Hier wird nur mit der Innenarchitektur und Bestandteilen der Ladeneinrichtungen gearbeitet und auf dekoratives Zubehör verzichtet.

■Architecture du *Caffe Esprit* à San Francisco et vue intérieure d'une boutique de Dallas avec la présentation typique des marchandises. On ne met ici en œuvre que l'architecture intérieure et les installations propres au magasin sans faire appel à des accessoires décoratifs.

Pentagram Design

Pentagram was commissioned to redesign the Corporate Identity of Faber & Faber, the long-established British publishing house. The program was aimed at reinforcing the company's prestige and position, especially in the visually competitive paperback market. Two related ligatures were adopted as logotypes for the book publishing company and the music publishing division, and these have been applied to a full range of stationery items. In addition, promotional material, catalogs, and displays have been designed, and Pentagram has also been appointed to plan and design jackets and covers for over 200 books each year.

There are two sides to the design that brings the writer and reader together. The first is attraction: the image and message of a book or magazine cover, or a newspaper's handling of the front page. The second is sympathy: the ease and interest experienced by the reader once inside. Designing for a book publisher is often not designing at all, but constantly advising on presentation strategy once design principles have been established. Designing for magazines and newspapers is again a matter of advice. With a format, typographical style, policy on photography and illustration well defined, the image and function mature, forming a special bond with regular readers.

Pentagram Design

Pentagram erhielt den Auftrag, das Erscheinungsbild von Faber & Faber, eines alteingesessenen britischen Verlagshauses, neu zu gestalten. Es ging darum, das Prestige und die Marktposition dieser Firma zu verstärken, und zwar speziell auf dem stark umkämpften Taschenbuchmarkt. Als Logo für den Buchverlag und den Musikverlag wurden zwei verwandte Ligaturen gewählt. Diese werden für sämtliche Geschäftspapiere verwendet. Ausserdem hat Pentagram Promotions- und Ausstellungsmaterial sowie Kataloge gestaltet und den Auftrag erhalten, Buchumschläge für über 200 Bücher pro Jahr zu entwerfen.

Es gibt zwei Voraussetzungen, die das Design erfüllen muss, um Autor und Leser zusammenzubringen. Die erste ist Anziehungskraft: Das Bild und die Botschaft eines Buch- oder Zeitschriftenumschlages bzw. die Gestaltung der Titelseite einer Zeitung. Die zweite ist Sympathie: das Behagen und Interesse, das der Leser nach dem Aufschlagen empfindet. Design für einen Buchverleger hat oft gar nichts mit Design zu tun, sondern mit Ratschlägen für die Präsentationsstrategie, sobald die Design-Prinzipien einmal festgelegt sind. Auch bei der Gestaltung von Zeitschriften und Zeitungen geht es nach dem ersten Entwurf vor allem um Beratung.

Pentagram Design

Pentagram Design s'est vu confier le lifting de l'image institutionnelle de Faber & Faber, éditeur britannique au bénéfice d'une longue tradition. Le programme devait renforcer le prestige de l'entreprise et consolider sa position sur le marché, notamment dans le secteur du livre de poche où la concurrence fait rage au plan visuel. Deux ligatures connexes ont été adoptées pour l'édition livres, d'une part, l'édition musicale, de l'autre. On les retrouve sur tous les imprimés maison. Pentagram Design a également élaboré les catalogues Faber & Faber, ainsi que le matériel de promotion et d'exposition.

Le design comporte deux aspects qui rapprochent l'auteur et le lecteur. Le premier, c'est l'attraction: l'image et le message d'un livre ou d'une couverture de magazine, ou la manière dont un quotidien traite la une. Le second, c'est la sympathie: l'intérêt et le plaisir du lecteur une fois qu'il est entré dans le jeu. Travailler pour un éditeur de livres consiste souvent à ne pas faire de design du tout, mais à rappeler continuellement la stratégie de la présentation une fois les principes de design admis. Travailler pour des magazines et journaux signifie à son tour une activité de conseil une fois le format, le style typographique, l'attitude face à la photo et à l'illustration sont bien définis.

DESIGN FIRM:
PENTAGRAM DESIGN LIMITED

ART DIRECTOR:
JOHN MCCONNELL

DESIGNER:
*JOHN MCCONNELL/
KAREN HOUSE*

CLIENT:
FABER & FABER LIMITED

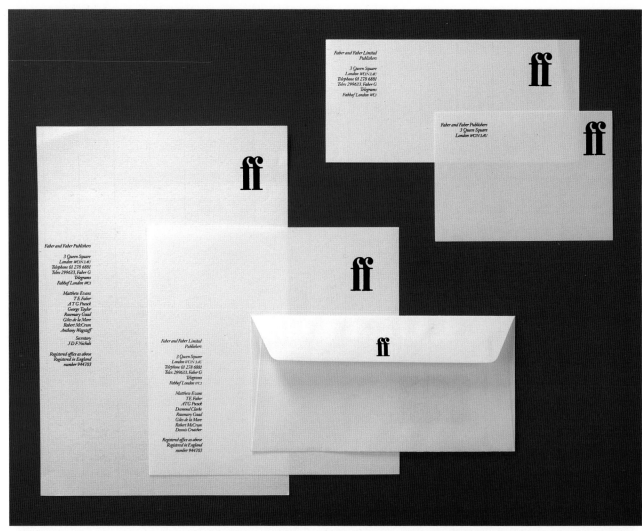

■ The restrained design of the letterheads for this book and music publisher allows the logo to come to the fore. The allusion to the clef is obvious in the version for the music publisher. Also in a more "volatile" sphere, such as book jackets, the logo loses nothing of its effect. In a more playful version, e.g. for wrapping paper and book jackets, the logo becomes a pattern.

■ Die zurückhaltende Gestaltung des Briefpapiers für den Buch- und den Musikverlag lässt das Logo voll zur Geltung kommen. Unübersehbar ist bei der Variante für den Musikverlag die Anspielung auf Notenschlüssel. Auch in einem «bewegteren» Umfeld, wie bei Buchumschlägen, verliert das Logo nichts von seiner Wirkung. In spielerischen Varianten, z.B. beim Packpapier und auch bei Buchumschlägen, wird das Logo zum Muster.

■ La conception discrète de l'en-tête des éditions (livres resp. musique) fait pleinement ressortir le logo, additionné pour les éditions musicales d'une référence aux clefs de sol, etc. Placé dans un environnement plus animé, sur des couvertures par exemple, le logo ne perd rien de son efficacité. Dans ses variantes ludiques, p. ex. sur le papier d'emballage et sur certaines couvertures, le logo se fait dessin décoratif.

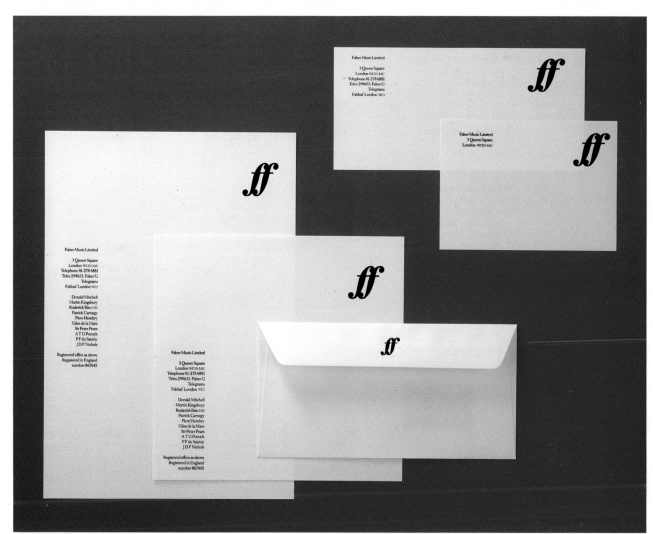

Hartmut Esslinger, frogdesign, Altensteig, (Black Forest) Germany

frogdesign is only 21 years old. It was founded on January 1, 1968. For a long time this date was part of the program - until the young people got too young to remember its significance... frogdesign has over 60 employees. frogdesign sells creativity: "Industrial Design for Money". In 1982 the company was given its current name. Old partners left and the present concept of a free team with a lateral management-structure was initiated. And frogdesign went "global", in 1982 to San Jose, California, and in 1986 to Toyko. frogdesign understands itself as being outside the establishment. The environment is left as free as possible and as disciplined as necessary. frogdesign must be the fondest dream of designers - then we'll be the fondest dream of our clients.

Industrial design is always an original - be it the idea, the model or the finished product. And this is the pivot. It is also the focal point of the frogdesign Corporate Identity. For this reason photography is depicted as original - as a slide from the camera. The motifs are freely selected, the photographer's story becomes the product i.e. "frogdesign". The layout is frugal, reduced to comments. The type is not Helvetica, but Univers condensed italic. A little more stylized, slightly ambivalent - that much more fun. Standard colors are green, red, and dark grey. No black. The logo - a frog - was reduced from an original photograph to black-and-white values and then manually stylized. The frog is the mascot of Altensteig a romantic small town in the Black Forest and home of the frogdesign studios.

Hartmut Esslinger, frogdesign, Altensteig/ Schwarzwald, Deutschland

frogdesign ist 21 Jahre jung – gegründet am 1. Januar 1968. Die Jahreszahl war lange auch Programm - bis die jungen Leute zu jung zum Erinnern wurden...frogdesign hat über 60 Mitarbeiter. frogdesign verkauft Kreativität: «Industrial Design for Money». 1982 wurde dem Unternehmen der heutige Namen gegeben, es schieden alte Partner aus, die heutige Konzeption eines freien Teams mit flacher Management-Struktur wurde angelegt. Und frogdesign ging «global»: 1982 nach San Jose/ Kalifornien sowie 1986 nach Tokio/Japan. frogdesign versteht sich als «nicht-etabliert» – die Umgebung ist so frei wie möglich, aber auch so diszipliniert wie nötig. frogdesign muss der Wunschtraum der Design-Talente sein, dann sind wir auch der Wunschtraum unserer Klienten.

Industrial Design ist immer ein Original: die Idee, das Modell, das fertige Produkt. Und dieses steht im Mittelpunkt. Auch im Mittelpunkt der frogdesign CI. Die Photographie zeigt sich deshalb ebenfalls als Original: als Dia aus der Kamera. Die Motive sind frei, der Photograph macht seine Geschichte zum Produkt bzw. «frogdesign». Das Layout ist sparsam, auf «Kommentare» reduziert. Die Schrift ist nicht Helvetica sondern Univers, condensed, italic. Etwas mehr stilisiert, etwas ambivalent, etwas mehr Fun. Standardfarben sind Grün, Rot und Dunkelgrau - kein Schwarz. Das Logo - ein Frosch - wurde von einem Original-photo auf Schwarz-Weiss-Werte reduziert und dann manuell stilisiert. Der «Frosch» ist das Maskottchen von Altensteig/Schwarzwald.

Hartmut Esslinger, frogdesign, Altensteig, (Forêt Noire), Allemagne

frogdesign était fondée le 1er janvier 1968. Ce millésime a longtemps servi de programme, jusqu'au jour où les jeunes ont été trop jeunes pour se souvenir... frogdesign vend de la créativité, «de l'esthétique industrielle pour de l'argent». La raison sociale date de 1982, année où des associés de longue date se sont retirés et où s'est mise en place la conception actuelle d'une équipe libre sans vraie structure hiérarchique verticale. frogdesign s'est étendu à la planète tout entière: San José en 1982, Tokyo en 1986. frogdesign récuse tout place au sein de l'establishment. Son environnement offre le plus grand degré de liberté possible compatible avec la discipline indispensable. frogdesign doit être le rêve de tout designers talentueux, alors nous serons aussi le rêve de nos clients.

Une création d'esthétique industrielle est toujours un original: l'idée, le modèle, le produit fini. Et c'est ce dernier qui occupe la place centrale. La photo se présente également sous l'aspect d'un original: une diapo sortie de l'appareil. Les motifs sont au choix, le photographe transforme son histoire en produit resp. en «frogdesign». La mise en pages est succincte, restreinte à des «commentaires». Les caractères employés ne proviennent pas de l'Helvetica, mais de l'Univers condensé, italique. Un peu plus stylisé, un peu ambivalent, un peu plus marrant. Couleurs standards: le vert, le rouge, le gris foncé - mais pas le noir. Le logo - une grenouille - a été réduit au noir et blanc à partir d'une photo originale, puis stylisé à la main. La «grenouille» est la mascotte d'Altensteig.

■ The frog is the mascot of the small town of Altensteig in the Black Forest *(above left)* - the seat of frogdesign in Germany. On a self-promotional advertisement it is allowed for once to go crazy *(previous double spread)*, otherwise it appears restrained in green as here on the business stationery and the advertising in which the product design – a robot – is in the foreground.

■ Der Frosch ist das Maskottchen des Städtchens Altensteig im Schwarzwald *(oben, links)*, Firmensitz von frogdesign in Deutschland. In einer speziellen Anzeige darf er sich für einmal austoben *(vorangehende Doppelseite)*, sonst erscheint er zurückhaltend in Grün wie hier auf den Geschäftspapieren und der Eigenwerbung, bei der das Produkt-Design – ein Roboter – im Vordergrund steht.

■ La grenouille est la mascotte d'Altensteig en Forêt-Noire *(en haut, à gauche)* où frogdesign a installé son quartier général. Pour une fois, elle peut s'en donner à cœur joie dans l'autopromotion de la double page précédente; autrement elle apparaît sous un jour plus réservé, en vert comme ici dans des en-têtes et dans l'autopromotion à base d'esthétique industrielle (étude de robot).

 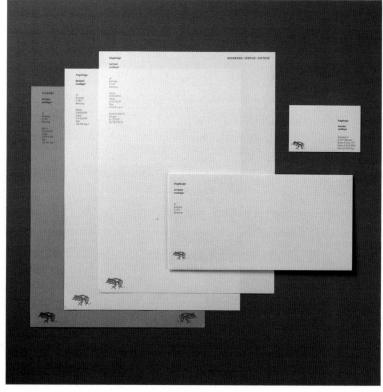

DESIGN FIRM:
FROGDESIGN

DESIGNERS:
HARTMUT ESSLINGER/
URS SCHWERZMANN/
CLEMENT MOK

PHOTOGRAPHERS:
VICTOR GOICO/
HANS HANSEN/
DIETMAR HENNEKA/
MANFRED RIEKER

CLIENT:
FROGDESIGN

Industrial Design for Bodenseewerk: µ–KROS by **frogdesign**, Germany (07453) 2740, California (408) 866–1801, Japan (03) 442–5558 (Photo by Dietmar Henneka)

Klatu barada nikto.

Industrial Design Study: WORKSTATION by frogdesign, Germany 0-7453/7071, California (408) 866-1801, Japan (03) 442-5558 (Photo by Dietmar Henneka)

Divide et impera.

Manfred Rieker fotografiert SONY Fergline von frogdesign, Grenzweg 33, D-7272 Atmostieg, Tel. 0 74 53/80 00, California (408) 3 79-01 32.

Alles frosch!

Dietmar Henneka fotografiert INDUSCO Rollerskate von frogdesign, Grenzweg 33, D-7272 Atmostieg, Tel. 0 74 53/80 00, California (408) 866-1801.

Viva California!

Industrial Design for The Helen Hamlyn Foundation by frogdesign, Germany (074 53) 7071, California (408) 8 66-18 01, Japan (03) 442-55 58 (Photo by V. Goico)

Cad the wave.

■Examples from an advertising campaign which, according to a consistent concept of uniform size and typography, introduces various products developed by frogdesign. The same concept also applies to the concertina brochure.

■Beispiele einer Anzeigenkampagne, die gemäss einem durchgehenden Konzept mit einheitlichem Format und Typographie verschiedene von frogdesign entwickelte Produkte vorstellt. Dasselbe Konzept hat auch für die mehrteiligen Leporello-Prospekte Gültigkeit.

■Exemples tirés d'une campagne d'annonces où divers produits étudiés par forgdesign sont présentés selon une conception homogène, dans un format et une typo identiques. La même conception régit également les prospectus pliés en accordéon.

DESIGN FIRM:
FROGDESIGN

DESIGNERS:
*HARTMUT ESSLINGER/
URS SCHWERZMANN/
CLEMENT MOK*

PHOTOGRAPHERS:
*VICTOR GOICO/
HANS HANSEN/
DIETMAR HENNEKA/
MANFRED RIEKER*

CLIENT:
FROGDESIGN

BREMER
MARZIPANSTOLLEN

ENTENLEBER
TERRINE MIT GRÜNEM PFEFFER
Grashoff
1872

Grashoff
187

PINEAU DES CHARENTES

PELLATION PINEAU DES CHAREN... ...EE SEIT GENERA-
...EN WIRD DIESE SPEZIALITÄT VON ...HN DER CHARENTE
...GESTELLT, FRISCH GEPRESSTER ...AUS DEM GESETZ-
... FESTGELEGTEN ANBAUGEBIET ... WIRD GLEICH NACH
...R ERNTE MIT ABGELAGERTEM C... ...INE ... IN LIMOUSIN-
...ENHOLZFÄSSERN WIRD ER MI... ...NE BIS ZUR REIFE
...PFLEGT. PINEAU DES CHARENTES 2... ...UNT ALS APERITIF
...BER ZUR GÄNSELEBERPASTETE. G... ...DER PINEAU DES
...ARENTES WURDE AUSGEBAUT U... ...VON NORMANDIN
...IER - CHATEAU DE LA PERAUD... ...IERRE, FRANKREICH.

Grashoff
187

...ORTIERT DURCH: GRASHOFF DE... ...EN, 2800 BREMEN.

Grashoff
1872

Jürgen Schmidt, Proprietor, B. Grashoff Nachf., Bremen, Germany

The company was founded in 1892 by Binne Grashoff and has been in the hands of the Schmidt family since 1900. Apart from wine and delikatessen retailing, the company's activities also include wholesale distribution and the production of jams, as well as a bistro restaurant. The reason for the creation of a new Corporate Identity design was the transfer of the firm's premises to a beautiful but less-frequented city location. With the emphasis on offering unmistakable top-quality products under the company's own label and specialty services to bind the clientele to the company, it also became imperative to create an individual, up-to-date image. The result of the design based on the firm's name and its year of founding is a positive company development and an upgrading of the company image.

Jürgen Schmidt, Inhaber, B. Grashoff Nachf., Bremen, Deutschland

Die von Binne Grashoff 1892 gegründete Firma ist seit 1900 im Besitz der Familie Schmidt. Zum Geschäftsbereich gehören ausser dem Einzelhandel mit Weinen und Delikatessen auch der Grosshandel und die Herstellung von Konfitüren sowie ein Bistro-Restaurant. Anlass für die Erstellung des neuen Corporate-Identity-Designs war die Verlegung der Geschäftsräume in eine weniger frequentierte City-Lage, in der es wichtig wurde, eigene, unverwechselbare Produkte von sehr guter Qualität und Dienstleistungen besonderer Art anzubieten, um die Kundschaft an das Geschäft zu binden und um ein individuelles, zeitgemässes Image zu schaffen. Das Ergebnis des auf dem Namen und dem Gründungsjahr basierenden Designs ist eine positive Geschäftsentwicklung und eine Aufwertung des Firmen-Images.

Jürgen Schmidt, Propriétaire, B. Grashoff Nachf., Bremen, Allemagne

L'entreprise fondée en 1892 par Binne Grashoff est depuis 1900 propriété de la famille Schmidt. Elle comprend aujourd'hui une boutique de vins et comestibles, un commerce de gros, une confiturerie et un restaurant-bistrot. C'est le transfert des locaux de vente dans un quartier moins passant de la ville qui a été l'occasion de la création d'une nouvelle image institutionnelle. Il apparaît désormais essentiel de mettre l'accent sur les produits maison de qualité inégalée et les services spécifiques qu'offre l'entreprise soucieuse de fidéliser sa clientèle. En même temps, il s'agissait de créer une image moderne et individualisée. La conception retenue se contente d'utiliser la raison sociale et l'année de fondation. Résultat de cette réalisation institutionnelle: un développement accéléré des affaires et une image publique revalorisée.

Sibylle Haase, Atelier Haase & Knels, Bremen, Germany

All marketing efforts of Grashoff Delikatessen are focused on the name of its founder. We have used this aspect for the design in that we have signed all printed matter with the initials that stem from his pen. Whether on photographs or illustrations, the signature is always a vital component because it means that everything that leaves the shop has his "seal of approval". The uniqueness and value of the products was carried to such extremes by the layout that, for example, with the marmalades almost every brush stroke is made to look different by a special print technique: gourmet art in print. Since enjoyment is only possible without effort, all printed matter should radiate ease and the joy of life. The layout is a combination of illustration and an upper-case typefont for typographic gourmets.

Sibylle Haase, Atelier Haase & Knels, Bremen, Deutschland

Die tragende Person von Grashoff Delikatessen ist der Firmengründer. Wir haben dies für das Design benutzt, indem wir alle Drucksachen mit dem Schriftzug, der aus der Feder kommt, signiert haben. Ob Photos oder Illustrationen eingesetzt werden, immer ist die Signatur wichtiger Bestandteil, denn sie bedeutet, dass alles, was aus dem Laden herausgeht, für gut befunden wurde. Die Einmaligkeit und Wertigkeit der Produkte wurde durch das Layout so auf die Spitze getrieben, dass z.B. bei den Marmeladen fast jeder Pinselstrich durch einen drucktechnischen Eingriff ein anderer ist. Da Genuss nur ohne Anstrengung möglich ist, sollten alle Drucksachen Leichtigkeit und Lebensfreude ausstrahlen. Das Layout ist eine Kombination von Illustration und einer Versalschrift für Typogourmets.

Sibylle Haase, Atelier Haase & Knels, Bremen, Allemagne

La vedette de Grashoff Delikatessen est son fondateur. D'où notre idée de signer tous les imprimés de son nom sorti d'une plume. Qu'il s'agisse de photos ou d'illustrations, la signature trône en bonne place, signifiant que tout ce qui sort de ce magasin a trouvé grâce aux yeux de son propriétaire. La mise en pages accentue encore l'originalité et la valence des produits en assurant p. ex. à la présentation des confitures une extrême variabilité des coups de pinceau par un artifice lors de l'impression – d'où un renforcement de l'idée de l'œuvre d'art gastronomique. Les plaisirs de la table ne se concevant qu'en l'absence de tout effort, tous ces imprimés sont censés communiquer en effet d'apesanteur et une réelle joie de vivre. La mise en pages combine l'illustration et une écriture majuscule de manière à satisfaire les gourmets de la typo.

DESIGN FIRM:
HAASE & KNELS

ART DIRECTOR:
SIBYLLE HAASE

DESIGNER:
SIBYLLE HAASE

ILLUSTRATOR:
KARIN HOLLWEG

CLIENT:
B. GRASHOFF DELIKATESSEN

■ The signature employed as a guarantee for quality, the simple and reduced design, and the coloring chosen for the articles (such as crockery, wine-card, boxes, packaging of foodstuffs, and bottle livery) used in the bistro and in retail are all totally in step with a business that, always conscious of quality and tradition, has moved with the times without rejecting past values.

■ Der Schriftzug, mit dem hier quasi für Qualität gebürgt wird, das einfache, reduzierte Design und die Farbgebung für die im Bistro sowie im Einzelhandel verwendeten Gegenstände und Material wie Geschirr, Weinkarte, Päckchen, Verpackungen von Lebensmitteln und Weinflaschen, entspricht ganz einem qualitäts- und traditionsbewussten Handelshaus, das mit der Zeit gegangen ist, ohne auf die Werte der Vergangenheit zu verzichten.

■ Le sigle garantie de qualité et les couleurs employées se conjuguent à la simplicité d'un design réduit à l'essentiel pour donner expression à l'esprit de tradition et au souci de qualité d'une maison de commerce branchée sur l'esprit du temps, mais désireuse de préserver les valeurs du passé. Image utilisée au bistrot ainsi que sur les matériaux utilisés dans la vente au détail - vaisselle, carte des vins, emballages, conditionnement des aliments etc.

Il Fornaio

Hilary Wolf, Design Director, Il Fornaio, San Francisco, CA/USA

After our logo had recently been updated by another design firm, Michael Mabry was asked in January of 1988 to redesign completely the retail packaging program. We needed an image that could convey our high quality bakery products and also work with the new products and restaurants we were creating. Michael visited our existing restaurant and spent time with the creative forces behind the company. Everyone instantly approved the Bakerman (= il fornaio). Because Il Fornaio has branched out into takeout foods, packaged goods, and restaurants, Michael felt we needed a system encompassing all these areas. His idea to change the basic illustration to represent the other products and services we provide gave way to the additional illustrations of the waiter, the pasta cook, and a bartender.

Hilary Wolf, Design Direktor, Il Fornaio, San Francisco, CA/USA

Nachdem unser Logo kürzlich von einem anderen Design-Studio überarbeitet worden war, baten wir Michael Mabry im Januar 1988 um eine völlige Neugestaltung unseres Verpackungsprogramms. Es sollte der hohen Qualität unserer Backwaren gerecht werden und auch für die geplanten neuen Produkte und Restaurants passen. Michael Mabry besuchte das bereits existierende Restaurant, sprach mit den kreativen Leuten und machte dann Vorschläge. Alle stimmten spontan für den Bäcker (= il fornaio). Michael fand, dass wir ein Konzept brauchten, das für alle Bereiche - neu auch verpackte Lebensmittel, Essen zum Mitnehmen und Restaurants - anwendbar ist. Seine Idee, die ursprüngliche Illustration entsprechend zu variieren, führte zu dem Kellner, dem Pasta-Koch und dem Barmann.

Hilary Wolf, Design Director, Il Fornaio, San Francisco, CA/USA

Après le lifting de notre logo entrepris par une autre société de design, Michael Mabry a été chargé de revoir de fond en comble le programme d'emballage. Il nous fallait une image capable de véhiculer la qualité supérieure de nos produits de boulangerie et de s'accorder aux nouveaux produits et restaurants en voie de création. Tout le monde a adhéré sur-le-champ au symbole du boulanger (=il fornaio). Il Fornaio s'étant diversifié en produits alimentaires à l'emporter, en produits livrés sous emballage et en restaurants, Michael a senti qu'il nous fallait un système englobant tous ces aspects. Son idée de transformer l'illustration de base de manière à représenter les autres produits et services que nous offrons a débouché sur les illustrations du garçon de restaurant, du cuisinier préparant la pasta, du barman.

Michael Mabry, Michael Mabry Design, San Francisco, CA/USA

Il Fornaio had referred to a book "Coffee Houses of Europe", as the inspiration for the interiors of the restaurant. Many of the interiors in this book had an unlikely charm. A mix of Beaux Arts frescos, Neo-Classical columns, Art Deco furniture, Futurist posters, and Bauhaus inspired espresso machines - a veritable smorgsbord of design - could be found in each interior, yet somehow it worked. My goal was to create an identity with the same illogical charm and capture the spirit of Il Fornaio. The primary image became the illustration of the Bakerman. Borrowing the basic form from futurism, and working with rich warm tones associated with bakery products, I created an image and a link to their past. The identity had to translate to packaging, the corporate image, and the restaurant itself.

Michael Mabry, Michael Mabry Design, San Francisco, CA/USA

Das Buch «Kaffeehäuser Europas» hatte laut Il Fornaio als Inspirationsquelle für die Einrichtung des Restaurants gedient. Die Mischung von Freskos, neoklassizistischen Säulen, Art-Deco-Bestuhlung, futuristischen Plakaten und Espresso-Maschinen im Bauhaus-Stil, die unwahrscheinlichsten Zusammenstellungen also bei allen diesen Ausstattungen, hatte einen unglaublichen Charme. Ich wollte einen ähnlich paradoxen Charme erzielen und den Geist von Il Fornaio einfangen. Das erste Bild war der Bäcker. Die Grundform ist eine Anleihe beim Futurismus, die warmen Farbtöne sind bezeichnend für Backwaren. So entstand ein neues Image und eine Verbindung zur Vergangenheit. Verpackungen, das Firmen-Image und das Restaurant selbst mussten in die Überlegungen mit einbezogen werden.

Michael Mabry, Michael Mabry Design, San Francisco, CA/USA

Il Fornaio s'est inspiré de l'ouvrage «Les Cafés d'Europe» pour l'aménagement intérieur du restaurant. Nombre des intérieurs présentés dans ce livre ont un charme inouï. Mélangeant allègrement les fresques des beaux-arts, les colonnes néoclassiques, le mobilier art nouveau, les machines à café style Bauhaus, le méli-mélo décoratif ne manquait pas de charme. J'ai cherché à créer une identité dotée du même charme illogique et à saisir sur le vif l'ambiance du Fornaio. L'image de base, c'est l'illustration du boulanger qui l'a fournie. Empruntant la forme fondamentale au futurisme et mettant en œuvre les tonalités chaudes associées aux produits de boulangerie, j'ai créé une image trait-d'union avec le passé. Cette identité devait être transposable aux emballages, à l'image institutionnelle et au restaurant même.

■In keeping with the name (il fornaio = the baker) this bakery and the restaurant belonging to it (both located in San Francisco) use the baker with a bread shovel as key motif for the new design program. Shown are some examples of bread bags, advertising articles, boxes, menus, and product packaging. The motif is modified in some cases: with a fork instead of the bread shovel for the foodstuffs packaging, with drinks tray or a coffee cup for beverage and dessert menus.

■Dem Namen dieser Bäckerei und des dazugehörigen Restaurants entsprechend (il fornaio = der Bäcker), ist der Bäcker mit der Brotschaufel das zentrale Motiv des neuen Design-Programms. Hier einige Beispiele von Brottüten, Werbeartikeln, Schachteln, Menukarten und Produktverpackungen. Das Motiv erscheint auch abgewandelt: mit einer Gabel statt der Brotschaufel auf den Lebensmittelpackungen, mit Getränke-Tablett oder Kaffeetasse für Getränke- und Dessert-Karten.

■Conformément au nom de cette boulangerie et du restaurant annexe (il fornaio = le boulanger) c'est au boulanger et à sa pelle à enfourner que revient la vedette au sein du nouveau programme de design. On voit ici quelques exemples de sachets à pain, d'articles-cadeaux, de boîtes, de menus et d'emballages produits. Le motif admet des variantes: une fourchette remplace la pelle sur les emballages alimentaires, un plateau de boissons ou une tasse de café décore les cartes de boissons et de desserts.

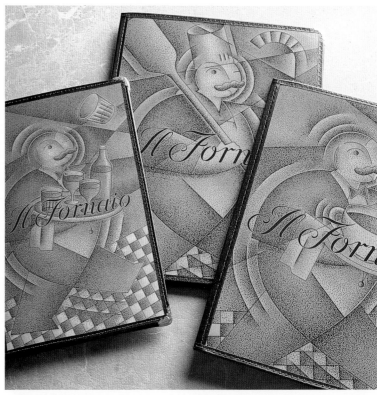

Design Firm:
Michael Mabry Design

Creative Director:
Hilary Wolf

Designer:
Michael Mabry/Margie Chu
Dyer/Kahn, Inc. (Logo)

Illustrator:
Michael Mabry

Photographer:
Monica Lee

Client:
Il Fornaio

ÍPSA

Jun Tashiro, Planning & Development Dept., IPSA Co., Ltd., Tokyo, Japan

We chose the name IPSA, the Latin expression for "you yourself", because our concept is to discover, in collaboration with the customer, a recipe for the sustenance of her natural beauty. Our products must appeal to women who wish to find their own style according to their own ideas and whose wisdom tells them to use the product that best suits their own personal wishes and desires. IPSA wants to give every woman the chance to choose and collect products that appeal to her personal character. The instinct for beauty inherent in every woman is the focal point. The IPSA range of products embraces care and decorative cosmetics, hair-cares and perfumes. In the IPSA boutiques a computer and counsellors are at the disposal of customers for the analysis of their skin type and, on the basis of computer data, a questionnaire and a direct skin analysis, a personal recipe is worked out with the customer. In counselling, importance is placed on information - never is a customer persuaded to buy a product. These aspects - the support of the woman's own personality, her creativity, and her beauty - as well as the expert counselling and a product range that fulfills all demands, is reflected in the Corporate Identity program for IPSA.

Jun Tashiro, Planning & Development Dept. IPSA Co., Ltd., Tokio, Japan

Wir wählten den Namen IPSA, den lateinischen Ausdruck für «sie selbst», denn unser Konzept basiert auf der Idee, zusammen mit unseren Kundinnen ein Rezept für die Unterstützung ihrer natürlichen Schönheit zu finden. Unsere Produkte sollen Frauen ansprechen, die einen eigenen Stil ganz nach ihren eigenen Vorstellungen finden wollen, die sich ein Wissen aneignen, das ihnen erlaubt, die Produkte ganz nach ihren persönlichen Wünschen und Bedürfnissen einzusetzen. Das IPSA-Programm umfasst pflegende und dekorative Kosmetik, Haarpflegemittel und Parfums. In den IPSA-Boutiquen stehen den Kundinnen sowohl ein Computer für die Analyse ihrer Haut als auch Beraterinnen zur Verfügung, die zusammen mit der Kundin auf der Basis der Computerdaten, eines Fragebogens und einer direkten Hautanalyse ein ganz persönliches Rezept erstellen. Wichtig dabei sind Beratung und Information, nie wird die Kundin zum Kauf eines Produktes überredet. Diese Aspekte, die Unterstützung der eigenen Persönlichkeit der Frau, ihrer Kreativität und Schönheit, wissenschaftlich fundierte, fachmännische Beratung und ein Produktprogramm, das allen Ansprüchen gerecht wird, werden im Corporate-Identity-Programm für IPSA reflektiert.

Jun Tashiro, département de planification et de développement, IPSA Co., Ltd., Tokyo, Japon

Nous avons opté pour le mot latin IPSA, qui veut dire «elle-même», parce que notre conception s'inspirait de la recherche, en accord avec les femmes, d'une recette magnifiant leur beauté naturelle. Nos produits sont destinés aux femmes désireuses de se créer un style personnel et d'acquérir le savoir nécessaire pour utiliser ces produits en fonction des besoins et nécessités du moment. IPSA aimerait donner à tout femme l'occasion de composer la gamme des produits convenant à sa personnalité. Le programme comprend des cosmétiques de soins et d'ornement, des produits de capilliculture et des parfums. Les boutiques IPSA mettent à la disposition de leurs clientes un ordinateur pour l'analyse de leur peau, ainsi que des conseillères qui aident la cliente à composer une recette hautement individuelle sur la base des données traitées par l'ordinateur, d'un questionnaire et des résultats de l'analyse cutanée. L'essentiel, c'est l'activité de conseils et renseignements. Ces aspects, le soutien apporté à l'affirmation de la personnalité féminine, de sa créativité et de sa beauté, les conseils spécialisés sur une base scientifique et un programme de produits satisfaisant aux plus hautes exigences, sont reflétés par le programme de publicité institutionnelle mis au point pour IPSA.

DESIGN FIRM:
IPSA Co., Ltd.

CREATIVE DIRECTORS:
Shunsaku Sugiura/Kanji Tanaka

ART DIRECTORS:
Tetsuo Hiro/Toshio Yamagata/
Jouji Yasuda

DESIGNERS:
Kazuya Takaoka/Helmut Schmid/
Yuiro Nakamura

PHOTOGRAPHERS:
Francis Giacobetti/
Yukio Shimizu

CLIENT:
IPSA Co., Ltd.

■ Warm yellow and gold tones were used for the cosmetic and fragrance flacons as well as for the cardboard boxes, carrier bags, brochures, notepaper, and shop interiors. The Latin name, the logotype and the contrasting blue used in the company's advertising, support the personalized, scientific approach of this product range. The motif with the hand - here seen as a poster - is also used in ads and brochures, etc. The photograph on the previous page is an example of the profile shots used for product promotion - this one is for perfume.

■ Warme Gelb- und Goldtöne wurden für die Kosmetik- und Parfumbehälter sowie auch für Kartonschachteln, Tragtaschen, Prospekte, Briefpapier und Ladeneinrichtungen verwendet. Der lateinische Name, der Schriftzug und die Farben verleihen der Kosmetiklinie etwas Kostbares, Wissenschaftliches. Das Motiv mit der Hand, das hier als Plakat zu sehen ist, wird auch für Inserate, Prospekte etc. verwendet. Die auf der vorangehenden Seite gezeigte Aufnahme ist ein Beispiel der für die Produktwerbung verwendeten Profilaufnahmen, diese z.B. für Parfum.

■ Des tons chauds, jaune et or, ont été employés pour les conditionnements des cosmétiques et des parfums, ainsi que pour les cartons, sacs à commissions prospectus, entêtes et agencement de magasin. Le nom latin, le sigle et les couleurs confèrent à ces produits un caractère précieux et scientifique. Le motif à la main, que l'on voit ici sur une affiche, se retrouve aussi dans les annonces, les prospectus, etc. La photo de la page précédente est un bon exemple des profils utilisés dans la publicité produits, ici pour un parfum.

Masayuki Shishizuka, Managing Director, JR Higashi-Nippon Kikaku, Inc., Tokyo, Japan

The original state railways (Japan National Railways) were privatized in 1987 under the name Japan Railway (JR). The C.I. program for this new management form had to be developed in a tremendously short period according to the reorganization schedule offered by the government. Therefore we focused on the two most necessary items. One was the creation of the corporate symbol; the other the development of a more memorable "marketing name" with which we could build awareness among the public. We expected that the symbol should have a simple look with a "safety and accuracy" image which is the most important in the railway business. Nippon Design Center assigned more than 10 excellent art directors to undertake our assignment which was very difficult because of the complex transition schedule. The design chosen is a strong figure symbolizing "JR". By choosing this design, "JR" also became our new "marketing name".

Masayuki Shishizuka, Managing Director, JR Higashi-Nippon Kikaku, Inc., Tokio, Japan

Die ursprünglich staatlichen Eisenbahnen (Japan National Railways) wurden 1987 unter dem Namen Japan Railway (JR) privatisiert. Das Corporate-Identity-Programm für diese neue Unternehmensform musste gemäss Zeitplan der Regierung innert kürzester Frist entwickelt werden. Deshalb konzentrierten wir uns auf die beiden notwendigsten Dinge: das Firmenzeichen und ein neuer «Marketing-Name», der leicht zu behalten und prägnant sein sollte. Wir wollten ein einfaches, schlichtes Logo, im Einklang mit dem «Sicherheit-und-Zuverlässigkeit»-Image, das für ein Eisenbahnunternehmen von äusserster Wichtigkeit ist. Das Nippon Design Center beauftragte zehn der besten Art Direktoren mit der Entwicklung dieses Zeichens, was äusserst schwierig war angesichts der knapp bemessenen Zeit, die zur Verfügung stand. Die eindrucksvolle Interpretation der Buchstaben JR (Japan Railway) wurde gleichzeitig zum neuen «Marketing-Namen».

Masayuki Shishizuka, directeur général, JR Higashi-Nippon Kikaku, Inc., Tokyo, Japon

La Société nationale des chemins de fer japonais (Japan National Railways) a été privatisée en 1987 sous la nouvelle appellation Japan Railway (JR). Le programme de publicité institutionnelle pour cette nouvelle forme d'entreprise a dû être mis au point en un laps de temps extrêmement réduit conformément aux délais imposés par le gouvernement. Nous nous sommes donc concentrés sur la cible essentielle, soit les deux nécessités indispensables. La première a consisté à créer le nouvel emblème du groupe; la seconde, à développer une nouvelle «raison sociale de marketing» qui s'imprime mieux à la mémoire et facilite la prise de conscience. Nous souhaitions que l'emblème soit à la fois simple et distinct et traduise l'image de la sécurité et de la ponctualité chère aux utilisateurs des chemins de fer. Le design retenu symbolise avec énormément de puissance le nouveau JR (Japan Railway). En même temps, ce JR est devenu la «raison sociale de marketing».

Yoji Yamamoto, Nippon Design Center, Toyko, Japan

With our C.I. program we mainly aimed at avoiding confusion and also convincing the Japanese that the company was very conscious of its commitment to the public. An aesthetic, clear, and vital emblem had to be found that had the same appeal for young and old, men and women, customers and employees alike. When the company started out – on April 1, 1987 – the new emblem appeared on all the trains, and on 5000 stations there were new signboards with the JR logo instead of the former JNR. New business stationery was also introduced. The new logo was announced as "news" in the print press and on television, as well as through multi-media advertising.

Yoji Yamamoto, Nippon Design Center, Tokyo, Japan

Mit unserem neuen C.I.-Programm verfolgten wir vor allem das Ziel, Verwirrung zu vermeiden und die Japaner zu überzeugen, dass sich die neue Gesellschaft ihrer Verantwortung der Öffentlichkeit gegenüber bewusst ist. Es sollte ein ästhetisches, klares, vital wirkendes Emblem gefunden werden, das Jung und Alt, Männer und Frauen, Kunden und Angestellte anspricht. Mit dem Start der Gesellschaft am 1. April 1987 erschien das neue Emblem auf allen Zügen; auf 5000 Bahnhöfen gab es neue Hinweistafeln mit dem JR-Logo, und neues Geschäftspapier wurde eingeführt. Die Bekanntgabe des neuen Logos erfolgte durch Presse, Fernsehen und Werbung in allen Medien.

Yoji Yamamoto, Nippon Design Center, Tokyo, Japon

Notre nouveau programme de publicité d'entreprise visait surtout à éviter toute confusion et à persuader les Japonais du caractère responsable de la nouvelle société, de son souci du bien collectif. Le symbole devait être esthétique, clair, vital et s'adresser aux jeunes comme aux moins jeunes, aux hommes comme aux femmes, aux clients comme aux employés. Lors de la mise en route de JR le 1er avril 1987, le logo a fait son apparition sur tous les trains; 5000 gares se sont enrichies de nouveaux panneaux explicatifs ornés du symbole JR, et un nouvel en-tête a été diffusé. La presse, la télévision et la publicité multimédias ont fait largement connaître le nouveau logo.

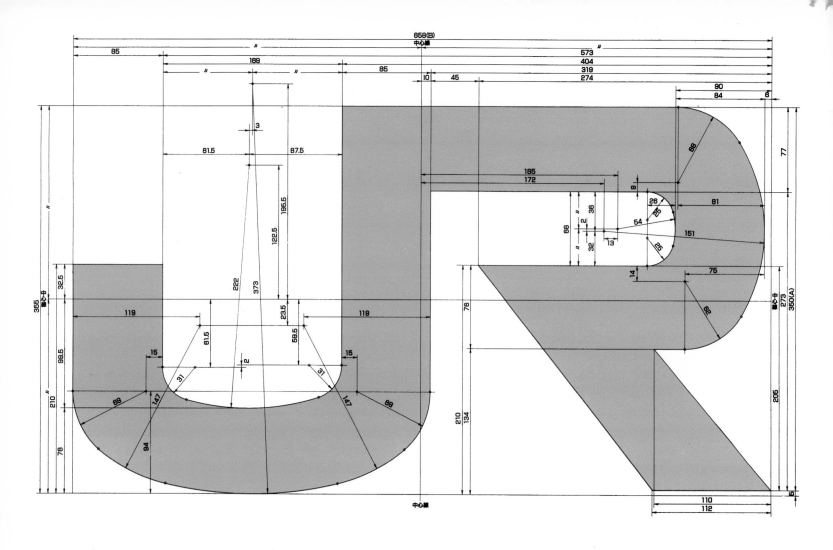

■Enamel-badge on the cap of a railway employee *(pre-vious double spread),* the construction of the new logo from the standard manual, color samples and their application on the business stationery. The presentation of the rail network shows the geographic allocation of the various standard colors which at the same time represent the respective regional headquarters. On the basis of the color coding the train as well as the corresponding letter-heading is ascribed to a certain region.

■Email-Medaillon auf der Mütze eines Bahnangestellten *(vorangehende Doppelseite),* die Konstruktion des neuen Logos aus dem Standard-Manual, Farbmuster und deren Anwendung. Die Darstellung des Schienennetzes zeigt die geographische Zuordnung der verschiedenen Standardfarben, welche gleichzeitig einem regionalen Hauptquartier angehören. Aufgrund der Farbkodierung können sowohl der jeweilige Zug als auch z.B. das entsprechende Briefpapier einer bestimmten Region zugeordnet werden.

■Insigne émaillé ornant la casquette d'un cheminot de la nouvelle société de chemins de fer Japan Railway *(double page précédente),* développement du nouveau logo dans le manuel standard, échantillons de couleurs et leur utilisation pour les en-têtes commerciaux. La représentation du réseau montre le code couleur des régions et des directions régionales correspondantes. Ce code couleur permet d'identifier l'appartenance régionale des trains et des en-têtes utilisés.

DESIGN FIRM:
NIPPON DESIGN CENTER

ART DIRECTOR:
YOJI YAMAMOTO

DESIGNER:
YOJI YAMAMOTO

PHOTOGRAPHER:
YOJI YAMAMOTO

CLIENT:
JAPAN RAILWAY COMPANY GROUP

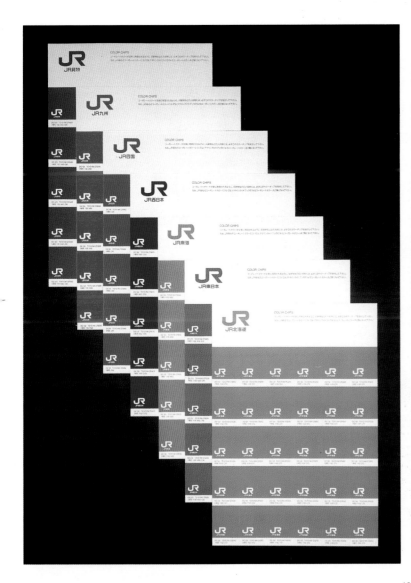

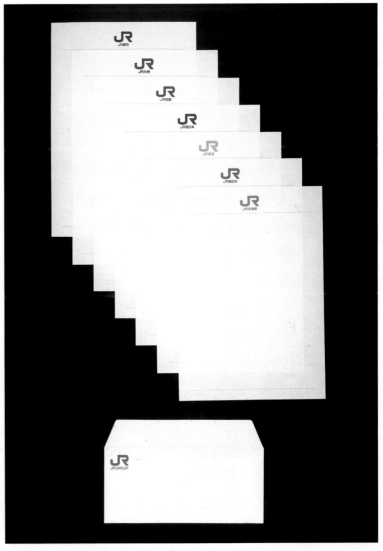

■ Double spreads from the standard manual for the new Corporate Identity for Japan Railway, which replaced the former sign of the Japan National Railways on all the 5,000 railway stations on April 1st, 1987.

■ Doppelseiten aus dem Standard Manual für das neue Corporate-Identity-Design der Japan Railway, das am 1. April 1987 auf allen 5'000 Bahnhöfen das alte Zeichen der Japan National Railways ersetzte.

■ Pages doubles du manuel standard publié à l'occasion du nouveau programme d'identité institutionnelle de Japan Railway, qui s'est substitué le 1er avril 1987 à l'image traditionnelle des Japan National Railways dans la totalité des 5'000 gares du réseau.

シンボルマーク
Symbol mark

A-1 シンボルマークは、JR各社やJRグループの理念や姿勢を視覚的に象徴するものです。ベーシックデザインの中でも最上位のもので、原則としてJR各社・JRグループに関するすべての表示物に、単独で、または呼称ロゴタイプと組み合わせたシグネチャーとして、積極的に用いていきます。
このシンボルマークは、これまでのJNRや動輪

などのマークに代わるもので、JRの文字をデザイン化したものです。
鉄道輸送の安全性・正確性などの固き伝統に加えて、新会社の多面的な発展性と新生感などをテーマに開発され、100年経ってもさびず、民営・分割の理念を具現化したものとして決定したものです。
このマークは、7社共一として、各社のカラーを変

えることで識別します。
ポジを基本にして、ネガタイプもありますが、表示物によってその使用方法が規定されていますので、それに準じて下さい。

ポジタイプ

ネガタイプ

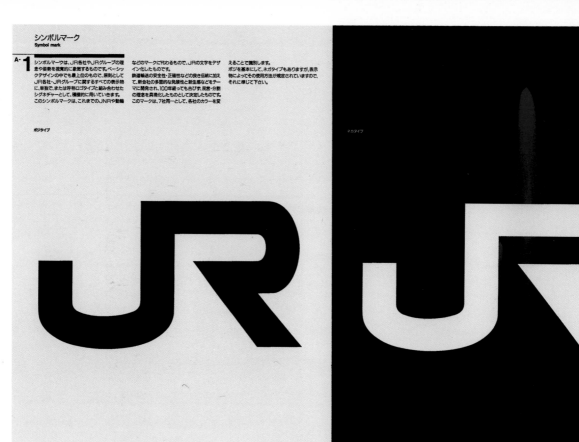

シグネチャー
Signature

A-4 シンボルマークと呼称ロゴタイプを組み合わせたものです。2つのエレメントの大きさや位置は、全体のバランスを考え、厳密な計算の上で設計されたものです。
各社が独自に呼称ロゴタイプのサイズを大きくしたり、位置を変えたりすると、JRグループ各社のイメージ統一が崩れ、お客様を混乱させる

一因ともなりかねません。規定にしたがって正しく表示して下さい。
シグネチャーの使用法については、「B-1シグネチャー使用規定」、「B-2シグネチャー使用禁止例」を参照して下さい。

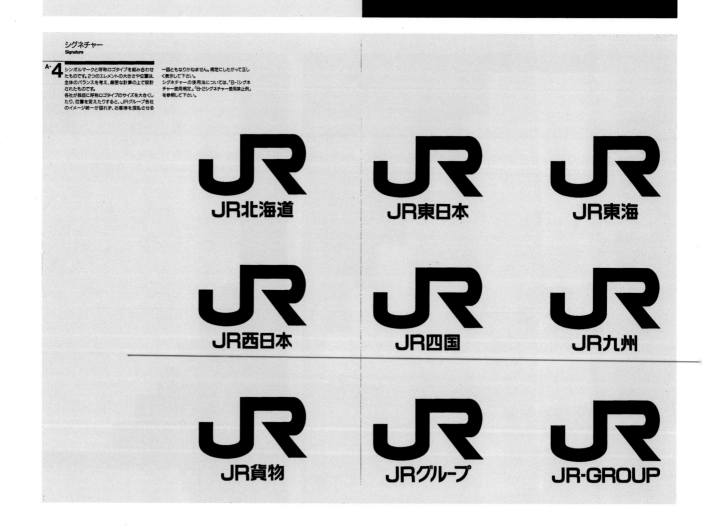

DESIGN FIRM:
NIPPON DESIGN CENTER

ART DIRECTOR:
YOJI YAMAMOTO

DESIGNER:
YOJI YAMAMOTO

PHOTOGRAPHER:
YOJI YAMAMOTO

CLIENT:
JAPAN RAILWAY COMPANY GROUP

コーポレートカラー
Corporate colors

A·5 コーポレートカラーは、JRグループ各社の企業姿勢や決意を色彩を通じてアピールしていくものです。いつも同一の色彩を意識的に、統一的に使用していくことで、他企業や同業他者との差別化を図ります。
JRグループ各社は、自社のコーポレートカラーを最も厳格に順守して下さい。他の色やJRグループ

他社のカラーを使用してはいけません。お客様の混乱を招き、企業イメージの異機効果を弱めることになります。

※コーポレートカラーを表示する場合、特色を使用することが望ましいが、それが不可能な場合は、分解色(近似色)の指定に従ってください。

JR北海道	JR北海道ライトグリーン	分解色(近似色)	掲示色 マンセル値 1.0G 6.8/12.2 DIC 130 TOYO INK CF8292 分解色(近似色) Y100 C70	ライトグリーン：真白な大地から一斉に芽生え、やがて野山を彩る鮮やかなライトグリーン。新会社の、さわやかで伸びやかなイメージを表現する色です。
JR東日本	JR東日本グリーン		マンセル値 1.7G 5.0/8.0 DIC 213 TOYO INK CF8305 分解色(近似色) Y100 M30 C90	グリーン：東北、信越、関東の豊かな緑色で、力強く発展していく新会社の未来をシンボライズしました。また、東北・上越新幹線のカラーでもあります。
JR東海	JR東海オレンジ		マンセル値 2.2YR 6.5/13.3 DIC 120 TOYO INK CF8135 分解色(近似色) Y100 M60	オレンジ：かぎりなく広がる東海の海と空の彼方を染める透明な白の色です。刻新ともした新会社のように、フレッシュな新会社を表わします。
JR西日本	JR西日本ブルー		マンセル値 4.6PB 4.1/13.0 DIC 182 TOYO INK CF8475 分解色(近似色) M50 C100	ブルー：日本の文化と歴史に彩られた地域にふさわしい色です。地域に密着した会社を表わし、また、豊かな海と湖を象徴するカラーでもあります。
JR四国	JR四国ライトブルー		マンセル値 6.2B 6.0/11.2 DIC 99 TOYO INK CF8460 分解色(近似色) C90	ライトブルー：太平洋の青さより、さらに鮮やかなブルーです。「青い国・四国」で知られる済みきった空のブルーで、新会社のフレッシュさを表現しました。
JR九州	JR九州レッド		マンセル値 6.6R 5.3/15.5 DIC 158 TOYO INK CF8096 分解色(近似色) Y90 M90	レッド：南の明るい太陽の国には、燃える熱意の色「赤」がふさわしく、全力で明るいスタートダッシュをきる新会社の積極的な姿勢を表わしています。
JR貨物	JR貨物コンテナブルー		マンセル値 1.4PB 4.5/6.5 DIC 423 TOYO INK CF8483 分解色(近似色) Y30 M50 C80	コンテナブルー：すでに、27万個のコンテナイメージの一粒を伝え、ブルー作業を展開しています。新会社のフレッシュさと信頼感を表出するカラーです。
JRグループ	JRグループ無彩色(黒、グレー、白)		無彩色：鉄道6社、貨物1社のJRグループを表わすマークです。グループとしての汎用性を考え、黒、グレー、白、3つの無彩色しました。(金、銀も可)

※DICはすべて11版の色番号、TOYO INKはすべて10版の色番号です。

社員証/氏名札/バッジ/社旗/フロア案内/屋外看板
ID cards, name cards, badges, corporate flags, floor direction boards and billboards

C·6 社員証：社員証は、社員一人一人の勤務先を示す身分証明書であり、無断で変更したりすることはできません。JRグループ全社、同一フォーマットとしてします。ここに掲示したものは、JR北海道の社員証デザイン規定ですが、各社、これに準じて製作して下さい。
シグネチャーや式式社名ロゴの大きさや位置、所

定書体(ゴナM)やコーポレートカラーなどに、特に留意して下さい。
氏名札：氏名札は、ふだんお客様の目に触れるものです。デザイン規定に準じたものを必ず使用して下さい。ここに示したものは、JR北海道とJR東海の氏名札デザイン規定ですが、各社、これに準じて製作して下さい。

社旗：社旗は、国にとっての国旗と同じです。きちんとデザイン統一がなされていなければなりません。JRグループ全社、同一のデザインとなっており、それぞれ各社ごとのシグネチャーとコーポレートカラーで識別します。旗のポジネガでは、シグネチャーのサイズが異なっていますので、特に注意して下さい。

フロア案内：フロア案内のデザインサンプル例でも、マークと呼称ロゴタイプを表示しますが2つの要素は、必ず例示のように離して下さい。近づけてはいけません。和文はゴナ、英文はヘルベチカの書体を使用して下さい。

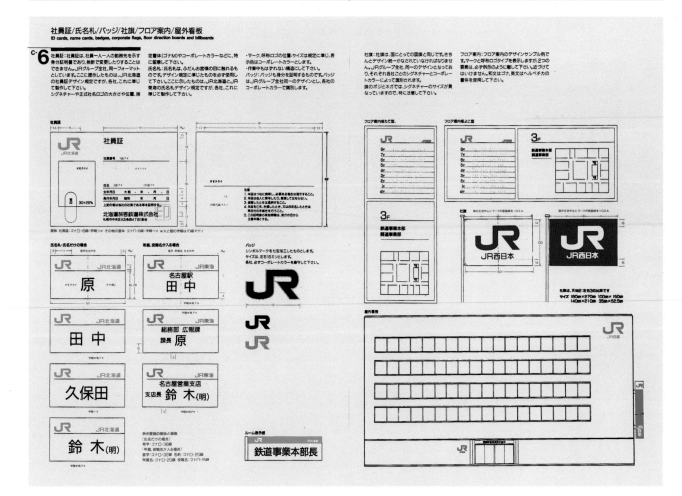

DESIGN FIRM:
NIPPON DESIGN CENTER

ART DIRECTOR:
YOJI YAMAMOTO

DESIGNER:
YOJI YAMAMOTO

PHOTOGRAPHER:
YOJI YAMAMOTO

CLIENT:
JAPAN RAILWAY COMPANY GROUP

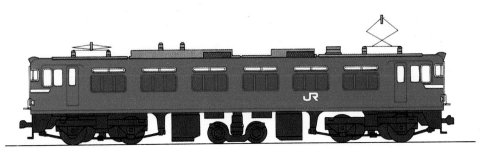

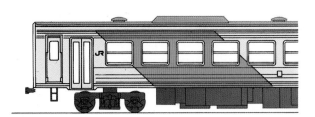

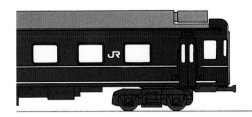

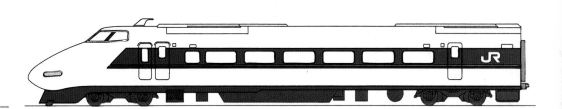

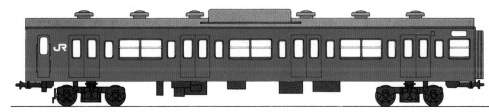

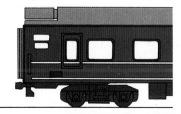

■Description for the use of the new sign for Japan Railway on the various types of trains, locomotives, and carriages, taken from the standard manual. On the set date (April 1st, 1987) the brand new sign made its debut on 10,000 trains.

■Darstellung der Anwendung des neuen Zeichens der Japan Railway auf den verschiedenen Zugtypen, den Lokomotiven und Wagons, dem Standard Manual entnommen. Am Stichtag (1. April 1987) wurden 10'000 Züge mit dem neuen Zeichen gekennzeichnet.

■Mode d'emploi du nouveau symbole de Japan Railway pour les divers types de train, les locomotives et les wagons, dans le manuel standard. Le 1er avril 1987, 10'000 trains ont été pourvus de la nouvelle image de marque.

Wolfgang Weber, Marketing Manager, C. Josef Lamy GmbH, Heidelberg, Germany

C. Josef Lamy GmbH, founded in 1930, has been occupied from its beginnings with the subject of "Writing by Hand". In 1952 the product name *Lamy* was brought onto the market for the first time. The current Corporate Identity program evolved from the new company concept. This began in 1966 with exclusive concentration on writing articles that were based on the functional design concept. In 1974 design guidelines were laid down for the first time, and these were redesigned in 1986. The Corporate Identity program in its present form has the task of giving this medium-sized business a distinct and unmistakable profile that is consistent and continually applied. The most important result of this program is certainly the company's success and the Design Prize awarded by the European Community in 1988.

Peter Vogt, Peter Vogt Grafik Design, Stuttgart, Germany

The archetype of the Lamy symbol was used for the first time in 1952. The black and silver house colors were added in 1966. A better understanding of product design and new up-to-date looks in communication design led to a total review of the whole visual image in 1985/86. The photographic concept runs throughout, and assists the unique Lamy image – from the advertisement and the brochure through to the store slides. The product illustrations are typical – almost without perspective – and the lack of oversophisticated style. Typical too in the photographs are the low-key tips on use, or user-target group. The form of the product itself should lend the photographs its main attributes. Typographic rules create an individual image in spite of restriction to the most elementary basics.

Wolfgang Weber, Marketingleiter, C. Josef Lamy GmbH, Heidelberg, Deutschland

Die C. Josef Lamy GmbH – 1930 gegründet – hat sich von Anfang an mit dem Thema «Schreiben von Hand» beschäftigt. 1952 kam zum ersten Mal auch die Produktmarke *Lamy* auf den Markt. Die neue Unternehmenskonzeption begann 1966 mit der ausschliesslichen Konzentration auf Schreibgeräte, die dem Konzept des «funktionalen Designs» folgten. 1974 wurden zum ersten Mal Gestaltungsrichtlinien festgelegt, die 1986 überarbeitet wurden. Das C.I. Programm hat die Aufgabe, einem mittelständischen Unternehmen durch eindeutige, konsequent verwirklichte und kontinuierlich angewendete Massnahmen ein unverwechselbares Profil zu geben. Wichtigstes Resultat sind sicherlich der unternehmerische Erfolg und 1988 die Verleihung des Designpreises der Europäischen Gemeinschaft.

Peter Vogt, Peter Vogt Grafik Design, Stuttgart, Deutschland

Eine Urform des Lamy-Zeichens wurde erstmals 1952 verwendet. Die Hausfarben Schwarz und Silber kamen 1966 dazu. Neue Formensprachen beim Produkt-Design und neue zeitgemässe Auftritte beim Kommunikations-Design führten 1985/86 zu einer Überarbeitung des gesamten visuellen Erscheinungsbildes. Ein durchgängiges Photokonzept verhilft zu Lamy-typischen Auftritten. Typisch ist die fast perspektivlose Abbildung der Produkte, der Verzicht auf überzogene Stilmittel. Typisch ist auch der im Photo immer «reduziert» gehaltene Hinweis auf Anwendung oder Benutzer-Zielgruppe. Die Form der Produkte selbst soll die formale Sensation des Bildinhalts sein. Die typographischen Vorgaben schaffen, trotz der Beschränkung auf elementarste Grundregeln, ein eigenständiges Erscheinungsbild.

Wolfgang Weber, Marketing Manager, C. Josef Lamy GmbH, Heidelberg, Allemagne

La C. Josef Lamy GmbH fondée en 1930 s'est investie d'emblée dans le matériel d'écriture manuelle. Vendant d'abord divers produits de marque, ce n'est qu'en 1952 que la firme s'est dotée de produits *Lamy*. Le nouveau programme de publicité institutionnelle résulte de la nouvelle conception d'entreprise élaborée depuis 1966: la spécialisation exclusive en ustensiles d'écriture étudiés selon les règles du design fonctionnel. Les premières directives en matière de création datent de 1974; elles ont été remaniées en 1986. Le programme d'identité vise à conférer un profil original à cette P.M.E. et de le concrétiser par un programme homogène, cohérent et continu. Ledit programme a grandement influencé le chiffre d'affaires de l'entreprise; il a été récompensé en 1988 du prix de design de la Communauté européenne.

Peter Vogt, Peter Vogt Grafik Design, Stuttgart, Allemagne

La première image institutionnelle de Lamy date de 1952. Elle s'enrichit en 1966 des couleurs maison, le noir et l'argent. L'avènement de nouveaux langages formels en matière de design de produits et l'élaboration du design de communication contemporain ont entraîné un rajeunissement visuel en 1985/86. Une conception photo homogène caractérise désormais la publicité institutionnelle de Lamy. Celle-ci se signale par une reproduction des produits qui se passe presque entièrement de la perspective et de moyens de style surfaits. Caractéristique également, la minimisation des indications d'emploi et des références aux utilisateurs-types accompagnant les photos. C'est la forme même du produit qui doit créer la sensation visuelle au plan formel. Le texte réduit à l'essentiel constitue néanmoins un élément visuel essentiel.

■ The logotype on business stationery, as display, on the cover and inside pages of a catalog with promotional articles, and in the standard manual. The design of the catalog is in line with the distinct product design.

■ Der Schriftzug auf Geschäftspapieren, als Display, auf dem Umschlag eines Katalogs mit Werbeartikeln und im Inhalt sowie im Standard-Manual. Die Gestaltung der Kataloge entspricht dem klaren Produkt-Design.

■ Sigle figurant dans les entêtes, en vitrine, sur la couverture d'un catalogue d'articles publicitaires et sur les pages intérieures, dans le manuel standard. La conception des catalogues s'inspire des règles de sobriété et de clarté.

DESIGN FIRM:
Peter Vogt Grafik Design

ART DIRECTOR:
Peter Vogt

DESIGNER:
Peter Vogt

PRODUCT DESIGN:
Gerd A. Müller/
Wolfgang Fabian/
Berndt Spiegel

PHOTOGRAPHERS:
Victor Goico/
Wolfgang Gscheidle

CLIENT:
C. Josef Lamy GmbH

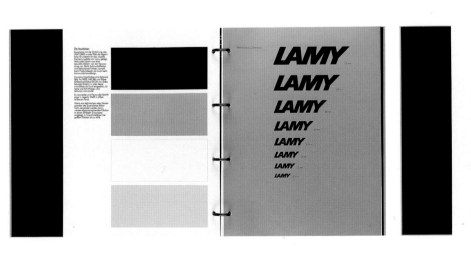

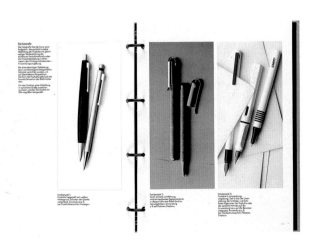

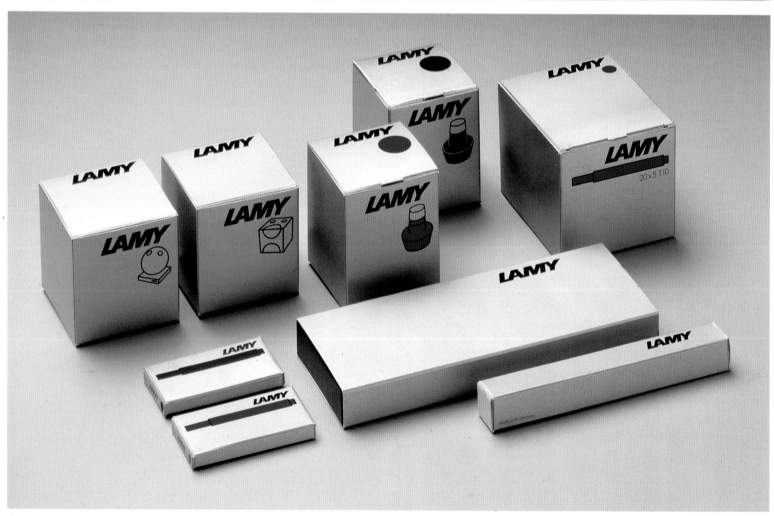

DESIGN FIRM:
PETER VOGT GRAFIK DESIGN

ART DIRECTOR:
PETER VOGT

DESIGNER:
PETER VOGT

PRODUCT DESIGN:
GERD A.MÜLLER/
WOLFGANG FABIAN/
BERNDT SPIEGEL

PHOTOGRAPHERS:
VICTOR GOICO/
WOLFGANG GSCHEIDLE

CLIENT:
C. JOSEF LAMY GMBH

■ The logotype as signage on the building, and examples of the packaging and product design that all uphold the concept of "functional design".

■ Der Schriftzug als Gebäudekennzeichnung, sowie Beispiele der Packungs- und Produktgestaltung, die dem Konzept des «funktionalen Designs» entsprechen.

■ Le sigle en façade et des exemples du design des emballages et des produits qui correspond au concept d'un «design fonctionnel».

LOV I NG

Shinichi Murayama, Planning Division Manager, Loving Corporation, Saitama, Japan

Loving Corporation was established on February 14, 1938. Our Corporate Identity program was initiated with the launch of our newest retail outlet – a unique concept shop that answers the needs of our multi-faced operations, including classroom facilities, a crafts gallery, a 60-seat restaurant, as well as sales and display counters. Our existing Corporate Identity did not mesh with this new and updated facility, designed to serve as "the base of a leisurely life". Our corporate philosophy aims at familiarizing more people with dyeing, thus our operation focuses on administration of classes and development of innovative products. The new CI program was designed to evoke the delicate and well-balanced nature of our operations, and has been highly successful. Consumer response has been overwhelmingly favorable.

Shinichi Murayama, Planning Division Manager, Loving Corporation, Saitama, Japan

Die Loving Corporation wurde am 14. Februar 1938 gegründet. Anlass für die Schaffung unseres C.I. Programms war unser neuster Laden – aufgebaut nach einem einzigartigen Konzept, das unseren vielfältigen Geschäftszweigen gerecht wird. Der Komplex umfasst Schulungsräume, eine Galerie für Kunsthandwerk, ein Restaurant mit 60 Plätzen sowie Verkaufs- und Ausstellungstresen. Unsere bisherige Firmenidentität passte nicht zu diesem neuen, modernen Komplex, der als «Grundlage für ein angenehmes Leben» dienen sollte. Unser Ziel ist es, mehr Leute mit dem Färben vertraut zu machen, deshalb konzentrieren wir uns vor allem auf Schulung und auf die Entwicklung neuer Produkte. Das neue C.I.-Programm sollte das Behutsame, Ausgewogene unserer Unternehmungen verdeutlichen.

Shinichi Murayama, Planning Division Manager, Loving Corporation, Saitama, Japon

La Loving Corporation a été fondé le 14 février 1938. Notre programme d'identité institutionnelle a vu le jour à l'occasion de l'inauguration d'un nouveau magasin dont la conception novatrice répond aux besoins de nos opérations polyvalentes. On y trouve des salles de cours, une galerie artisanale, un restaurant, des points de vente et d'exposition. La publicité d'entreprise n'était pas assortie à ces installations au modernisme destinées à fournir «la base d'une vie de tout repos». La philosophie de notre entreprise vise à familiariser un plus grand nombre de personnes avec les techniques de la teinture, d'où l'accent mis sur les cours et le développement de produits novateurs. Le nouveau programme de publicité corporate a été conçu de manière à évoquer la nature délicate et équilibrée de nos opérations.

Hiromi Inayoshi, Inayoshi Design Inc., Tokyo, Japan

Loving belongs to Seiwa Corporation, a manufacturer of dyeing materials, and is designed to provide proposals on life style ranging from shopping, galleries, dining and creative activities (dyeing classes). As the shop is targeted to women, the letter I out of Loving symbolizes a woman's figure. The name itself was chosen with regard to this target group and also implies the idea of doing things with love. The building was designed and constructed by architect Hirokazu Matsunaga, suggesting an unconventional, free life style. Purple, being the most noble color and closely linked with dyeing, was selected as the corporate color. For the opening campaign posters, guidebooks for events planned to mark the start of the shop, PR magazines etc. were unified under the Corporate Identity program.

Hiromi Inayoshi, Inayoshi Design Inc., Tokio, Japan

Loving gehört zur Seiwa Corporation, einem Hersteller von Färbemitteln. Der Laden enthält ein breitgefächertes Angebot: Einkaufsmöglichkeiten, Galerien, Restaurants und kreative Anregungen (Färbeklassen) – Vorschläge für die Gestaltung des Lebens. Zielpublikum sind Frauen, deshalb symbolisiert der Buchstabe I des Namens die Gestalt einer Frau. Der Name selbst wurde im Hinblick auf das Zielpublikum gewählt sowie auf die verschiedenen Tätigkeiten, die mit «Liebe» getan werden sollen. Auch das von Hirokazu Matsunaga entworfene Gebäude soll einen unkonventionellen, freien Lebensstil suggerieren. Die kostbarste und mit dem Färben am engsten verbundene Farbe – Purpur – wurde als Standardfarbe für die Marke ausgewählt. Zur Eröffnung gab es Plakate, Veranstaltungsführer, PR-Magazine etc.

Hiromi Inayoshi, Inayoshi Design Inc., Tokyo, Japon

Loving est un centre commercial de la Seiwa Corporation. Ce fabricant de colorants y propose un grand choix de styles de vie à travers des boutiques, des galeries d'art, des retaurants et des activités créatrices. Le public visé, ce sont les femmes, d'où la silhouette féminine qui constitue l'I de Loving. Cette raison sociale a été choisie en fonction du public féminin et des activités proposées. Le bâtiment a été conçu et construit par l'architecte Hirokazu Matsunaga dans un style peu conventionnel symbole de liberté. Le pourpre, la plus noble des couleurs et celle que l'on associe de plus près à la teinture, a accédé au rang de coloris institutionnel. Le nouveau programme de publicité d'entreprise a fourni pour l'inauguration du centre Loving les affiches, les calendriers de manifestations, les magazines de RP, etc.

DESIGN FIRM:
INAYOSHI DESIGN INC.

ART DIRECTOR:
HIROMI INAYOSHI

DESIGNERS:
MIHA TAKAGI/HIROMI INAYOSHI

CLIENT:
LOVING CORPORATION

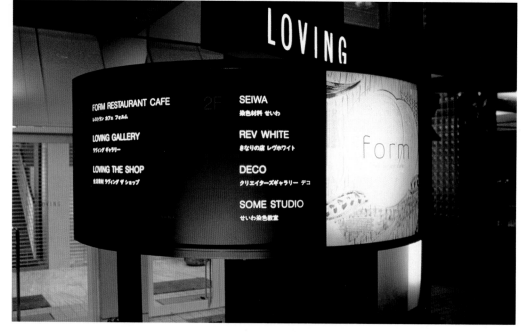

■The women is the focus of interest – not only seen as a silhouette in the logotype but also with regard to the range of this center (shops, galleries, restaurants, workshops). Shown are examples of labels, paper carrier bag, video presentation of topical information, a complete view of the building and a view of the interior – all under the precept of an unconventional, enlightened attitude towards life.

■Die Frau steht im Mittelpunkt – nicht nur als Silhouette im Schriftzug, sondern auch im Hinblick auf das Angebot (Läden, Galerien, Restaurants, Werkräume) dieses Zentrums. Hier Beispiele von Etiketts, Papiertragetasche, die Video-Präsentation von aktuellen Informationen, eine Gesamtansicht des Gebäudes und eine Innenansicht – alles unter dem Motto einer unkonventionellen, aufgeschlossenen Lebenseinstellung.

■Tout est ramené à la femme, qu'elle soit silhouettée à l'intérieur du sigle, qu'elle soit le public visé par les boutiques, galeries, restaurants, ateliers de ce centre. Exemples choisis ici: étiquettes, sac à commissions en papier, présentation vidéo d'informations d'actualité, vue générale de l'immeuble, vue intérieure – le tout obéissant à une conception de vie peu conventionnelle, ouverte sur les problèmes contemporains.

Steve Marsel Studio

Steve Marsel, Steve Marsel Studio, Cambridge, MA/USA

When I opened Steve Marsel Studio in January of 1986, I faced a real image problem. I was branching out on my own for the first time and needed a way to communicate my independence to my target market – Boston art directors and designers. The identity Bruce Crocker designed for me is original, witty, and sophisticated. Since I do mostly advertising and annual report photography, I'd like my business to be perceived as a place to expect the unexpected. And the logo clearly communicates both my penchant for innovative solutions and my willingness to take risks. Most important, it projects a sense of self-effacing humor that makes Steve Marsel Studio appear friendly and approachable, yet very professional. By the way, the illustration in my logo bears no resemblance to the real Steve Marsel.

Bruce Crocker, Crocker Inc., Advertising & Design, Boston, MA/USA

After separation from his partner, Steve Marsel needed to create an awareness of his own personality and photographic talent. Simply put, he is a first-rate photographer who is friendly and easy to work with. The thinking behind Steve's identity and marketing materials addresses these two points. I hoped to develop a mark that was as unique and distinct as the photographer himself. After developing the "photographer bust" concept, I contacted *New Yorker* cartoonist Michael Maslin to execute the final artwork. The result is a perfect marriage of "human and sophisticated" while it also promotes Steve's photography in an unconventional und unexpected way. Design considerations included the subtle use of color, open space and serif type juxtaposing the whimsical quality of the final art to help convey the message.

Steve Marsel, Steve Marsel Studio, Cambridge, MA/USA

Als ich im Januar 1986 mein Photostudio eröffnete, stand ich vor einem Problem. Ich stellte mich zum ersten Mal ganz auf eigene Beine und musste diese Unabhängigkeit meinen potentiellen Kunden – den Art Direktoren und Graphikern in Boston – irgendwie mitteilen. Das Erscheinungsbild, das Bruce Crocker für mich entwarf, ist originell, witzig und anspruchsvoll. Da ich vor allem für Werbung und Jahresberichte photographiere, möchte ich, dass man von mir das Unerwartete erwartet. Das Logo zeigt sowohl meine Vorliebe für ungewöhnliche Lösungen als auch meine Bereitschaft, Risiken einzugehen. Am allerwichtigsten ist dabei der Humor, der das Steve Marsel Studio freundlich, zugänglich und doch sehr professionell erscheinen lässt. Übrigens, die Illustration hat überhaupt keine Ähnlichkeit mit mir.

Bruce Crocker, Crocker Inc., Advertising & Design, Boston, MA/USA

Nach der Trennung von seinem Partner musste Steve Marsel sich selbst und sein photographisches Talent bekanntmachen. Er ist ein erstklassiger Photograph, freundlich und umgänglich. Um diese beiden Punkte ging es bei unseren Überlegungen für das Erscheinungsbild und das Marketing. Ich hoffte, ein Zeichen zu finden, das so einmalig wie Steve ist. Nachdem ich das Konzept für die «Photographenbüste» entwickelt hatte, bat ich den *New Yorker*-Cartoonisten Michael Maslin um die Ausführung. Das Resultat ist eine perfekte Verbindung von «menschlich und kultiviert» und ausserdem eine unkonventionelle Werbemöglichkeit. Die graphischen Überlegungen führten zu vorsichtigem Einsatz von Farbe, viel freiem Raum und einer Typographie mit Serifen als Gegenpol zum komischen Element des Erscheinungsbildes.

Steve Marsel, Steve Marsel Studio, Cambridge, MA/USA

En inaugurant mon studio en janvier 1986, je me suis trouvé dans l'embarras: quelle image adopter? C'était bien la première fois que je me posais en indépendant, et il fallait que j'informe de cette nouvelle indépendance les directeurs artistiques et les designers bostoniens. L'identité que Bruce Crocker a réalisée pour mon compte s'est avérée originale, spirituelle, sophistiquée. Aussi me paraissait-il important de signaler qu'on peut attendre de moi l'inattendu. Le logo donne clairement expression à ma prédilection pour les solutions novatrices et mon goût de risque. En plus il incarne un humour pince-sans-rire qui fait apparaître le Steve Marsel Studio sous un jour amène et familier, mais en souligne l'aspect professionnel. L'illustration utilisée dans mon logo ne ressemble du reste pas du tout au vrai Steve Marsel.

Bruce Crocker, Crocker Inc., Advertising & Design, Boston, MA/USA

La force, de Steve Marsel est l'étendue de son talent et l'affabilité et la gentillesse de son caractère, deux points qu'il s'agissait de faire ressortir dans le logo aussi bien que dans le matériel destiné au marketing. Je souhaitais trouver un symbole aussi exceptionnel que le photographe lui-même. Après avoir réalisé le concept du «buste du photographe», j'ai contacté le caricaturiste Michael Maslin, du *New Yorker*, pour le mettre à exécution. Le résultat est un mariage réussi entre «l'humain et le sophistique» et, qui plus est, un moyen de promotion de l'art de Steve à la fois peu conventionnel et insolite. Des considérations de design motivent l'emploi circonspect de la couleur, la surface aérée et la typo à empattements pour faire contrepoids à la qualité fantasque de la composition finale et faciliter la transmission du message.

DESIGN FIRM:
CROCKER INC.

ART DIRECTOR:
BRUCE CROCKER

DESIGNER:
BRUCE CROCKER

ILLUSTRATOR:
MICHAEL MASLIN

CLIENT:
STEVE MARSEL STUDIO

■ The bust, which has become photographer Steve Marsel's hallmark, is shown here three dimensional with neon tubes and in printed form on business stationery, on a mug, on the case with the photographic equipment, on an automobile *(previous page),* on T-shirts, and as a partially punched-out silhouette for business cards.

■ Die Büste, die zum Markenzeichen des Photographen Steve Marsel wurde, hier dreidimensional mit Neonröhren gestaltet und in gedruckter, zweidimensionaler Form auf Geschäftspapier, einer Tasse, dem Koffer mit der Photoausrüstung, einem Auto *(vorangehende Seite),* auf T-Shirts und als teilweise ausgestanzte Silhouette für Visitenkarten.

■ Le buste qui s'est imposé comme marque distinctive du photographe Steve Marsel apparaît ici dans les trois dimensions en tubes néon ainsi que comme motif sur les en-têtes, une tasse, la mallette avec l'equipement photo, la voiture *(page précédente),* des tee-shirts et des cartes de visite sous forme de silhouette partiellement découpée.

ONE
SHIRT
IS
WORTH
A
THOUSAND
WORDS

617·547·4445

Steve Marsel Studio

215 First Street
Cambridge, Mass. 02142

Kevin Donovan, Director of Food & Beverage, Hyatt On Collins, Melbourne, Vic., Australia
Max's Seafood Restaurant is characterized by fine food and magnificent interior design treatments. The symbol design utilizes the interior elements to create an image that is in harmony with the restaurant operation and at the same time promotes aspects of individuality and style. The Max's Restaurant Corporate Identity program is very extensive for a single restaurant. However, Hyatt On Collins recognizes the importance of creating a distinctive image throughout its various venues to enhance the Hotel's tradition of excellence. The images created are used in all promotional and marketing activities.

Richard Henderson, Flett Henderson & Arnold, Abbotsford, Victoria, Australia
Max's Seafood Restaurant is one of Melbourne's finest. Located at the Hyatt On Collins hotel, the design contains as its central element a "gold crack" in a marble surface. This was developed from the interior design of the restaurant which features large areas of brass "cracks" inserted for effect into the marble and stone wall and floor surfaces. The typography, layout, and the use of special papers and printing finishes are designed to reinforce aspects of quality and the opulent style of the restaurant. The design is usually reproduced in full color using marble texture and gold foil stamping. It is applied to all restaurant collateral such as menus, matches, invitations, stationery, etc. and, because it is complete in its configuration, does not require additional descriptive text or other elements.

Kevin Donovan, Director of Food & Beverage, Hyatt On Collins, Melbourne, Vic., Australien
Max's Seafood Restaurant zeichnet sich aus durch hervorragendes Essen und prachtvolle Innenarchitektur. Das entworfene Design, das auf der Innenarchitektur basiert, harmoniert mit der Funktionsweise des Restaurants und unterstreicht gleichzeitig die Aspekte der Individualität und des Stils. Wenn man bedenkt, dass es sich bei Max's Seafood Restaurant nur um ein einziges Restaurant handelt, ist das Corporate-Identity-Programm äusserst weitreichend. Das Hyatt-On-Collins-Hotel hat jedoch erkannt, wie wichtig es ist, bei jeder Gelegenheit ein unverwechselbares Erscheinungsbild zu haben.

Richard Henderson, Flett Henderson & Arnold, Abbotsford, Victoria, Australien
Max's Seafood Restaurant im Hyatt-On-Collins-Hotel ist eines der exklusivsten Lokale Melbournes. Das Hauptelement des neuen Designs ist ein «goldfarbener Riss» in einer Marmoroberfläche. Die Idee wurde abgeleitet von der Innenarchitektur des Restaurants: Auf dem Boden, an den Wänden und im Marmor sind zur Dekoration «Messingrisse» eingelassen. Die Typographie, das Layout, die Verwendung von hochwertigem Papier und eine spezielle Drucktechnik dienen dazu, den Qualitätsanspruch und den exklusiven Stil des Restaurants zu unterstreichen. Meistens erscheint das Design mehrfarbig, mit Marmorstruktur, im Prägedruck. Es wird auf sämtlichen Drucksachen sowie für das Werbe- und Promotionsmaterial des Restaurants verwendet, wie z.B. Speisekarten, Streichhölzer, Einladungen, Briefpapier usw.

Kevin Donovan, Director of Food & Beverage, Hyatt On Collins, Melbourne, Vic., Australie
Max's Seafood Restaurant est réputé pour la qualité de sa cuisine et son décor exceptionnel. L'emblème a été étudié en fonction de cette décoration intérieure de manière à refléter harmonieusement le mode opératoire du restaurant tout en mettant en vedette ses caractéristiques d'individualisme et de style. Pour un seul et unique établissement, le programme de publicité institutionnelle développé pour Max's Seafood Restaurant est exceptionnellement ambitieux. Toutefois, l'hôtel Hyatt On Collins a réalisé l'importance qui revient dans l'image globale de l'hôtel à ce restaurant nec plus ultra dont l'ensemble de haute tradition ne peut que profiter.

Richard Henderson, Flett Henderson & Arnold, Abbotsford, Victoria, Australie
Max's Seafood Restaurant est l'un des plus huppés de Melbourne. Installé à l'hôtel Hyatt On Collins, il exhibe comme élément central d'un design renouvelé une «craquelure or» dans une surface marbrée. Cette conception a pour point de départ l'intérieur du restaurant sillonné de craquelures en laiton dans les murs et sols de marbre et de pierre pour obtenir un effet décoratif. La typo, la mise en pages et le recours à des qualités de papier et techniques d'impression spéciales sont destinés à mettre en évidence les impératifs de qualité et le style exclusif du restaurant. Les éléments du design apparaissent généralement en polychromie avec une structure marbrée et un gaufrage or. L'image institutionnelle se retrouve sur tous les imprimés, les menus, les pochettes d'allumettes, les invitations, le papier à lettres, etc.

■The huge brass "cracks" in the marble, on the stone walls, and on the floors distinguish the interior decor of this exclusive restaurant and also dominate the graphic Corporate Identity. Shown are some examples of the graphic application on business stationery and promotional articles, and also various interior elements that are all integral to the company image.

■Die durch grosszügige Messing-«Risse» im Marmor, an den Steinwänden und auf Fussböden gekennzeichnete Innenarchitektur dieses exklusiven Restaurants dominiert auch das graphische Erscheinungsbild. Hier einige Beispiele der Anwendung auf Geschäftspapieren und Promotionsartikeln und verschiedene Elemente der Innenausstattung, die zu diesem Erscheinungsbild gehören.

■L'architecture intérieure de ce restaurant de luxe, caractérisée par les larges «fissures» de laiton dans le marbre, les murs de pierre et le sol, domine aussi l'image graphique. Ici quelques exemples de l'emploi de cette image dans les en-têtes commerciaux, les articles promotionnels et divers éléments de la décoration intérieure qui sont tous traités comme éléments intégrés de l'image globale.

DESIGN FIRM:
FLETT HENDERSON & ARNOLD

ART DIRECTOR:
*FLETT HENDERSON & ARNOLD/
DON STRANDELL*

DESIGNER:
FLETT HENDERSON & ARNOLD

CLIENT:
MAX'S SEAFOOD RESTAURANT

Seizo Shimamura, President, Meiji Milk Products Co., Ltd., Tokyo, Japan

In its long history, Meiji has matured from a producer of dairy products to a manufacturer and distributor of a full range of food products. Just recently, we have also initiated expansion plans in exciting new areas of non-food products and services. As the company's business has grown, and all throughout its history, we have always been guided and inspired by our high concern for people. It is of paramount importance to Meiji to provide those products and services which will enhance and contribute to the better health and well-being of all the people we serve. We have been cognizant of the continous changes in the condition of the environment and in the public's growing awareness and appreciation of health values. We have made continuous and concerted efforts to fill those needs and expectations.

Takenobu Igarashi, Igarashi Studio, Tokyo, Japan

Meiji Milk Products instituted a new Corporate Identity system in 1986 in anticipation of the 1987 celebration of the 70th anniversary of its founding. The design of the first initial "M" of the Meiji name is intended to communicate the company's vitality and prospects for continued growth in the years leading up to the 21st century. It also expresses Meiji's corporate sturdiness and reliability. The six stripes represent the human body, life, culture, medicine, food, and health, standing for Meiji Milk Products' roles and the areas of business in which it is active. The corporate color – red – signifies "verve", "warmth", and "humanity". The logo has been applied for stationery, printed matters, brochures, cars, signage, uniforms, packaging of products, and many others.

Seizo Shimamura, Präsident, Meiji Milk Products Co., Ltd., Tokio, Japan

Meiji, ursprünglich Hersteller von Milchprodukten, entwickelte sich im Laufe der langen Firmengeschichte zu einem Hersteller und Verteiler von einer ganzen Reihe von Lebensmitteln. Seit kurzem bestehen Expansionspläne in anderen Produktbereichen sowie auf dem Dienstleistungssektor. Die Sorge um das Wohl der Menschen war von Anfang an unser Leitgedanke und hat unsere Geschäftspolitik sehr geprägt. Für Meiji ist es von grösster Wichtigkeit, Produkte und Dienstleistungen anzubieten, die der Erhaltung und Förderung der Gesundheit und des Wohlbefindens der Verbraucher dienen. Wir haben die ständigen Veränderungen der Umwelt und das wachsende Bewusstsein für die Bedeutung der Gesundheit erkannt und uns immer bemüht, den Bedürfnissen und Erwartungen gerecht zu werden.

Takenobu Igarashi, Igarashi Studio, Tokio, Japan

Im Hinblick auf den 70sten Jahrestag der Gründung von Meiji Milk Products wurde ein Jahr zuvor, 1986, ein neues Corporate Design eingeführt. Das Design sollte die Vitalität und die guten Aussichten für ständiges Wachstum zum Ausdruck bringen. Ausserdem steht es für Meijis Stabilität und Zuverlässigkeit. Die sechs Streifen repräsentieren den menschlichen Körper, Leben, Kultur, Medizin, Nahrungsmittel und Gesundheit – Begriffe, die mit dem Geschäftsbereich und der Rolle der Firma im Zusammenhang stehen. Die Firmenfarbe – Rot – bedeutet «Elan», «Wärme», «Menschlichkeit». Das Logo wurde für Geschäftspapiere, Drucksachen, Broschüren, Fahrzeuge, Hinweisschilder, Uniformen, Produktverpackungen und viele andere Bereiche verwendet.

Seizo Shimamura, président, Meiji Milk Products Co., Ltd., Tokyo, Japon

Meiji, à l'origine simple producteur de produits laitiers, a accédé au rang d'une importante entreprise de production et de distribution d'une vaste gamme de produits alimentaires. Tout récemment nous avons commencé notre expansion dans des secteurs très prometteurs concernant des produits et services non alimentaires. Il est essentiel que Meiji fournisse les produits et services appropriés pour améliorer et renforcer la santé et le bien-être de toutes les personnes au service desquelles nous nous sommes mis. Nous sommes pleinement conscients des transformations continuelles qui affectent notre environnement, ainsi que de l'intérêt et de l'estime que le public porte dans une mesure croissante aux valeurs inhérentes à la santé. Nous avons fourni des efforts continus et concertés pour satisfaire ces besoins et ces attentes.

Takenobu Igarashi, Igarashi Studio, Tokyo, Japon

La société Meiji Milk Products a entrepris en 1986 le lifting de son système d'identité institutionnelle en prévision des cérémonies du 70e anniversaire de l'entreprise en 1987. Le design doit exprimer la vitalité et les perspectives de croissance continue de Meiji et mettre l'accent sur la robustesse et la stabilité de ses structures. Les six bandes se réfèrent au corps humain, à la vie, à la civilisation, à la médecine, à l'alimentation et à la santé, six domaines qui ressortissent au rôle et aux activités de Meiji Milk Products. La couleur de l'image institutionnelle – le rouge – exprime le dynamisme, la chaleur et l'humanité. Ce logo illustre les imprimés maison, les en-têtes, les brochures, les panneaux de signalisation, la décoration des véhicules, les uniformes, les emballages, pour ne citer que ceux-là.

DESIGN FIRM:
IGARASHI STUDIO

ART DIRECTOR:
TAKENOBU IGARASHI

DESIGNER:
YUKIMI SASAGO/
DEBI SHIMAMOTO/
ICHIRO TAKAHASHI/
KAZUHIRO HAYASE/
HONAMI MORITA

CLIENT:
MEIJI MILK PRODUCTS, LTD.

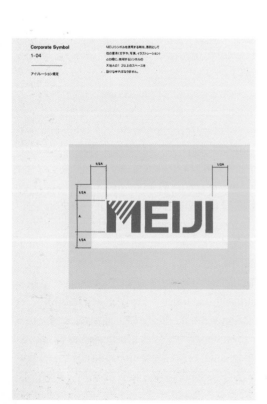

■ Building identification *(previous double spread)*, covers and sections from the brochures "CI Graphic Design Program" and "Basic Standards Manual", with reproduction pages and examples showing use of the logo, negative and positive, and as an endless pattern. *(Below)* Examples of the business stationery.

■ Gebäudekennzeichnung *(vorangehende Doppelseite)* und Umschläge und Teile der Broschüren «CI Graphic Design Program» und «Basic Standards Manual» mit Reproduktionsseiten und Beispielen der Anwendung des Logos - negativ und positiv - und als Endlosmuster. *(Unten)* Beispiele des Geschäftspapiers.

■ Identification du bâtiment *(double page précédente)*, couvertures et pages intérieures des brochures «CI Graphic Design Program» et «Basic Standards Manual» avec des pages de reproduction et des exemples d'application du logo - négatif, positif, - en continu. *(En bas)* Exemples d'en-têtes.

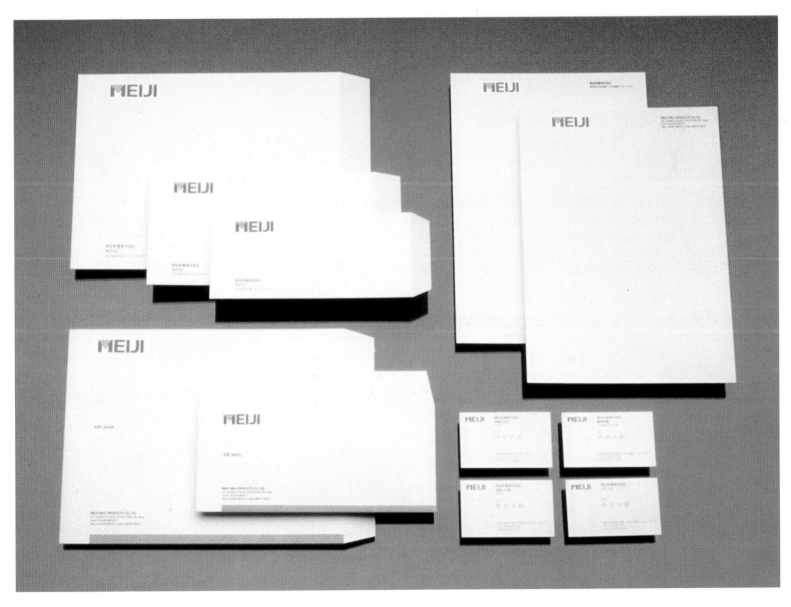

DESIGN FIRM:
IGARASHI STUDIO

ART DIRECTOR:
TAKENOBU IGARASHI

DESIGNER:
YUKIMI SASAGO/
DEBI SHIMAMOTO/
ICHIRO TAKAHASHI/
KAZUHIRO HAYASE/
HONAMI MORITA

CLIENT:
MEIJI MILK PRODUCTS, LTD.

■Photographs from a brochure about the graphic-design program for *Meiji* foodstuffs: on a flag, carrier bags, vehicles, wrapping paper, mail packaging, advertising material, products, and uniform. The cross-strokes of the M always serve as a design element, either as triangles or as stripes.

■Aufnahmen aus einer Broschüre über das Graphik-Design-Programm für *Meiji*-Lebensmittel: die Anwendung auf einer Fahne, Tragtaschen, Fahrzeugen, Einwickelpapier, Versandverpackung, Werbematerial, Produkten und Uniform. Die Querstreifen des M dienen immer wieder als Design-Element, als Dreiecke oder als Streifen.

■D'une brochure consacrée au programme graphique des produits alimentaires *Meiji:* drapeau, sacs à commissions, véhicules, papier d'emballage, emballage d'expédition, matériel publicitaire, produits et uniforme. Les bandes transversales du M se retrouvent régulièrement comme élément de design, sous forme de triangles ou de rayures.

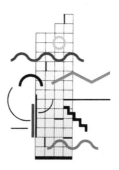

David Sainsbury, Director, Millar Smith Partnership, Abbotsford, Victoria, Australia

Millar Smith Partnership is an architectural design practice established four years ago by a group of young architects. They work in the very competitive area of commercial and industrial architecture. A specific aspect of the Corporate Identity program was to create a distinctive image that would identify the practice as a dynamic and innovative firm. The design was also required to be non-specific to allow for any change to the firm's business activity and range of services. Because of its unique configuration, visual reference to the firm's offices, and wide appeal, the C.I. program has played an important role in assisting Millar Smith Partnership to stand out in the marketplace in which it operates.

David Sainsbury, Direktor, Millar Smith Partnership, Abbotsford, Victoria, Australien

Millar Smith Partnership ist ein Architekturbüro, das vor vier Jahren von einer Gruppe junger Architekten gegründet wurde und hauptsächlich kommerzielle und industrielle Architektur entwirft. Ein wichtiger Aspekt des Corporate-Identity-Programms war es, ein unverwechselbares Signet zu schaffen, das die Firma als dynamisch und innovativ kennzeichnen würde. Ebenfalls musste darauf geachtet werden, ein flexibles Signet zu entwerfen, das der Firma erlaubt, ihre Aktivitäten und Dienstleistungen jederzeit auszudehnen. Dank diesem Corporate-Identity-Programm ist es Millar Smith Partnership gelungen, sich auf dem hart umkämpften Markt in ihrem Gebiet zu behaupten.

David Sainsbury, Directeur, Millar Smith Partnership, Abbotsford, Victoria, Australie

Millar Smith Partnership est un bureau d'architectes fondé il y a quatre ans par une jeune équipe d'architectes. Leur travail se concentre sur le secteur très concurrentiel de l'architecture commerciale et industrielle. Un aspect essentiel du nouveau programme institutionnel consistait à réaliser un emblème original porteur de dynamisme et d'innovation. En même temps, cet emblème devait pouvoir s'adapter aux nouvelles orientations éventuelles de l'entreprise et aux services qu'elle s'adjoindrait. L'image exceptionnelle mise au point, la référence visuelle aux locaux de la société et l'impact de cette publicité institutionnelle ont fortement contribué à asseoir la réputation de Millar Smith Partnership.

Richard Henderson, Flett Henderson & Arnold, Abbotsford, Victoria, Australia

The pictogram developed as the central motive for the design program contains visual reference to their offices, and also alludes to the interface of architecture with the landscape. The graphic element is more dominant than the type matter and is usually reproduced in full color. Applications of the design to stationery and other promotional material has resulted in a distinctive image for the architectural practice. A special neon sign was manufactured to identify the company's offices.

Richard Henderson, Flett Henderson & Arnold, Abbotsford, Victoria, Australien

Das Piktogramm, das als zentrales Motiv für das Design-Programm entwickelt wurde, bezieht sich u.a. auf die Büroräumlichkeiten des Architekten-teams. Das graphische Element ist dominanter als die Schrift und wird meist mehrfarbig dargestellt. Die Anwendung des Designs auf Briefpapier und Promotionsmaterial resultierte in einem unverwechselbaren Erscheinungsbild für dieses Architekten-Team. Zur Kennzeichnung der Büros wurde ein spezielles Neonsignet ausgearbeitet.

Richard Henderson, Flett Henderson & Arnold, Abbotsford, Victoria, Australie

Le pictogramme contient des références visuelles aux locaux de ce bureau d'architectes, mais aussi à l'interaction entre l'architecture et le paysage. L'élément graphique, dominant par rapport à la typo, est généralement reproduit en polychromie. L'application de ce design aux en-têtes et autres matériels promotionnels compose une image institutionnelle hautement originale pour cette équipe d'architectes. Une enseigne néon a été étudiée spécifiquement pour la signalisation des bureaux.

DESIGN FIRM:
FLETT HENDERSON & ARNOLD

ART DIRECTOR:
FLETT HENDERSON & ARNOLD

DESIGNER:
FLETT HENDERSON & ARNOLD

CLIENT:
MILLAR SMITH PARTNERSHIP

■ The architecture of the business headquarters was the determining factor for the design, whereby the surrounding countryside also plays a role. A special neon sign was created for the exterior identification of the offices; the many design possibilities are clearly seen in the business stationery and promotional articles. In most cases the logo is printed in polychrome.

■ Bestimmend für das Erscheinungsbild dieses Architekten-Teams war die Architektur des Geschäftssitzes, wobei auch auf die landschaftliche Umgebung angespielt wird. Für die Aussenkennzeichnung der Büros wurde ein spezielles Neon-Zeichen geschaffen; die vielfältigen Gestaltungsmöglichkeiten werden hier anhand der Geschäftspapiere und Promotionsartikel deutlich.

■ L'image de cette équipe d'architectes s'est orientée vers l'architecture du siège et son environnement. Un signe néon spécial caractérise à l'extérieur l'accès des bureaux; les multiples possibilités d'application sont démontrées ici par l'exemple des en-têtes commerciaux et des articles promotionnels. Dans la plupart des cas, le logo apparaît en polychromie.

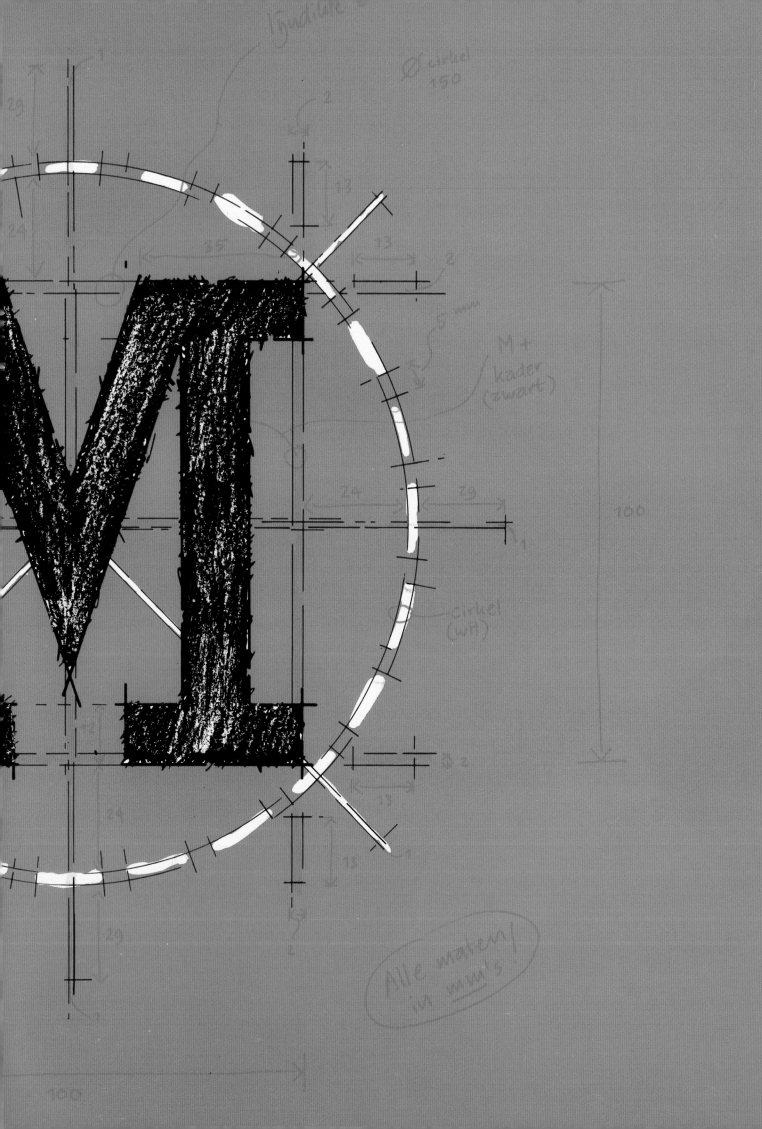

MORS

Jeroen Damen, Partner, Mors Systeemplafonds, Opmeer, The Netherlands

Mors is a young company, founded in 1980, and engaged in ceiling construction. With a total of 100 employees, there are 33 directors who occupy various functions. We took the decision to create a new corporate identity program in order to differentiate ourselves from the competition. When our rapid growth forced us to move to new premises, it tipped the balance in favor of a new image. In proportions the logo is based on the architectural elements of the new building. We had to find a strong logo that would be easily recognizable by our customers i.e. building societies, architects, builders, ministries, and the public. We believe that we have found a suitable logo.

André Toet, Samenwerkende Ontwerpers, Amsterdam, The Netherlands

How do you present a Corporate Identity program for a ceiling-construction company with 33 directors? Even though, naturally, the design itself is decisive, the mode of presentation should also be allotted adequate significance. We decided to make a flipbook by which the whole design process could be followed just by quickly flipping through the pages. The logo is based on the architectural proportions of the impressive new factory designed by Benthem Crouwel. The standard color scheme chosen was orange – and black and silver-grey for the buildings and company vehicles.

Jeroen Damen, Partner, Mors Systeemplafonds, Opmeer, Niederlande

Mors ist ein junges Unternehmen, 1980 gegründet, das sich mit der Konstruktion von Decken befasst. Zu den insgesamt 100 Angestellten gehören 33 Direktoren. Wir haben uns für ein neues Corporate-Identity-Programm entschieden, um uns von der Konkurrenz abzusetzen. Als angesichts des schnellen Wachstums ein neues Gebäude notwendig wurde, gab dies den Ausschlag für ein neues Erscheinungsbild. Das Logo basiert in seinen Proportionen auf der Architektur des neuen Gebäudes. Wir mussten ein starkes Logo finden, das für unsere Kunden - Bauherren, Architekten, Bauunternehmen, Ministerien – leicht erkennbar sein sollte.

André Toet, Samenwerkende Ontwerpers. Amsterdam, Niederlande

Wie präsentiert man 33 Direktoren eines Herstellers von Deckenkonstruktionen ein Corporate-Identity-Programm? Obgleich natürlich das Design selbst ausschlaggebend ist, sollte auch der Form der Präsentation genügend Beachtung geschenkt werden. Wir beschlossen, ein Flip-Buch zu machen, bei dem man die ganze Entwicklung des Designs verfolgen kann. Das Logo basiert auf der Architektur des neuen Werkgebäudes (von den Architekten Benthem Crouwel) für Mors. Die Standard-Farben sind Orange und Schwarz und Silbergrau für das Gebäude und die Firmenwagen.

Jeroen Damen, Associé Mors Systeemplafonds, Opmeer, Pays-Bas

Mors est une entreprise de création récente (1980) spécialisée dans la construction de plafonds. La centaine de personnes qu'elle occupe comprend 33 directeurs travaillant à divers niveaux. Notre nouveau programme de publicité institutionnelle devait nous singulariser par rapport à la concurrence. C'est la construction d'un nouveau bâtiment nécessitée par notre croissance rapide qui a entraîné la décision en faveur d'une image renouvelée. Le logo s'inspire des proportions de ce bâtiment. Il lui fallait la puissance et la lisibilité nécessaires pour que nos clients, les entrepreneurs, les architectes, les ministères et le grand public l'identifient sans problème.

André Toet, Samenwerkende Ontwerpers, Amsterdam, Pays-Bas

Comment présente-t-on un programme d'identité globale de marque aux 33 directeurs d'un fabricant de plafonds? S'il est bien évident que c'est le design qui compte avant tout, la forme adoptée pour sa présentation a son importance. Nous avons donc décidé de préparer un flip-book retraçant les étapes de l'élaboration de la nouvelle image. Le logo est basé sur l'architecture du nouveau bâtiment d'exploitation dû aux architectes Benthem Crouwel. Les couleurs standards sont l'orange, le noir et le gris argenté (ce dernier pour le building et le parc de véhicules).

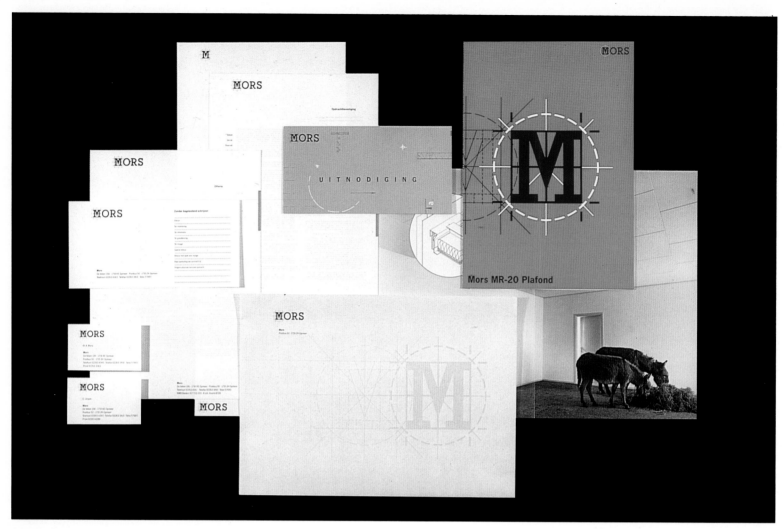

DESIGN FIRM:
SAMENWERKENDE ONTWERPERS

ART DIRECTOR:
ANDRÉ TOET

DESIGNERS:
ANDRÉ TOET/
STELLA LINDERS

CLIENT:
MORS SYSTEEMPLAFONDS

■The M based on the architectural proportions of the new factory building stands alone or is used in combination as a logotype ("Mors"), as shown here on stationery, the company's cars and on the building. Orange, silver-gray, and black are the standard colors of the company. The typefaces used are Rockwell and News Gothic.

■Das auf den Proportionen des neuen Fabrikgebäudes basierende M wird isoliert oder kombiniert als Schriftzug («Mors») verwendet, wie hier auf dem Briefpapier, den Firmenwagen und dem Gebäude gezeigt. Orange, Silbergrau und Schwarz sind die Standardfarben der Firma. Die verwendeten Schrifttypen sind Rockwell und News Gothic.

■Le M dérivé des proportions architecturales de la nouvelle usine s'emploie isolément ou en combinaison avec les autres lettres de «Mors», comme on le voit ici sur l'entête, le véhicule d'entreprise et le bâtiment. L'orange, le gris argenté et le noir sont les coloris standards adoptés. Les caractères utilisés sont le Rockwell et le News Gothic.

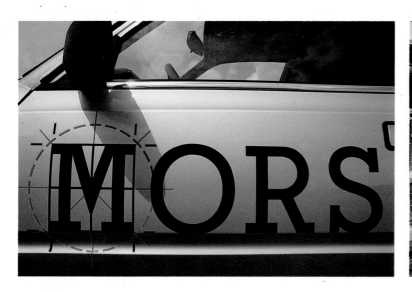

NASA

Robert Schulman, Chief, Special Services Branch, NASA, Washington D.C., USA

NASA was mandated in 1958 and employs approx. 22,000 people at 10 Space Centers. Before the Unified Visual Communications System was introduced in 1975, NASA's graphics material was fragmented, had no family resemblance, no style and therefore poorly communicated the agency's message. The main objective was to provide a cost effective system which would project a strong, vital, and cohesive image. The design system focuses on the NASA logotype in that the letters N-A-S-A are reduced to their simplest form, giving a feeling of unity, technological precision, thrust, and orientation toward the future. The visual communications system has made it possible for NASA to achieve maximum communication of the agency's program objectives, both internally and externally and we have received many highly favorable comments.

Robert Schulman, Chef der Special Services Branch, NASA, Washington D.C., USA

Die NASA, 1958 ins Leben gerufen, beschäftigt heute ca. 22'000 Mitarbeiter in zehn Raumfahrtzentren. Bevor das neue vereinheitlichte visuelle Kommunikationssystem 1975 eingeführt wurde, war das graphische Material der NASA fragmentarisch, es hatte keine «Familienähnlichkeit», keine Linie und war für die Vermittlung unserer Botschaft somit ungeeignet. Das Hauptziel war ein kosteneffektives System, das ein starkes, vitales und geschlossenes Bild ergeben würde. Mittelpunkt des Design-Systems ist der Schriftzug, in welchem die Buchstaben N-A-S-A auf die einfachste Form reduziert sind. Es wird ein Gefühl der Einheit, technologischer Präzision, Kraft und zukunftsorientierter Einstellung vermittelt. Mit diesem visuellen Kommunikationssystem ist es der NASA gelungen, ihr Programm und ihre Ziele nach innen und aussen effizient mitzuteilen.

Robert Schulman, Chief, Special Services Branch, NASA, Washington D.C., USA

La NASA, qui a vu le jour en 1958, occupe aujourd'hui quelque 22'000 personnes. Avant l'introduction d'un système unifié de communications visuelles en 1975, les matériels graphiques de l'Agence étaient fragmentés, ne présentaient aucun air de famille, n'avaient pas de style et transcrivaient par conséquent très mal le message au public. L'objectif principal a consisté à élaborer un système rentable projetant une image forte, vitale, cohérente. Ce système de design est centré sur le logo qui réduit à sa plus simple expression la séquence N-A-S-A. Il en résulte une sensation d'unité, de précision technologique, de dynamisme et d'ouverture sur l'avenir. Le nouveau système de communications visuelles a permis à la NASA de faire pleinement comprendre les données et les objectifs de ses programmes, tant sur le plan intérieur que dans la communication avec l'extérieur.

Richard Danne, Richard Danne & Associates, New York, NY/USA

The NASA identity program was considered a breakthrough when it was introduced. Its success helped encourage other U.S. Agencies to redesign. Danne & Blackburn was awarded the NASA contract in 1974.. The objective was to produce a program which would be contemporary, convey the proper spirit of innovation, and symbolically embody the Agency's achievement and goals. Because NASA graphics are produced primarily by their internal staff, the overall system needed to be simple and easy to maintain. We applied many of the proven principles of the Corporate Identity process to this complicated institutional program. The NASA program has been widely cited and published. In 1985 it was awarded one of the first Presidential Awards for Design Excellence.

Richard Danne, Richard Danne & Associates, New York, NY/USA

Das Identitätsprogramm für die NASA wurde zu einem echten Durchbruch. Der Erfolg dieses Programms spornte auch andere US-Behörden zur Erneuerung ihres graphischen Erscheinungsbildes an. Danne & Blackburn erhielten den NASA-Auftrag 1974. Aufgabe war es, ein Programm zu schaffen, das zeitgemäss ist, dem Geist von Innovation entspricht und die Leistungen und Ziele der Behörde symbolisiert. Da das NASA-Design-Programm in erster Linie von internen Mitarbeitern umgesetzt wird, musste das Gesamtsystem einfach und leicht einzuhalten sein. Wir bedienten uns bei diesem komplizierten institutionellen Programm vieler bei Firmenerscheinungsbildern erprobter Prinzipien. Das NASA-Programm wird immer wieder zitiert und gezeigt.

Richard Danne, Richard Danne & Associates, New York, NY/USA

Le programme d'identité de la NASA a été salué comme une nouveauté de poids lors de son introduction. Ce succès a incité d'autres agences gouvernementales américaines à tenter un lifting de leur image insitutionnelle. Pour Danne & Blackburn il s'agissait en 1974 de mettre au point un programme d'aspect contemporain, porteur de l'esprit d'innovation et symbolisant les réalisations et les objectifs de l'agence. Les applications graphiques étant essentiellement le fait de l'équipe de design permanente de la NASA, le nouveau système global devait être simple et facile à observer. Pour la mise en œuvre de ce programme institutionnel complexe, nous avons eu recours à un grand nombre de principes éprouvés dans la création du capital-image des entreprises.

NASA Spacecraft Markings

The marking of NASA spacecraft vehicles is essential, critical, and difficult. It is quite important that any identification or markings which appear on spacecraft be consistent with the overall goals of the NASA Unified Visual Communications System. These vehicles represent tangible evidence of many of NASA's most interesting programs. As such, they are the focus of considerable public and media attention and should be marked in simple but effective ways.

Another important consideration is that the vehicle be marked so that it can be identified from different angles, whether in a launch mode or in outer space.

Of course, the overriding consideration is that the markings not interfere or impede the scientific mission of the craft. This principle applies to maintenance as well as the operational qualities of the craft when performing in space. This objective is very achievable as demonstrated on the Space Shuttle shown below.

Only a few isolated areas were designated for graphics by flight engineers and scientists. Working within these serious constraints, the Shuttle Orbiter is fully marked with all of the basic identifiers: The NASA Logotype, the American flag, United States, plus the name of the particular craft. Helvetica Medium is the typeface used on the spacecraft.

Note that the NASA Logotype appears in NASA Gray so as not to conflict with the red of the American flag. The flag is equal to the height of the capital letters on the side, top, and bottom of the craft. The placement of these identifying elements is responsive to technical requirements as well as being harmonious with the basic shape and form of the Shuttle.

On the following gatefold you will see examples of other spacecraft which

employ one or several of the available markings. Though they vary in size, shape, and configuration, they nevertheless maintain a strong overall relationship within the NASA Unified Visual Communications System.

Columbia
United States
NASA
USA

7.10

NASA Aircraft Markings

The marking scheme adapts well to the wide range of aircraft shapes and sizes that comprise the NASA fleet. Shown below are approved paint and marking schemes for eight aircraft.

a) Grumman Gulfstream I: The windows determine the width and placement of the blue stripe. Fuselage markings align with the top edge of the windows.

b) Northrop T-38: The top of the blue stripe aligns with the top edge of the jet engine nacelle. Fuselage markings are flush with the trailing edge of the wings.

c) Lockheed F-104: The blue stripe aligns with the width of the jet engine inlet cone and the nose of the fuselage. Fuselage markings align with the top of the wings.

d) Beech Queenair 80: The blue stripe is positioned under the windows. Fuselage markings meet the 12" cap height requirement, aligning with the rear edge of the window above.

e) Lockheed P-3: The blue stripe includes the round windows on the fuselage. An American flag, required on this aircraft, is flush right with the logotype. Wing and horizontal stabilizer tips are red for high visibility against white backgrounds.

f) Lockheed F-106: The bottom of the blue stripe aligns with the leading edge of the wings. Fuselage markings are flush left with the tail markings.

g) Beech C-45: The blue stripe aligns with the top and bottom of the windows. Fuselage markings meet the 12" cap height requirement, centered within the blue stripe.

h) Bell UH-1B Helicopter: The top of the blue stripe aligns with the bottom of the cockpit window and angles up the tail. The logotype and numeral are in a horizontal configuration, flush left under the door markings.

These eight schemes serve also as guides for developing marking applications for other aircraft in the NASA fleet. Leased or loaned aircraft may have a minimum marking of a red logotype with black Helvetica

Medium numerals. This type of aircraft (when repainted by NASA) is painted following the white/blue/gray scheme shown here.

Complete detailed specification drawings (including color specifications) on all aircraft shown on these pages, are available from the NASA Aircraft Office.

7.9

NASA Uniform Patches

Personnel identification is an important facet of the NASA identification program. An embroidered patch incorporating the logotype is available for application on a wide variety of uniforms and clothing. Two patch designs, shown to the right, are available.

For general personnel, a white patch with a NASA Red logotype is available. This achieves the simplest and most effective identification on various types and colors of clothing that may include other badges or name tags. The patch is applied on the right front side of the garment approximately 1½" (3.8 cm) directly above the breast pocket or in a comparable position on garments without pockets. On a blazer (fig. e), the top edge of the patch aligns with the left breast pocket.

A few specific color recommendations are made for NASA uniforms: royal blue for flight suits; white for lab coats, hardhats, and helmets. A 7" wide (17.8 cm) logotype may be embroidered in NASA Red centered on the back of a white lab coat (fig. d). On a white hardhat or helmet, a 5" wide (12.7 cm) NASA Red decal of the logotype may be centered on the front (fig. g).

To distinguish emergency/security personnel (security guards, firemen, etc.) a distinctive NASA Red patch with a white border, white logotype and the installation identification in black is available. The name of the emergency/security service (i.e. Fire Department) appears in white centered within a smaller black patch that is positioned ⅜" (.9 cm) under the red patch. This configuration is worn on both shoulders of the uniform, on both shirts (fig. f) and outer-jackets. A light blue shirt and hat with dark blue trousers or skirt is recommended.

NASA
General personnel patch

NASA
National Space
Technology Labs

Fire Department
Emergency/security patches

9.2

Going to Work in Space

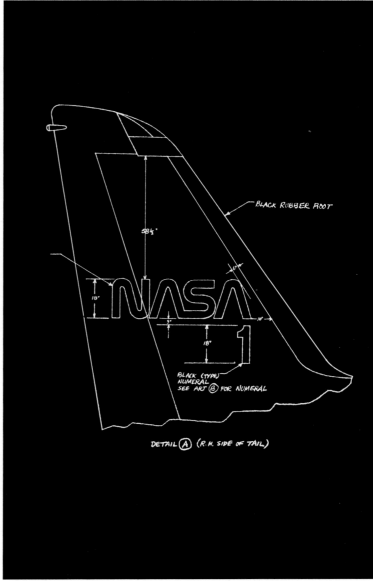

BLACK RUBBER ROOT

DETAIL Ⓐ (R.H. SIDE OF TAIL)

DESIGN FIRM:
DANNE & BLACKBURN INC.

ART DIRECTOR:
RICHARD DANNE

DESIGNERS:
RICHARD DANNE/
BRUCE BLACKBURN/
STEPHEN LOGES/
GARY SKEGGS

GRAPHICS COORDINATOR:
ROBERT SCHULMAN/NASA

PHOTOGRAPHER:
RENÉ BURRI/MAGNUM

CLIENT:
NASA NATIONAL AERONAUTICS
& SPACE ADMINISTRATION

■ Pages from NASA's standard manual. NASA not only had to consider the design from a graphic viewpoint, but also had to take into consideration the technical aspects – for instance the application of the logo on space craft. This logo can be seen, among other things, on the cover of NASA's house organ. The manual serves as a model for many private and state enterprises, and the Corporate Identity design as such has received many awards.

■ Seiten aus dem Standard Manual der NASA, in dem nicht nur die graphischen Gesichtspunkte, sondern auch die technischen Überlegungen im Zusammenhang mit der Anbringung des Logos auf den Raumschiffen berücksichtigt werden. Auf den Umschlägen der Hauszeitschrift der NASA ist u.a. diese Beschriftung zu erkennen. Das Manual gilt als Musterbeispiel, und auch das Corporate-Identity-Design als solches wurde mehrfach ausgezeichnet.

■ Pages du manuel standard de la NASA où l'on trouve non seulement les instructions relatives à l'image graphique, mais aussi les indications techniques concernant l'emploi du logo sur les véhicules spatiaux. La même inscription figure entre autres aussi sur les couvertures de la revue d'entreprise de la NASA. Le manuel sert de modèle du genre à de nombreuses entreprises étatisées ou privées. L'image institutionnelle de la NASA a été souvent primée.

Bob Bradford, Director, The National Aviation Museum, Ottawa, Ontario, Canada

The National Aviation Museum was founded in Canada in the 1930s and today has one of the best collections of aircraft in the world. The exhibits were housed for many years in World War I hangars in Toronto, but the need to provide a safe, more modern interpretive environment for the collection eventually led to the opening of a new building in June 1988. The Museum wished to celebrate the new building and focus public attention on this hitherto little-known Canadian treasure. As Canada has made significant contributions to the development of aviation at home and abroad, the selection of the Silver Dart as the main design element was particularly appropriate. We consider the design image created by Neville Smith and Aviva Furman a success. It generated a great deal of excitement in the cultural community.

Bob Bradford, Direktor, The National Aviation Museum, Ottawa, Ontario, Kanada

Das National Aviation Museum wurde während der dreissiger Jahre in Kanada gegründet. Heute beherbergt es eine der besten Flugzeugsammlungen der Welt. Nachdem es viele Jahre in Flugzeughallen aus dem Ersten Weltkrieg in Toronto untergebracht war, führte das Bedürfnis nach einem sicheren, moderneren Unterbringungsort 1988 zur Eröffnung eines neuen Gebäudes. Dieses Ereignis wollte das Museum feiern und gleichzeitig die Aufmerksamkeit des Publikums erwecken. Kanada hat zur Flugzeugentwicklung auf nationaler und internationaler Ebene viel beigetragen. Deshalb schien die Wahl des Silver Dart als wichtigstes Design-Element besonders passend. Wir betrachten das Corporate-Design-Programm von Neville Smith und Aviva Furman als Erfolg. Beim Publikum wurde es mit Begeisterung aufgenommen.

Bob Bradford, Directeur, The National Aviation Museum, Ottawa, Ontario, Canada

Le National Aviation Museum a été fondé dans les années 1930 dans des hangars de Toronto datant de la Première Guerre mondiale. Ce n'est qu'en 1988 que la volonté d'en moderniser la présentation dans une enceinte offrant toute garantie de sécurité s'est traduite par le transfert dans un nouvel immeuble inauguré au mois de juin. Le Musée entendait faire d'une pierre deux coups en attirant l'attention du grand public sur ce trésor national lors de l'inauguration officielle du bâtiment. Le Canada ayant compté des avionneurs de grand mérite, le choix de l'élément central de l'image institutionnelle à créer s'est porté tout naturellement sur le Silver Dart. Le design créé par Neville Smith et Aviva Furman est à nos yeux un grand succès qui n'a pas manqué d'enthousiasmer la communauté culturelle nationale.

Neville Smith, Neville Smith Graphic Design, Aylmer, Quebec, Canada

The visual identity was created for the opening of The National Aviation Museum of Canada. All of the print applications include the Silver Dart symbol. This was the first airplane to make a powered flight in Canada in 1909. Print applications also include graphic references to the building structure as well as to other aircraft in the collection. A complete press kit was delivered to aviation dignitaries and media sources in advance of the opening. The "Cleared for Takeoff" program booklet was given to everyone attending the official opening ceremonies. The poster, available in both English and French, is used for promotion at the Museum as well as in other locations inside and outside Canada.

Neville Smith, Neville Smith Graphic Design, Aylmer, Quebec, Kanada

Das visuelle Erscheinungsbild wurde anlässlich der Eröffnung des National Aviation Museums von Kanada gestaltet. Auf allen Drucksachen wurde das Silver Dart Symbol angewendet (das Flugzeug machte 1909 den ersten motorbetriebenen Flug Kanadas) sowie graphische Elemente, die von der Architektur des Gebäudes und von anderen Flugzeugen aus der Sammlung abgeleitet wurden. Vor der Eröffnung wurde eine Pressemappe an Honoratioren aus der Luftfahrt und an die Presse verschickt. Die Broschüre «Cleared for Takeoff» wurde an alle Gäste der offiziellen Eröffnungsfeier verteilt. Das Plakat, erhältlich in Englisch und Französisch, ist für den Innenaushang im Museum und für die Aussenwerbung bestimmt.

Neville Smith, Neville Smith Graphic Design, Aylmer, Quebec, Canada

La publicité institutionnelle a été créée à l'occasion de l'inauguration du Musée national canadien de l'aviation. Tous les imprimés sont illustrés du symbole du Silver Dart, l'avion qui réalisa le premier vol moteur au Canada en 1909. Les autres éléments graphiques utilisés font référence à l'architecture du musée et à d'autres types d'avions figurant dans ses collections. Un press-book complet a été remis aux représentants des médias et de l'aviation dès avant l'inauguration du bâtiment. La brochure intitulée «Cleared for Takeoff» (Prêt à décoller) était destinée aux participants de la journée officielle. L'affiche est destinée à la promotion à l'interieur du musée, ainsi qu'à la publicité au Canada et à l'étranger.

DESIGN FIRM:
NEVILLE SMITH GRAPHIC DESIGN

ART DIRECTORS:
NEVILLE SMITH/AVIVA FURMAN

EDITORIAL DIRECTOR:
WENDY McPEAKE

DESIGNERS:
NEVILLE SMITH/ AVIVA FURMAN

CLIENT:
*THE NATIONAL AVIATION
MUSEUM OF CANADA*

■ The "Silver Dart", Canada's first successful aircraft, is shown in gold tones in all the printed matter as the symbol of the National Aviation Museum. The graphic design of the printed matter is based on the architecture of the museum itself (opened in 1988). Other veterans from the museum's collection are used as subjects for the printed material. The poster is intended both for inside and outside advertising for the museum.

■ Der «Silver Dart» (Silberpfeil), Kanadas erstes erfolgreiches Motorflugzeug taucht in allen Drucksachen als Symbol für das Museum auf. Ferner spielt die graphische Gestaltung der Drucksachen auf die Architektur des 1988 eröffneten neuen Gebäudes an, und auch andere Veteranen aus der Kollektion sind immer wieder Gegenstand der Drucksachen. Das Plakat ist für den Innen- und Aussenaushang bestimmt.

■ La Flèche d'argent (Silver Dart), le premier avion à moteur canadien, apparaît sur tous les imprimés comme emblème du National Aviation Museum, exécuté en or. L'image graphique des imprimés fait également référence à l'architecture du nouveau bâtiment dont le musée s'est doté en 1988. Les imprimés font aussi régulièrement connaître d'autres vétérans des collections du musée. L'affiche est destinée à l'affichage intérieur et extérieur.

Betty Hudson, Vice President, Corporate and Media Relations, NBC Inc., New York, NY/USA

In 1926, the National Broadcasting Company became the nation's first radio network. Today, NBC is a multi-faceted communications company. NBC has had a number of service marks over the years. Improved performance and the company's 60th Anniversary gave us both the means and the reason to introduce the new design. Our main objectives were to simplify the existing design while attaching minimum notice to the change. We have tested the new design against the old and more than 90% of the respondents could correctly indentify the new design as being NBC and did not notice the difference. The final visual solution was embraced because it simplified the peacock – initially a symbol for "living color" and later associated with the slogan "NBC - Proud as a Peacock" – and included a return to the full use of our corporate initials (NBC) as our logo.

Stephan Geissbuhler, Chermayeff & Geismar, New York, NY/USA

The symbol and logotype designed by our firm in 1980 were finally introduced and aired in 1986. The most recent identity, prior to our design, was a combination of two different ideas, neither of which was satisfactory by itself and in combination became cluttered, unreadable, and nonfunctional. (The original peacock, designed by Herb Lubalin, was a symbol for color television; the Diamond "N" by Lippincott & Margulies; the combination was designed by the NBC in-house design department.) As part of the identification program we redrew the letters NBC, News, Sports, etc. and consequently three weights of the Futura typeface. We believe that the simplicity, strength, and appropriateness of the symbol, logo, typeface, and the colors have made this solution successful.

Betty Hudson, Vice President, Corporate and Media Relations, NBC Inc., New York, NY/USA

Die National Broadcasting Company war 1926 die erste Radiostation der USA. Heute ist NBC ein breitgefächertes Kommunikationsunternehmen. Im Laufe der Jahre hatte NBC verschiedene Logos. Besserer Geschäftsgang und der 60. Geburtstag des Unternehmens waren Anlass für die Einführung des neuen Designs. Unser Hauptanliegen war, das bestehende Logo zu vereinfachen, und zwar ohne allzu grosse Änderungen. Im Vergleichstest des neuen und alten Logos konnten 90% der Befragten die neue Lösung eindeutig als NBC-Logo identifizieren, ohne sich einer Änderung bewusst zu sein. Für die neue Lösung sprach vor allem, dass sie den Pfau – ursprünglich Symbol für Farbfernsehen und später im Zusammenhang mit dem Slogan «NBC - stolz wie ein Pfau» eingesetzt – vereinfachte und dass das Logo wieder die vollständigen Firmeninitialen NBC enthielt.

Stephan Geissbuhler, Chermayeff & Geismar, New York, NY/USA

Das 1980 entworfene Symbol und Logo wurden schliesslich 1986 eingeführt. Das vorherige Erscheinungsbild war eine Kombination aus zwei Design-Ideen, von denen keine für sich allein funktionierte, während die Kombination überladen, unleserlich und nicht funktionell war. (Der Original-Pfau war ein von Herb Lubalin entworfenes Symbol für Farbfernsehen; das «N» stammt von Lippincott & Margulies; die Kombination wurde von der Graphikabteilung der NBC gestaltet.) Teil der Neugestaltung war eine Überarbeitung der Typographie für NBC, Nachrichten, Sport etc. in drei Stärken der Futura. Wir glauben, dass die Schlichtheit, Stärke und Eignung des Symbols, Logos und der Typographie sowie die Farben diese Lösung so erfolgreich machen.

Betty Hudson, Vice-président, Relations institutionnelles et médiatiques, NBC Inc., New York

En 1926, la National Broadcasting Company devenait la première société de radiodiffusion américaine. Aujourd'hui, la NBC est une société de communications aux multiples facettes. Au fil des années, nombre de logos ont vu le jour. Le développement des affaires et le 60e anniversaire de la création de la NBC nous ont fourni les moyens et l'occasion d'introduire une nouvelle image institutionnelle. Nous avions procédé à une évaluation de la nouvelle image et de l'ancienne: plus de 90% des téléspectateurs ont nettement identifié la nouvelle comme symbolisant la NBC sans même être conscients des changements opérés. La solution retenue se recommandait parce qu'elle simplifiait le paon, à l'origine symbole de la «couleur vivante», par la suite associé à la devise «NBC - fier comme un paon»; par ailleurs, elle impliquait le retour à nos trois initiales NBC.

Stephan Geissbuhler, Chermayeff & Geismar, New York, NY/USA

Le symbole et le logo ont été introduits et télévisés en 1986. L'image institutionnelle dont nous devions assurer le lifting combinait deux idées dont aucune n'était suffisante et dont la combinaison produisait un ensemble brouillé, peu lisible et non fonctionnel. (Le paon d'origine était l'œuvre de Herb Lubalin; le caractère «N» Diamond venait de chez Lippincott & Margulies. C'est au département graphique de NBC qu'était revenue la combinaison des deux éléments.) Une partie du lifting a consisté à redessiner les lettres NBC, ainsi qu'à revoir la typo des sous-titres News, Sport, etc. en utilisant trois forces de corps Futura. Nous estimons que la sobriété, la force et le caractère adéquat du symbole, du logo, de la typo et des couleurs font cette solution un réel succès.

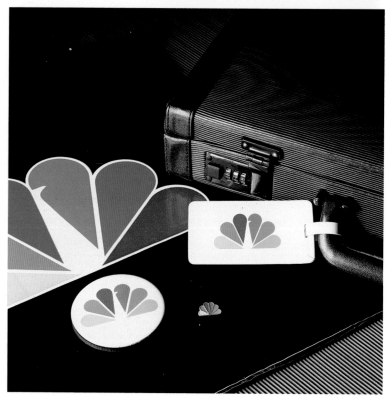

■The reworked logo for NBC – introduced in 1986 – on business stationery (on which the stylized peacock also appears in monochrome), promotional material, and pages from the standard manual. The peacock was, in another form, used by NBC for the first time when color TV was introduced, but as color became a matter of course, it was dropped. Because of the pleasurable association of this symbol in the minds of viewers (established by market research) the peacock was again taken into the NBC logo in the late seventies.

■Das 1986 eingeführte, neu überarbeitete Logo für NBC auf Geschäftspapieren, auf denen der stilisierte Pfau auch einfarbig erscheint, Promotionsmaterial und Seiten aus dem Standard Manual. Der Pfau wurde – in anderer Form – erstmals von NBC bei Einführung des Farbfernsehens benutzt; als Farbe zur Selbstverständlichkeit wurde, verschwand er. Aufgrund der positiven Erinnerung der Zuschauer an dieses Symbol, die in einer Marktstudie festgestellt wurde, wurde der Pfau in den späten 70er Jahren wieder in das NBC-Logo aufgenommen.

■Le logo de la NBC issu du lifting de 1986 figure ici sur des en-têtes commerciaux où le paon stylisé apparaît également monochrome, sur du matériel promotionnel et des pages du manuel standard. Le paon a été employé sous une autre forme pour la première fois lorsque la NBC a lancé la télévision couleur. Il a disparu lorsque la couleur s'est généralisée. Des études de marché ayant révélé que nombre de téléspectateurs s'en souvenaient avec nostalgie, le motif du paon a été repris pour le logo NBC à la fin des années 70.

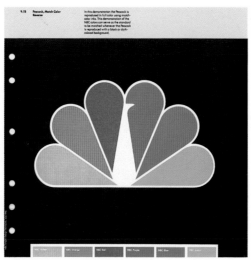

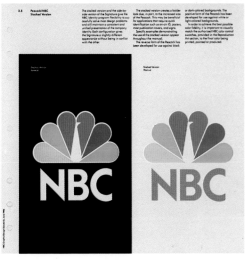

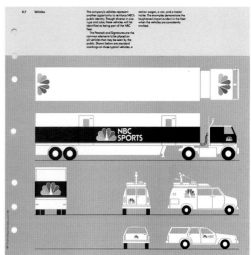

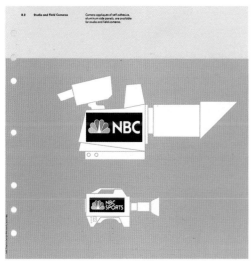

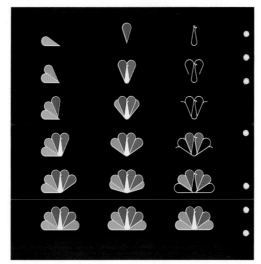

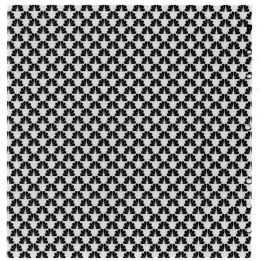

DESIGN FIRM:
*CHERMAYEFF & GEISMAR
ASSOCIATES*

ART DIRECTORS:
*STEFF GEISSBUHLER/
IVAN CHERMAYEFF*

DESIGNER:
*CHERMAYEFF & GEISMAR
ASSOCIATES*

PHOTOGRAPHER:
JÜRG KLAGES (PEACOCK)

CLIENT:
*NBC NATIONAL
BROADCASTING COMPANY*

DESIGN FIRM:
CHERMAYEFF & GEISMAR ASSOCIATES

ART DIRECTORS:
STEFF GEISSBUHLER/ IVAN CHERMAYEFF

DESIGNER:
CHERMAYEFF & GEISMAR ASSOCIATES

CLIENT:
NBC NATIONAL BROADCASTING COMPANY

■ Signboard for an NBC television station, T-shirts with monochrome and polychrome prints, detail of a uniform, and signboards at a studio in California.

■ Hinweisschild für eine NBC-Fernsehstation, T-Shirts mit ein- und mehrfarbigem Aufdruck, Detail einer Uniform und Hinweisschilder an einem Studio in Kalifornien.

■ Panneau indicateur pour une station de télévision NBC, tee-shirts avec impression en une ou plusieurs couleurs, détail d'uniforme et panneaux.

OBOURG

J.P. Bouillon, Manager of Advertising and Documentation, Ciments d'Obourg SA, Belgium

The corporation Ciments d'Obourg was founded in Obourg in 1911. The company at first limited itself exclusively to the production of portland cement. In the course of time, however, the production was extended to include furnace cement, puzzolane-portland cement, and permetallurgy cement in response to the multiple needs of the market. In 1988 production from the Obourg Cement Factory and the cement mill Ciments de Haccourt SA (100% owned by Obourg) amounted to 1,974,000 tons of cement goods. In view of the growth and rapid development of our company, we decided to modernize our visual identity without losing the friendly impact of the old symbol which refers to the village of Obourg.

J.P. Bouillon, Leiter des Werbe- und Dokumentationsdienstes, Ciments d'Obourg SA, Belgien

Die Ciments d'Obourg SA wurde 1911 in Obourg gegründet. Die Firma beschränkte sich zunächst auf die Produktion von Portland-Zement. Mit der Zeit aber wurde die Produktion auf Hochofen-Zement, Puzzolan-Portland-Zement und Permetallurgie-Zement ausgedehnt, um den vielfältigen Anforderungen der Verbraucher zu entsprechen. 1988 betrug der Ausstoss des Obourger Zementwerkes sowie der Zementmühle Ciments de Haccourt SA (zu 100% im Besitz von Obourg) 1'974'000 t Zementwaren. Angesichts dieser Entwicklung entschlossen wir uns zu einer Modernisierung unseres visuellen Erscheinungsbildes, ohne dabei auf die freundliche Wirkung des auf den Ort Obourg bezogenen alten Symbols zu verzichten.

J.P. Bouillon, Le Chef du Service Publicité et documentation, Ciments d'Obourg SA, Belgique

La société mère du Groupe, la s.a. Ciments d'Obourg fut constituée en 1911. Cette société s'est tout d'abord exclusivement intéressée à la fabrication du ciment de type portland. Par la suite, elle diversifia sa production en l'étendant aux ciment de haut fourneau, ciment portland à la pouzzolane et ciment permétallurgique. En 1988, la cimentorie d'Obourg et la station de mouture de la s.a. Ciments de Haccourt, filiale à 100% d'Obourg, ont livré 1'974'000 t de ciments. Etant donné le développement rapide et la croissance soutenue de notre entreprise, nous avons décidé de moderniser notre identité visuelle sans pour autant renoncer à la note chaleureuse qui accompagnait l'ancien symbole évoquant le village d'Obourg.

Philippe Lemmers, Design Board/Behaeghel & Partners, Brussels, Belgium

The existing concept of the village and the rising sun has been kept and so have the colors. The red stands for rising spirits, warmth and sympathy, the blue refers to a quiet, stable, comfortable location. In order to express the double message of tradition and modernity, the symbol has been simplified reducing the roofs to a double line. Also the type has been modernized; the U and the R have been linked for the sake of a stronger personality and impact. On stationery and other printed matters the logo and the symbol are always positioned in the top left corner. On signs inside and outside of buildings only the symbol appears. In corporate communications, each message to clients has to carry the "Mr. Obourg" sign, which is a pictogram of a little man "smiling and saluting".

Philippe Lemmers, Design Board/Behaeghel & Partners, Brüssel, Belgien

Das auf das Dorf und die aufgehende Sonne anspielende bestehende Symbol wurde modernisiert: aus den Dächern wurde eine doppelte Linie, um gleichzeitig Tradition und Fortschrittlichkeit auszudrücken. Die Farben Rot und Blau wurden beibehalten, wobei das warme Rot der Sonne neuen Elan, Wärme und Anteilnahme ausdrückt, während das Blau der Dächer auf eine ruhige, stabile, angenehme Lage hindeutet. Die Typographie wurde geändert, modernisiert. Um eine einprägsamere Identität zu erreichen, wurden das U und das R miteinander verbunden. Auf den Geschäftspapieren und anderen Drucksachen sind das Logo und das Symbol in der linken oberen Ecke positioniert. Auf Hinweisschildern in und an Gebäuden erscheint nur das Symbol.

Philippe Lemmers, Design Board/Behaegel & Partners, Bruxelles, Belgique

La conception ancienne du village au soleil levant a été maintenue tout comme les couleurs: le rouge incarnant l'enthousiasme, la chaleur et la sympathie, le bleu reflétant la solidité, le calme et le confort des lieux. La tradition alliée à la modernité a trouvé expression dans la réduction des toits à un double trait. La typo a été transformée et modernisée; la ligature du U et du R sert à souligner la personnalité de l'entreprise et à ancrer son image dans les esprits. Pour les imprimés et en-têtes, le logo et le symbole sont renvoyés dans le coin gauche supérieur. La signalisation extérieure et intérieure des bâtiments ne fait appel qu'au symbole. Les communications d'entreprise destinées aux clients s'enrichissent du pictogramme de «Mr. Obourg», un petit homme qui «salue en souriant».

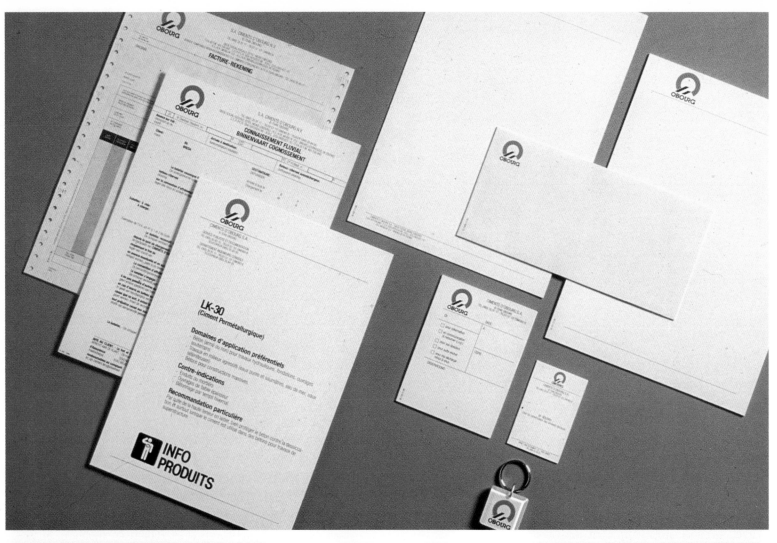

Design Firm:
Design Board/
Behaeghel & Partners
Art Director:
Julien Behaeghel

Designer:
Denis Keller/Erik Vantal

Client:
Ciments d'Obourg S.A.

■ The red and blue colors in the symbol for the Obourg Cement Factory represent the rising sun and the roofs of the City of Obourg. The symbol is placed alone on signs only, in other applications it is always placed along with the logotype "Obourg". Announcements and letters to customers additionally bear the pictogram of a smiling, saluting man.

■ Das in den Farben Rot und Blau gehaltene Zeichen symbolisiert die aufgehende Sonne und die Dächer der Stadt Obourg. Das Symbol wird nur auf Schildern alleine gezeigt, in den anderen Anwendungsbereichen jeweils zusammen mit dem Schriftzug «Obourg». Mitteilungen und Briefe an Kunden tragen zusätzlich das Piktogramm eines lächelnden, salutierenden Männchens.

■ L'emblème rouge et bleu de la cimenterie d'Obourg symbolise le soleil levant et les toits de la ville d'Obourg. Il n'apparaît seul que sur les enseignes, autrement on le voit associé à la mention «Obourg». Les communications d'entreprise et les lettres à la clientèle sont en plus dotées d'un pictogramme représentant un petit bonhomme souriant qui salue.

Ippei Inoh, President, OUN International Ltd., Tokyo, Japan

Since our establishment in May 1986, we have been dedicated to two major areas of the design business, one of which is to design and market our original products and the other to coordinate projects between the world's prominent designers and Japanese clients. Feeling the need for a logomark that would represent our philosophy and determination, we asked Mr. Takenobu Igarashi to take charge of a Corporate Identity program. The result is an ever-unique logomark which flexibly grows as our business expands. We are more than satisfied and are proud of the design.

Ippei Inoh, Präsident, OUN International Ltd., Tokio, Japan

Seit Gründung dieser Gruppe im Mai 1986 haben wir uns hauptsächlich mit zwei Design-Bereichen befasst: Wir entwerfen und verkaufen eine Reihe von Büroartikeln unter der Marke OUN und vermitteln japanischen Kunden internationale Designer. Um den Charakter unseres Geschäftes und unser Ziel - hervorragendes Design - auszudrükken, benötigten wir ein Logo, das den höchsten Ansprüchen gerecht wird. Wir beauftragten Takenobu Igarashi mit der Entwicklung eines Corporate-Identity-Programmes und sind mit dem Ergebnis in jeder Hinsicht zufrieden.

Ippei Inoh, Président, OUN International Ltd., Tokyo, Japon

Depuis notre fondation en mai 1986, nous nous sommes investis dans deux grands secteurs du design. Nous concevons et commercialisons des produits qui nous sont propres sous la marque OUN et nous assurons la coordination de projets associant les grands designers internationaux et des clients japonais. Notre philosophie et notre engagement exigeaient la création d'un logo de poids. C'est à M. Takenobu Igarashi que nous devons notre programme de publicité institutionnelle basé sur un logo d'une rare puissance expressive qui s'adapte aisément à nos besoins.

Takenobu Igarashi, Igarashi Studio, Tokyo, Japan

The company was set up by Suntory Ltd. and Dentsu Inc. with the aim to develop and market original designed products and selected items from around the world. Under the advice of three leading international designers, Alan Fletcher, Takenobu Igarashi, and Massimo Vignelli as executive directors, OUN started their activities with them taking the lead in designing and generating new ideas. The corporate symbol is represented through a myriad of variations (51 distinct types at present which have already been developed and put to actual use each time a new product or materials for the company are introduced). The symbols are developed around a standard designed base of the letters OUN. From this base, a limitless number of symbols are created. The intent of this concept is to represent the organization as modern and as a growing design enterprise. It calls attention to both the company's future expansion and their aim for originality, quality, and imagination.

Takenobu Igarashi, Igarashi Studio, Tokio, Japan

Die Firma wurde von Suntory Ltd. und Dentsu Inc. mit dem Ziel gegründet, neu entworfene Produkte und ausgewählte Gegenstände aus aller Welt zu fördern und zu vermarkten. Firmenberater und Executive Directors sind drei führende internationale Designer: Alan Fletcher, Takenobu Igarashi und Massimo Vignelli, deren Design-Ideen die Anfänge der Aktivitäten von OUN begründeten. Das Firmensymbol kann in unzähligen Varianten erscheinen (zur Zeit stehen 51 verschiedene Arten zur Auswahl, die bei Neueinführungen von Produkten verwendet wurden). Basis der einzelnen Symbole ist eine Standardform der Buchstaben OUN. Auf dieser Basis lässt sich eine unendliche Anzahl von Symbolen gestalten. Zweck des Konzeptes ist es, die Organisation als modernes und ständig wachsendes Design-Unternehmen darzustellen. Es unterstreicht sowohl das Streben der Firma nach Expansion als auch ihre Originalität, Qualität und ihren Erfindungsgeist.

Takenobu Igarashi, Igarashi Studio, Tokyo, Japon

La société OUN a été mis en place par Suntory Ltd. et Dentsu Inc. afin de développer et de commercialiser des produits nouveaux au design original, ainsi que des objets choisis dans le monde entier. Les trois designers internationaux appelés à fonctionner comme directeurs exécutifs, Alan Fletcher, Takenobu Igarashi et Massimo Vignelli, ont contribué au démarrage d'OUN par leurs idées et leurs créations. Le symbole de l'entreprise apparaît dans une myriade de variantes: actuellement, 51 versions distinctes ont vu le jour pour caractériser les produits de matériaux nouveaux lors des campagnes de lancement. Ces symboles sont élaborés à partir d'une forme standard des lettres composant la raison sociale, OUN, qui autorise une énorme variété de dérivés. Ce concept a pour but de souligner l'aspect moderne de cette société en expansion constante, l'originalité de sa démarche, la qualité de ses produits et son pouvoir d'imagination.

■Business stationery, examples of business cards of the members belonging to this international group of designers, and variations of the logo – of which there are now 51 in all. The company is also active as a counsellor and mediator between customers and designers for the development of products.

■Geschäftspapiere, Beispiele der Visitenkarten der zu dieser internationalen Gruppe von Designern gehörenden Mitglieder sowie Varianten des Logos, von dem bis jetzt insgesamt 51 existieren. Die Firma tritt ausserdem als Beraterin und Vermittlerin zwischen Kunden und Designern bei der Entwicklung von Produkten auf.

■En-têtes commerciaux et cartes de visite des membres de ce groupe international de designers et variantes du logo – il en existe en tout déjà 51. L'entreprise fait également fonction de conseillère et d'intermédiaire entre les clients et les designers dans le domaine du développement de produits.

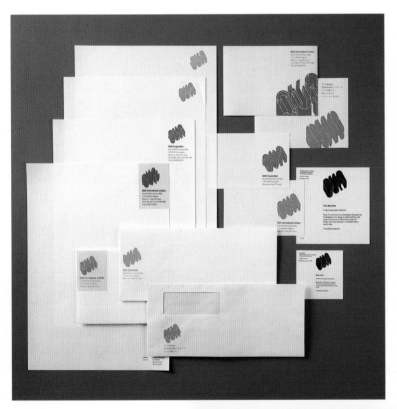

DESIGN FIRM:
IGARASHI STUDIO

ART DIRECTOR:
TAKENOBU IGARASHI

DESIGNER:
DEBI SHIMAMOTO

CLIENT:
OUN CORPORATION

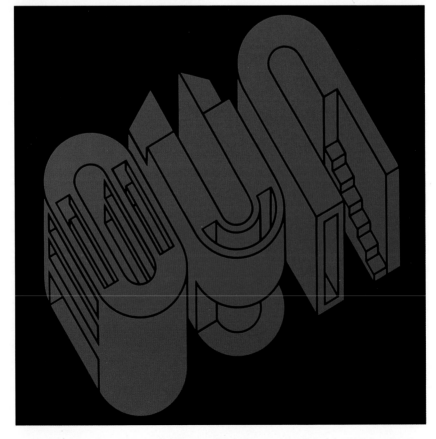

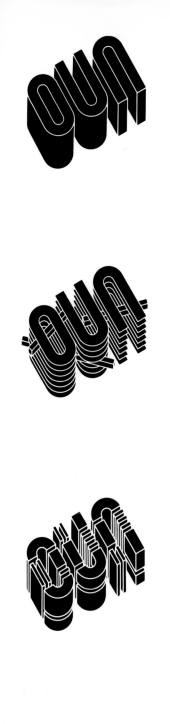
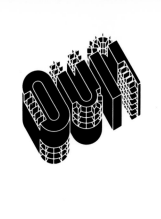
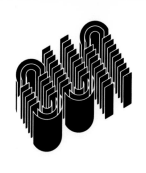

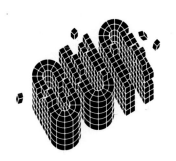

DESIGN FIRM:
IGARASHI STUDIO

ART DIRECTOR:
TAKENOBU IGARASHI

DESIGNER:
DEBI SHIMAMOTO

CLIENT:
OUN CORPORATION

■A different symbol is used for every new publication or new article (mainly office items in the broadest sense) which is created by the designers under the name of OUN. The logo with its numerous variations is in step with the creative prowess of this group.

■Für jeden neuen Artikel – es handelt sich vor allem um Büroartikel im weitesten Sinne, die von den Designern unter dem Namen OUN entworfen werden – oder jede neue Publikation wird ein anderes Zeichen verwendet. Die zahlreichen Spielarten des Logos entsprechen dem kreativen Anspruch der Gruppe.

■Pour tout nouvel article (il s'agit principalement de matériel de bureau conçu par ces designers sous la marque OUN) ou toute nouvelle publication, un nouveau signe entre en application. Les nombreuses variantes du logo correspondent au profil créatif revendiqué par le groupe.

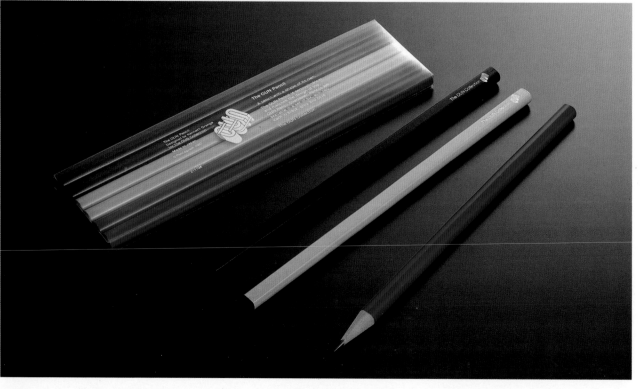

Jane Fincke Ellis, Asst. Vice President, Special Projects, Rockefeller Center, New York, NY/USA
Rockefeller Center is the world's largest privately owned business and entertainment center, comprised of 19 buildings on 22 acres in the heart of midtown Manhattan. Market research revealed that despite world-wide name recognition, there was no clear, correct image of Rockefeller Center. As part of a marketing communications program Chermayeff & Geismar Associates were asked to develop a symbol – a logo and related graphic elements – that instantly said "new" but was respectful of and compatible with the Center's architecture. The symbol had to be classic so as to have longevity yet simple enough to be incorporated and reproduced on items as diverse as bronze plaques in sidewalks, flags and awnings, stationery, and advertising. The logo fits all of our criteria and has been enormously well-received.

Jane Fincke Ellis, Asst. Vice President, Special Projects, Rockefeller Center, New York, NY/USA
Das Rockefeller Center ist weltweit das grösste Geschäfts- und Unterhaltungszentrum in privater Hand. Es besteht aus 19 Gebäuden auf 22 Morgen im Zentrum Manhattans. Gemäss einer Marktforschungsstudie bestand trotz der Bekanntheit des Namens keine klare Vorstellung des Centers. Im Rahmen eines Marketing-Programms wurden daraufhin Chermayeff & Geismar beauftragt, ein Symbol zu schaffen – ein Logo mit entsprechenden graphischen Elementen – das neu sein, aber auch die Architektur berücksichtigen sollte. Es musste klassisch und damit langlebig sein, aber einfach genug, um für die verschiedensten Dinge wie Bronzetafeln auf Bürgersteigen, gestickte Abzeichen auf Uniformen, bunte Fahnen, Markisen etc., Geschäftspapier und Werbung zu passen. Das Logo erfüllt alle diese Kriterien.

Jane Fincke Ellis, Asst. Vice President, Special Projects, Rockefeller Center, New York, NY/USA
Le Rockefeller Center est le centre d'affaires et de loisirs privé le plus important du monde. Des études de marché ont établi que malgré la notoriété mondiale du nom du Rockefeller Center, celui-ci n'avait pas de capital-image clairement identifiable. Chermayeff & Geismar ont été chargés de mettre au point un symbole – un logo et les éléments graphiques associés – donnant l'impression immédiate de la nouveauté tout en prenant en compte l'architecture du Centre. Le symbole en question devait adopter un look classique et pérenne; sa simplicité devait se prêter à l'intégration et à la reproduction dans des matériaux aussi divers que les plaques de bronze des allées, les badges brodés des uniformes, les bannières hautes en couleur, les drapeaux, les marquises, les en-têtes et les matériels publicitaires.

Tom Geismar, Chermayeff & Geismar Associates, New York, NY/USA
In spite of the size of the Rockefeller Center, each of us had a relatively clear idea, even if incorrect, of what The Center is. The problem in designing the visual identification was to incorporate a number of those feelings into a simple visual statement, and to do so in a way that would be absolutely appropriate to The Center, even to seem as if it had always been part of it. The tall vertical lines of the symbol suggest the architecture of the centerpiece RCA building. The round form connotes the idea of the all-encompassing nature of The Center, and its place in the heart of Manhattan. Overall, the geometric form and even-weight lines reflect the Art Deco style of the architecture and artwork, and allow the mark to be reproduced in a wide variety of materials from bronze to fiber to gold leaf, throughout Rockefeller Center.

Tom Geismar, Chermayeff & Geismar Associates, New York, NY/USA
Trotz der Grösse des Rockefeller Centers hatte jeder von uns eine klare, wenn auch nicht immer richtige Vorstellung, was das Center ist. Bei der Entwicklung des Symbols lag unser Problem darin, eine Anzahl von Vorstellungen in einer einfachen visuellen Aussage zu vereinen und zwar so, dass es dem Center gerecht werden würde. Die langen vertikalen Linien des Symbols beziehen sich auf die Architektur des zentralen RCA-Gebäudes. Die runde Form soll die Komplexität des Centers und seine Lage im Herzen Manhattans zum Ausdruck bringen. Darüber hinaus entsprechen die geometrische Form und die ausgewogenen Linien dem Art-Deco-Stil der Architektur und der Dekorationen. Sie erlauben eine Umsetzung des Zeichens in verschiedenen Materialien, von Bronze über Stoffe bis zu Blattgold.

Tom Geismar, Chermayeff & Geismar Associates, New York, NY/USA
Nonobstant les dimensions du Rockefeller Center, chacun de nous avait une idée relativement claire, peut-être inexacte, de ce qu'est le Centre. Le problème à solutionner en créant une identité visuelle était d'intégrer un certain nombre de ces impressions personnelles dans un message visuel simple et de le faire de manière à rendre entièrement justice au Centre. L'orientation verticale du symbole évoque l'architecture du building de la RCA qui en constitue l'élément central. La forme ronde exprime le caractère global des activités du Centre et sa situation au cœur même de Manhattan. De manière générale, la forme géométrique et les lignes équilibrées reflètent le style Art nouveau de l'architecture et de la décoration. Tous ces éléments font que ce symbole se prête à la reproduction dans toute une série de matériaux.

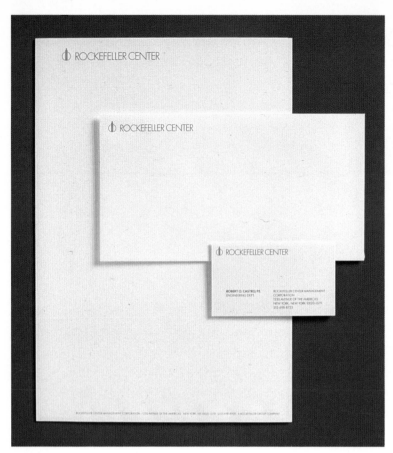

DESIGN FIRM:
CHERMAYEFF & GEISMAR
ASSOCIATES

ART DIRECTOR:
TOM GEISMAR

DESIGNER:
TOM GEISMAR

CLIENT:
ROCKEFELLER CENTER

■ The logo, based on the architectural elements of the Rockefeller Center, is shown here in different sizes for various applications, such as business stationery, carpeting, a banner, guards uniforms, a flag, windowpanes, and the cover of the *Rockefeller Center Magazine.*

■ Das auf der Architektur des Rockefeller Centers basierende Logo hier für die diversen Anwendungsbereiche wie Geschäftspapier, Teppich, Standarte, Uniform der Wachmänner sowie als Fahne, auf Fensterscheiben und auf dem Umschlag des *Rockefeller Center Magazine.*

■ Le logo du Rockefeller Center inspiré de son architecture est visible ici pour diverses applications telles qu'en-têtes commerciaux, tapis, bannières, uniformes des gardiens, drapeaux, décoration de vitres, couverture de la publication maison, le *Rockefeller Center Magazine.*

Catie White, Public Relations Manager, Sanctuary Cove, Hope Island, Queensland, Australia
Located at the main entrance to the Marine Village retail center, the Sanctuary Cove brewery is a prominent feature of the resort in terms of structure, beer production, and tourism appeal. The complex includes an out-door beer garden and a retail area selling souvenirs and merchandise featuring the brewing logo. The brewery combines the finest traditions of German beer production with colonial features of Australian architecture. The brewery manufactures *Island Lagers* – a beer exclusive to Sanctuary Cove. The name was derived from the fact that the resort is located on an island – and it was a name thought to evoke a resort feel. The logo had to fulfill the requirements of representing a "real" beer brewed in the traditional way, with all the history of the brewing industry, as well as illustrating a casual resort theme.

Catie White, Public Relations Manager, Sanctuary Cove, Hope Island, Qld., Australien
Am Hauptzugang einer Ladenstadt des Ferienzentrums Sanctuary Cove gelegen, ist diese Brauerei ein wichtiger Teil des Ortes, als Bau- und Touristenattraktion ebenso wie als Bierhersteller. Zur Anlage gehören ein Biergarten und Läden, in denen Souvenirs und verschiedene Gegenstände mit dem Brauereilogo verkauft werden. Das Bier wird nach der besten Tradition der deutschen Brauereikunst hergestellt, während die Architektur des Gebäudes an den australischen Kolonialstil erinnert. Das Bier *Island Lagers* ist eine exklusive Marke von Sanctuary Cove. Der Markenname impliziert, dass der Ort auf einer Insel liegt, und er vermittelt ein Feriengefühl. Das Logo sollte sowohl die grosse Tradition der Brauereikunst unterstreichen als auch das Ferienortthema berücksichtigen.

Catie White, directrice des relations publiques, Sanctuary Cove, Hope Island, Qld., Australie
La brasserie de Sanctuary Cove représente l'une des majeures attractions du site touristiques de par son architecture, sa production de bière et son intérêt pour le tourisme. L'ensemble comprend un débit de bière en plein air et des boutiques de souvenirs et articles frappés du logo de la brasserie. La bière est fabriquée dans la tradition éprouvée des brasseurs allemands dans un bâtiment du plus pur style colonial australien. L'*Island Lagers* est une bière exclusivement brassée à Sanctuary Cove, la mention «island» rappelant qu'on se trouve sur une île et que le climat y est à la détente. Le logo devait à la fois évoquer l'authenticité de la bière fabriquée selon les canons de la tradition et mentionner le site touristique. Il a trouvé usage sur toutes les étiquettes, dans la signalisation et le matériel publicitaire.

Barrie Tucker, Barrie Tucker Design, Eastwood, South Australia, Australia
The Sanctuary Cove Brewing Company, established within the Sanctuary Cove Resort, brews its own beer under the name *Island Lagers.* In developing a visual identity for the company, we were mindful of the broad range of applications the logo would be required to fulfill. The name of the company adorns the top of the building and was treated in an industrial manner to lend weight to the credibility of the working brewery concept. The brand logo is highly flexible to meet the requirement of scale. It was applied to labels, six-packs, and wooden crates; it was embossed with foil for stationery items; it features on a range of merchandising items such as steins, bar mirrors, and T-shirts; and it was applied directly to the building's exterior corrugated iron walls in large scale using traditional signwriting methods.

Barrie Tucker, Barrie Tucker Design, Eastwood, South Australia, Australien
Die Sanctuary Cove Brewing Company stellt Bier unter dem Markennamen *Island Lagers* her. Als wir das visuelle Erscheinungsbild für die Firma entwickelten, waren wir uns bewusst, dass das Logo vielen Anwendungsbereichen gerecht werden muss. Der Firmenname wurde zuoberst am Brauereigebäude angebracht, in einer industriegemässen Ausführung, um die Glaubwürdigkeit einer eigenen Brauereitätigkeit zu unterstützen. Das Logo für die Biermarke musste allen Grössen gerecht werden: es wurde für Etiketten, Sechser-Packungen und Holzkisten verwendet; für Geschäftspapiere wurde es im Prägedruck appliziert; es ist auf einer Reihe von Werbeartikeln wie Masskrügen, Barspiegeln und T-Shirts zu finden, und es wurde in riesigem Format auf die äusseren Wellblechwände des Gebäudes gemalt.

Barrie Tucker, Barrie Tucker Design, Eastwood, South Australia, Australia
La brasserie Sanctuary Cove Brewing Company installée sur le site touristique de Sanctuary Cove fabrique sa propre bière sous l'appellation *Island Lagers*. En élaborant une identité visuelle pour cette société, nous avons eu en vue la multiplicité des applications envisagées pour le nouveau logo. La raison sociale étalée au sommet de l'immeuble est traitée dans un style industriel propre à souligner les aspects actifs de la fabrication de bière. Le logo du produit s'adapte à tous les formats requis, de l'étiquette au six-pack en passant par les harasses; on le retrouve gaufré à chaud sur les imprimés de l'entreprise; il pare toute une série d'articles publicitaires, chopines, miroirs de bars, tee-shirts et figure en lettres surdimensionnées sur les murs extérieurs de l'immeuble de la brasserie Sanctuary Cove en tôle ondulée.

DESIGN FIRM:
BARRIE TUCKER DESIGN

ART DIRECTOR:
BARRIE TUCKER

DESIGNER:
BARRIE TUCKER/
ELIZABETH SCHLOOZ/
MARK JANETZKI

CLIENT:
SANCTUARY COVE RESORT

■ The logo designed for the beer *Island Lagers* produced by the Santuary Cove Brewing Company must be suitable for the most diverse uses. On the business stationery it appears in relief; on the corrugated wall it was applied in the usual sign-painting method. The palm emphasizes the holiday image of the "island", while the typography and colors (gold, silver, blue, and green) allude to the old brewery tradition.

■ Das Logo für das Bier *Island Lagers* musste für die verschiedensten Bereiche anwendbar sein. Auf den Geschäftspapieren erscheint es im Prägedruck, auf die Wellblechwand wurde es in den herkömmlichen Schildermalmethoden aufgetragen. Die Palme unterstreicht das im Namen wiedergegebene Ferien-Image des Ortes, während die Typographie und Farben (Gold, Silber, Blau und Grün) auf die alte Brautradition anspielen.

■ Le logo conçu pour la bière *Island Lagers* de la Sanctuary Cove Brewing Company devait être transposable aux domaines les plus divers. Il apparaît gaufré sur les entêtes, peint selon les méthodes traditionnelles sur la paroi de tôle ondulée. Le palmier souligne l'image touristique du site conformément au nom de la brasserie; la typo et les couleurs, soit l'or, l'argent, le bleu et le vert, évoquent la longue tradition du brasseur.

Catie White, Public Relations Manager, Sanctuary Cove, Hope Island, Queensland, Australia
The locality of Sanctuary Cove, a world-class international resort, is known as Hope Island - Qland area of some 2000 hectares which is separated from mainland Australia only by rivers and creeks. It combines a host of retail, recreational, hotel, and sporting facilities with a private residential community. Barry Tucker was commissioned to design all Corporate Identity logos for Sanctuary Cove, prior to its opening in January 1987, including a main Sanctuary Cove logo, and separate logos for each of its key components. All the logos had to demonstrate the quality and sophistication of the resort community, complement each other in design and character, yet stand alone as a recognized symbol of the individual component they represented. The Yacht Club is the focal point for all nautical activities of the resort. Its logo had to represent the quality and substance of an exclusive club and the casual nautical atmosphere.

Catie White, Public Relations Manager, Sanctuary Cove, Hope Islands, Qld., Australien
Sanctuary Cove, ein internationales Ferienzentrum von Weltklasse, liegt auf der Insel Hope Island - ein Gebiet von ca. 2000 Hektar, das nur durch Flüsse und Bäche vom australischen Festland getrennt ist. Es gibt hier zahlreiche Einkaufs-, Erholungs-, Unterkunfts- und Sportmöglichkeiten und auch ein Wohngebiet. Barry Tucker erhielt den Auftrag, vor Eröffnung des Zentrums im Januar 1987 das Erscheinungsbild zu gestalten und darüber hinaus verschiedene Logos für die wichtigsten Bereiche zu entwerfen. Alle sollten die Qualität und Eleganz des Ferienzentrums widerspiegeln, sich gegenseitig in Bezug auf Design und Eigenart ergänzen und doch jeweils ein selbständiges Symbol sein. Der Yacht Club ist der Mittelpunkt für alle nautischen Aktivitäten des Ortes. Das Logo sollte dem Anspruch eines exklusiven Yacht Clubs gerecht werden und gleichzeitig die ungezwungene Atmosphäre eines solchen Clubs wiedergeben.

Catie White, directrice des relations publiques, Sanctuary Cove, Hope Island, Qld., Australie
La localité de Sanctuary Cove, site touristique de grand classe internationale, est située sur l'île Hope, quelque 2000 ha séparés du continent australien par un lacis de cours d'eau petits et grands. On y trouve une foultitude de commerces, d'installations de loisirs, de logements et d'aménagements sportifs, ainsi qu'une importante zone résidentielle. Barry Tucker a été chargé de réaliser toute la publicité institutionnelle de Sanctuary Cove avec un logo central et des logos séparés pour les principaux secteurs d'activité. Tous ces éléments graphiques devaient faire la démonstration de la qualité et de la sophistication de la vie à Sanctuary Cove tout en assurant une identification précise de la composante à laquelle ils se rapportaient. Le Yacht Club est le pivot de toutes les activités nautiques locales. Son logo incarne donc la qualité et la substance d'un club exclusif, mais insiste à juste titre sur l'ambiance bon vivant.

Barrie Tucker, Barrie Tucker Design, Eastwood, South Australia, Australia
The Sanctuary Cove Yacht Club was established to cater for the boating activities enjoyed by residents and visitors alike. The logo we designed for the club is in the form of a traditional yachting image; a ship's bell, ropes and ensign were all incorporated into the circular design which was then adapted in three dimensions for all design applications. The main outdoor sign was executed in enamelled colors on cast gun metal and is 1200 mm in diameter. Covers of the visitor's book and menu display the logo as an enamel badge. Both items were bound using traditional materials to coordinate with the overall yachting theme.

Barrie Tucker, Barrie Tucker Design, Eastwood, South Australia, Australien
Der Sanctuary Cove Yacht Club wurde für die einheimischen Wassersportfreunde sowie für die Feriengäste gegründet. Das für den Club entwikkelte Logo entspricht dem traditionellen Image eines Yacht-Clubs: eine Schiffsglocke, Taue und Flagge sind die Bestandteile des runden Emblems, das dann auch in dreidimensionaler Form für verschiedene Zwecke ausgeführt wurde. Die Kennzeichnung des Gebäudes in Form des Emblems wurde aus gegossenem Geschützmetall (ø 120 cm) hergestellt und in Emailfarben ausgeführt. Der Umschlag des Gästebuches und der Menu-Karte zeigt das Emblem als Email-Plakette.

Barrie Tucker, Barrie Tucker Design, Eastwood, South Australia, Australie
Le Sanctuary Cove Yacht Club regroupe les activités nautiques des résidents et des visiteurs. Le logo mis au point pour le Club affecte la forme traditionnelle de ce genre d'association: une cloche, des cordages et un pavillon insérés dans l'image circulaire, qui connaît aussi une version tridimensionnelle pour les diverses applications envisagées. L'enseigne du Club en fonte de canon de 1200 mm de diamètre reproduit le logo en couleurs émail. Les couvertures du livre d'or et de la carte du restaurant s'ornent d'une plaquette émaillée représentant l'emblème du Club. Ces matériaux traditionnels font honneur à l'image du Club.

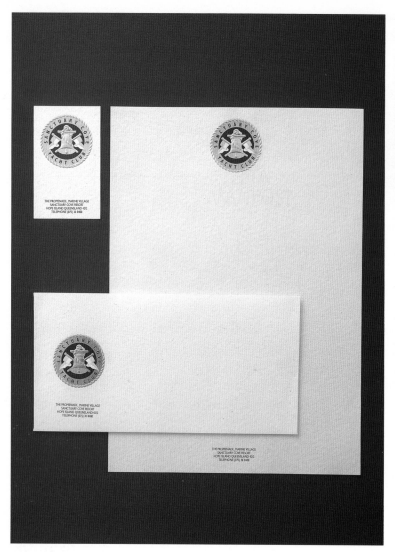

DESIGN FIRM:
BARRIE TUCKER DESIGN

ART DIRECTOR:
BARRIE TUCKER

DESIGNERS:
BARRIE TUCKER/
ELIZABETH SCHLOOZ/
NICOLA LLOYD

ILLUSTRATOR:
ELIZABETH SCHLOOZ

CLIENT:
SANCTUARY COVE RESORT

■Modern architecture and the emblem convey a traditional image of a yacht club and together form a harmonic unity. The same impression is gained from the elegance and solidity of the business stationery (with embossed print) and the cover of the guest book and menu with an enamel badge. The emblem on the exterior wall has a diameter of 1.2 meters and is constructed out of enamelled gunmetal.

■Moderne Architektur und das dem traditionellen Bild eines Yachtclubs entsprechende Emblem bilden eine harmonische Einheit. Den gleichen Eindruck von Gediegenheit und Solidität vermitteln auch die Geschäftspapiere (mit Prägedruck) und die Umschläge des Gästebuchs und des Menus (Emailausführung des Emblems). Das an der Aussenwand angebrachte Emblem hat einen Durchmesser von 1,2 m und ist aus emailliertem Geschützmetall.

■L'architecture moderne et l'emblème représentatif de l'image traditionnelle d'un yacht-club composent un ensemble harmonieux. La même impression de tradition de bon aloi et de solidité se dégage des en-têtes gaufrés et des couvertures du livre d'or et du menu (où l'emblème apparaît émaillé). L'emblème de ce yacht-club exclusif est placé sur la façade et a 1,2 m de diamètre. Il est exécuté en fonte de canon émaillée.

SUNTORY HALL

Kaoru Hirayama, Deputy General Manager, Suntory Hall, Tokyo, Japan

With the new concert hall which opened in October 1986 Suntory wanted to contribute to the development of art and culture in Japan. Takenobu Igarashi, a designer of international renown, was asked to design the logo. We briefed him on the characteristics of the hall and its architecture as well as on our management policy. Our logo was to be beautiful and unique and was meant to represent the idea of music, art, and pleasure. We discussed nearly 100 drafts before the idea of using the Japanese ideogram for sound "hibiki" (implying different aspects of sound) and modifying it with the help of the computer came up. This sign is also the basis for Mr. Igarashi's sculpture at the entrance of the hall. The reactions of both the audience and the musicians have been extremely positive.

Kaoru Hirayama, Deputy General Manager, Suntory Hall, Tokio, Japan

Mit der im Oktober 1986 eröffneten Konzerthalle möchte Suntory zur Entwicklung der Kunst und Kultur in Japan beitragen. Der international bekannte Designer Takenobu Igarashi wurde mit der Gestaltung des Logos beauftragt. Wir informierten ihn über die Besonderheiten der Konzerthalle und ihrer Architektur sowie über unsere Firmenpolitik. Das Logo sollte einzigartig sein und Musik, Kunst und Freude zum Ausdruck bringen. Wir diskutierten fast 100 Entwürfe, bis schliesslich die Idee auftauchte, das Schriftzeichen «hibiki» (ein umfassender Begriff für Ton) zu verwenden und mit Hilfe des Computers zu verfremden. Das Logo ist ebenfalls die Basis für die von Mr. Igarashi entworfene Skulptur vor dem Eingang der Halle. Die Reaktionen des Publikums und der Musiker auf das Erscheinungsbild sind äusserst positiv.

Kaoru Hirayama, directeur général adjoint, Suntory Hall, Tokyo, Japon

En inaugurant sa nouvelle salle de concerts en octobre 1986, Suntory désirait apporter une contribution de poids au développement des arts et de la culture au Japon. Takenobu Igarashi, un designer de réputation internationale, a été chargé de créer le logo idoine. Nous l'avons instruit des caractéristiques de l'auditorium et de son architecture, ainsi que de notre politique d'entreprise. Le logo devait allier la beauté à l'unicité et donner expression au concepts de musique, d'art et de plaisir sensoriel. Nous avons débattu d'une bonne centaine d'esquisses avant que ne prenne corps l'idée d'utiliser l'idéogramme japonais «hibiki» (terme qui englobe tous les aspects du son) et de le modifier à l'aide d'un logiciel d'ordinateur. Ce signe est aussi à la base de la sculpture de M. Igarashi à l'entrée de la salle.

Takenobu Igarashi, Igarashi Studio, Tokyo, Japan

Suntory Ltd., one of the major Japanese beverage manufacturers and prominent figures in the world market, celebrated 20 years of beer brewing and 60 years in the whisky business in 1983. That year, their own concert hall was constructed to commemorate the two anniversaries. It was planned in consultation with leading figures in the music world together with Herbert von Karajan, the renowned conductor. The project was undertaken with the vision of making it the world's most acoustically perfect concert hall. Its identifying logo was developed on the theme of "echo or reverberation", designed around the Chinese character "hibiki". This motif has been reproduced as a sculpture, in signage, advertising, promotional materials, as well as merchandise such as scarves, glasses, and neckties.

Takenobu Igarashi, Igarashi Studio, Tokio, Japan

Suntory Ltd., einer der grössten japanischen Getränkehersteller, der auch auf dem internationalen Markt grosse Bedeutung hat, feierte 1983 das 20jährige Jubiläum seiner Bierbrauerei und 60 Jahre im Whisky-Geschäft. Eingedenk dieser beiden Jubiläen liess die Firma in jenem Jahr eine eigene Konzerthalle bauen. Beraten wurde Suntory bei diesem Projekt von berühmten Fachleuten aus der Welt der Musik, u.a. von Herbert von Karajan. Man wollte die akustisch perfekteste Konzerthalle der Welt schaffen. Das Logo für diese Halle wurde auf der Basis des Themas «Echo oder Widerhall» bzw. des chinesischen Schriftzeichens «hibiki» geschaffen. Dieses Motiv wurde als Skulptur, Signalisierung, in der Werbung und für Promotionsmaterial umgesetzt. Hinzu kamen Produkte wie Tücher, Brillen und Krawatten.

Takenobu Igarashi, Igarashi Studio, Tokyo, Japon

Suntory Ltd., l'un des grands producteurs de boissons japonais au rôle déterminant sur le marché mondial, a commémoré en 1983 les 20 ans d'existence de sa brasserie et le 60e anniversaire de son opération de distillation de whisky, en construisant entre autres une salle de concerts Suntory. A cet effet, les dirigeants de la société s'entourèrent de conseillers de poids dans le monde international de la musique, dont Herbert von Karajan, afin d'assurer à l'édifice l'étiquette flatteuse d'enceinte acoustique nec plus ultra du monde. Le logo pour cette salle interprète le thème de «l'écho ou la réverbération» à l'aide du caractère chinois «hibiki». Ce motif a trouvé usage dans la sculpture, la signalisation, la publicité et la promotion des ventes, sans parler du marchandisage de foulards, lunettes, cravates, etc.

グリッドスケール マーク/ロゴタイプ

演題の使用や写真による拡大が不可能な場合
は、下図に従って正しく作図してください。

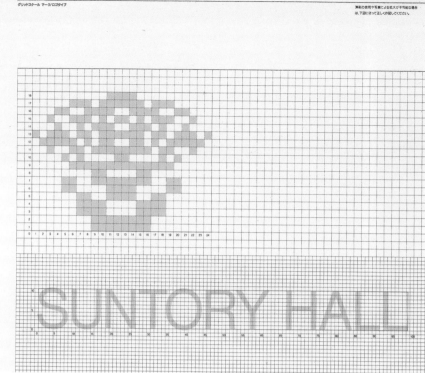

SUNTORY HALL

6

Suntory Hall Logo
Standard Type サントリーホールロゴ基本形

マーク/ロゴタイプを組み合わせたものをサン
トリーホールロゴと呼び サントリーホールロゴに
は基本形A、展開形A、展開形B、展開形Cの4種
が用意されています。スペース、メディアに合わ
せてふさわしいものを選択してください。
サントリーホールロゴの使用カラーは、シンボル
マークワインレッド、ロゴタイプチャコール
グレーの2色配色をなします。
また、ワインレッド、チャコールグレイ、黒、銀、銀
の5色は単色表示色の基本となりますが、使用

するメディア、印刷色等に加刷のある場合は、コ
ンサートホールシンボルのイメージを損なわな
い範囲での他の使用が可能です。
ベースに濃い色がある場合、白ヌキで使用する
ことができますが白とベースとの十分なコント
ラストが必要です。

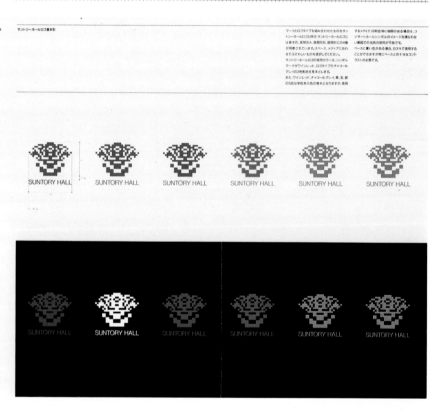

SUNTORY HALL

1

■The logo for this concert hall sponsored by Suntory is based on the Chinese character "hibiki" (echo or resonance). The sculpture that decorates the entrance to the simple hall was also developed from this basic character, as shown here on the model. Construction and coloring are set out in the standard manual.

■Das Logo für diese Konzerthalle basiert auf dem chinesischen Schriftzeichen «hibiki» (Echo oder Widerhall). Auch die Skulptur, die den Eingang zur Halle schmückt, wurde auf der Basis dieses Schriftzeichens entwickelt, wie anhand des gezeigten Models deutlich wird. Konstruktion und Farbgebung sind im Standard Manual festgelegt.

■Le logo de cette salle de concerts s'inspire du caractère chinois «hibiki» qui veut dire «écho». Même la sculpture installée à l'entrée de la salle a été développée à partir de la configuration de ce caractère, comme on le voit par le modèle présenté ici. La construction et les couleurs sont standardisées dans le manuel de design idoine.

DESIGN FIRM:
IGARASHI STUDIO

ART DIRECTOR:
TAKENOBU IGARASHI

DESIGNERS:
DEBI SHIMAMOTO/
YUKIMI SASAGO/
KAZUHIRO HAYASE/
HONAMI MORITA

CLIENT:
SUNTORY HALL

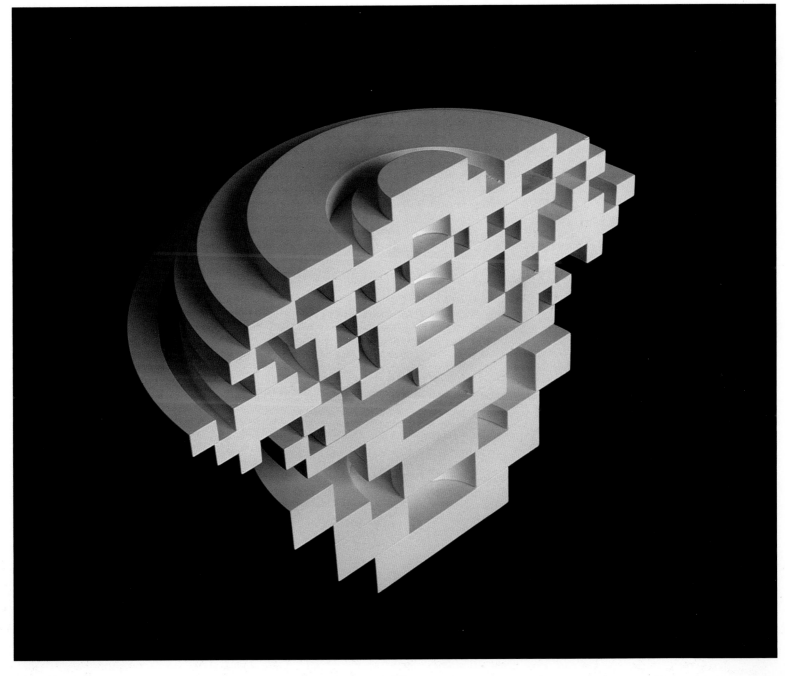

The Cold Chain
Your double guarantee of freshness

Patrick J. Broad, Managing Director, The Cold Chain, Sandton, South Africa

The company specializes in the distribution and marketing of branded quality, perishable food products. The previous identity of the company was not descriptive of its core activity, and because it incorporated the name of its holding company, it caused confusion among its various publics. In structuring the logo, the typographical elements selected were the generic name for frozen distribution "The Cold Chain" along with the promise "Your Double Guarantee to Freshness", to emphasize the dual endorsement of quality distribution and quality branded food products. The selected pictorial interpretation of the name identification was that of three penguins linked together with wing tips touching as if in a chain. The animals represent a warm, friendly way of representing an otherwise rather cold business.

Patrick J. Broad, Managing Director, The Cold Chain, Sandton, Südafrika

Die Firma ist spezialisiert auf die Verteilung und das Marketing von erstklassigen, leicht verderblichen Esswaren. Sie ist die grösste ihrer Art in Südafrika und hat verschiedene Verteilerzentren in diesem Land. Aus dem ursprünglichen Erscheinungsbild gingen die Aktivitäten der Firma nicht klar hervor und der Name – eine Ableitung des Namens der Holdinggesellschaft – stiftete Verwirrung im Markt. Der neue Name «The Cold Chain» lässt erkennen, dass sich die Firma mit der Verteilung von tiefgefrorener Ware beschäftigt und unterstreicht das Versprechen «Doppelte Garantie für Frische». Bildlich wird das Logo unterstützt durch drei Pinguine mit sich berührenden Flügeln. Auf warmherzige Art wird dadurch ein eher kaltes Geschäft dargestellt. Nachträgliche Untersuchungen ergaben überwältigend positive Resultate.

Patrick J. Broad, Managing Director, The Cold Chain, Sandton, Afrique du Sud

L'entreprise est spécialisée dans la distribution et le marketing de produits alimentaires de marque facilement périssables. L'ancienne image institutionnelle de la société ne se rapportait pas à l'essentiel de ses activités; de surcroît, on y mentionnait la holding du groupe, ce qui entraînait une certaine confusion dans les divers segments du public-cible. Lors de l'élaboration du logo, les éléments typo retenus ont été le nom générique de la distribution de produits congelés, «The Cold Chain», et la promesse «Votre double garantie de fraîcheur». Le logo est complété par une interprétation visuelle de la raison sociale sous forme de trois pingouins faisant la chaîne par le contact de leurs ailes. Ces animaux apportent une note chaleureuse et amicale à ce qui dégage nécessairement une impression de froid glacial.

Clive H. Gay, Trademark Design Ltd., London, Great Britain

The Cold Chain, a member of the ICS Group (Imperial Cold Storage) is a British company resident in Southern Africa and established since 1900. Previously being named ICS Distributors, the company had little or no identity to the retail trade as a refrigerated distribution network. The new naming exercise and visual identity required a consumer-friendly approach. The solution of groups of penguins with touching wing tips, as a symbolic vehicle, realized this need and the proposed company name of "The Cold Chain" was accepted as being appropriate and descriptive of both the company services and the identity. Many opportunities have been applied by using groups of three penguins from a varied combination of six master poses. The program has proved to be an innovative and highly recognized identity.

Clive H. Gay, Trademark Design Ltd., London, Grossbritannien

The Cold Chain gehört zur ICS Gruppe (Imperial Cold Storage), eine 1900 gegründete britische Firma mit Sitz in Südafrika. Unter dem Namen ICS Distributors war sie als Verteiler von Tiefkühlprodukten im Handel wenig bis gar nicht bekannt. Um die Konsumenten besser anzusprechen, mussten ein neuer Name und ein entsprechendes visuelles Konzept gefunden werden. Die Lösung war eine Gruppe von Pinguinen, deren Flügel sich berühren, symbolisch auch für den neuen Firmennamen «The Cold Chain», der als Umschreibung der Firmentätigkeit gutgeheissen wurde. Es wurden verschiedene Varianten von Pinguinen in Dreiergruppen – ausgewählt aus sechs unterschiedlichen Posen – ausgearbeitet. Das neue Erscheinungsbild wurde als äusserst innovativ und leicht identifizierbar beurteilt.

Clive H. Gay, Trademark Design Ltd., London, Grande-Bretagne

La Cold Chain fait partie du groupe ICS (Imperial Cold Storage), entreprise britannique fondée en 1900 en Afrique du Sud. Sous sa première raison sociale, ICS Distributors, la Cold Chain ne s'était guère fait connaître en tant que fournisseur du commerce de détail en produits réfrigérés. Une nouvelle raison sociale et une image visuelle appropriée devaient permettre de sensibiliser davantage les consommateurs. L'image trouvée réunit des pingouins dont les ailes se touchent; elle symbolise ce qui, désormais, s'appelle la Chaîne du froid en parfaite adéquation aux objectifs de l'entreprise et aux services qu'elle rend à la communauté. Les pingouins groupés par trois ont servi de base à diverses solutions de rechange à partir de six poses différentes. L'identité globale de marque qui en est résultée s'est avérée percutante et novatrice.

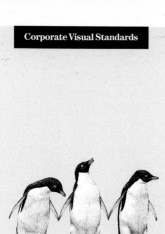

The Cold Chain
Your double guarantee of freshness

DESIGN FIRM:
TRADEMARK DESIGN (PTY) LTD.

ART DIRECTOR:
CLIVE H. GAY

DESIGNERS:
CLIVE H. GAY/
TREVOR FLIGHT/
GARY JONES

ILLUSTRATOR:
TREVOR FLIGHT

CLIENT:
THE COLD CHAIN

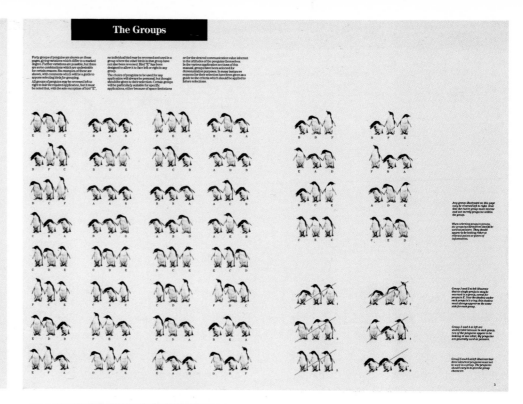

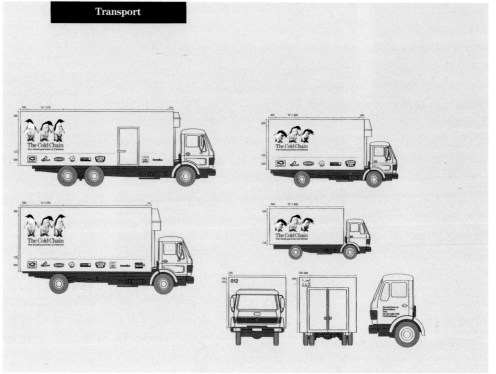

■Penguins in trios form the symbol for this company specializing in deep-frozen food. Shown are examples of its use in the company sign; in the standard manual (in which, among other things, the various positions and presentation on vehicles is shown); on business stationery and - in a long row - on a Christmas card.

■Pinguine in Dreiergruppen sind das Signet dieser auf den Vertrieb von Tiefkühlprodukten spezialisierten Firma. Hier Beispiele der Anwendung auf dem Firmenschild; im Standard Manual, in dem u.a. die verschiedenen Positionen und die Darstellung auf Fahrzeugen gezeigt werden; auf Geschäftspapieren und auf einer Weihnachtskarte.

■Des pingouins allant par trois incarnent ce distributeur de produits alimentaires surgelés. Voici des exemples d'application: sur l'enseigne; dans le manuel standard qui précise entre autres les différentes positions et la décoration des véhicules; dans les en-têtes et - en alignement impeccable - sur une carte de Noël.

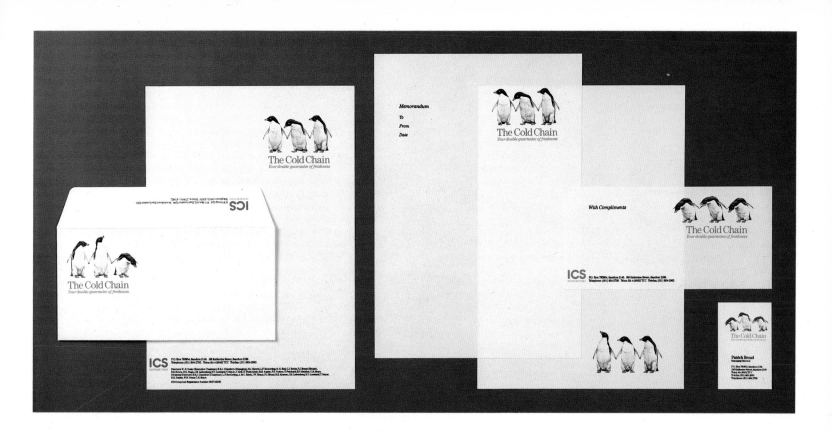

*Nicholas Negroponte, Professor of Media Techno-
logy, The Media Laboratory, Cambridge, MA/USA*
The purpose of the Media Laboratory is to enrich
human and computer communications technology with sensory as well as cognitive apparati.
The lab is built on the idea that publishing, broadcasting, and computer technology will merge. The
Lab's graphic identity was conceived by expand-
ing the presence of Kenneth Noland's painting.
The color coding has been carried forward onto all
of our business media, from calling to Christmas
cards, from correspondence to videodisc envelo-
pes. The striking use of color has caused people to
read our correspondence, which they claim they
otherwise might not have done. Everybody looks
for a code in the bars; and they are still looking.
The Lab has derived enormous benefit from this
unique and abstracted identity. It helps keep
people wondering what we will do next.

*Nicholas Negroponte, Prof. für Media Technolo-
gie, The Media Laboratory, Cambridge, MA/USA*
Zweck des Media Laboratory ist die Bereicherung
der menschlichen und der Computer-Kommuni-
kationstechnologie mit einem sowohl sensori-
schen als auch kognitiven Apparat. Das Labor
basiert auf der Vorstellung, dass Verlagswesen,
Rundfunk und Computer zusammengehören. Die
graphische Identität des Labors wurde auf der
Basis des Wandbildes von Kenneth Noland entwickelt. Die Farbkombination wurde für alle
Geschäftsbereiche übernommen, von Visiten- bis
zu Weihnachtskarten, von der Korrespondenz bis
zu Hüllen für Videodisketten. Die Farben haben die
Leute veranlasst, unsere Korrespondenz zu lesen,
was sie sonst wahrscheinlich nicht getan hätten.
Jeder sucht in diesen Streifen nach einem Code.
Das Labor hat von dieser einzigartigen, abstra-
hierten Identität enorm profitiert.

*Nicholas Negroponte, Professeur de technologie
des médias au MIT, Cambridge, MA/USA*
Le Media Laboratory a pour objectif d'enrichir la
technologie des communications humaines et
informatiques sur un plan aussi bien sensoriel que
cognitif. Les travaux du labo se fondent sur la con-
vergence entre l'édition, la radiodiffusion/télévi-
sion et l'informatique. L'image institutionnelle du
labo a été conçu en amplifiant les informations
contenues dans un mural de Kenneth Noland. Le
code couleur a été appliqué à tous nos supports
média. L'usage percutant de la couleur stimule la
lecture de nos envois et évite qu'ils passent inaper-
çus. Chacun est intrigué par la signification possible des bandes et cherche à y repérer un code. Le
Laboratoire a grandement profité de cette identité
abstraite exceptionnelle. Le public s'attend en per-
manence à d'autres trouvailles de ce genre de
notre part.

*Jacqueline S. Casey, Massachusetts Institute of
Technology, Cambridge, MA/USA*
The MIT Media Lab Dedication Box and other
coordinated publications were all based on the
design of the building which is a square in itself
and is made up of square tiles. The multi-colored
stripes are used on all related publications and
were inspired by the mural created by the painter
Kenneth Noland; they seemed the perfect solution
for the building's logo. The stripes with their
never-ending color combinations express the
research, experimentation, and activity that is
related to the Lab. The box contained five large
and two small booklets describing the activities of
the Media Lab plus two jackets containing a compact disc and a hologram created especially for the
occasion. The building was designed by I.M. Pei &
Partners. Steve Rosenthal took all the photographs
as shown.

*Jacqueline S. Casey, Massachusetts Institute of
Technology, Cambridge, MA/USA*
Die Einweihungs-Box des MIT Media Labors und
die damit zusammenhängenden Publikationen
basieren alle auf der Architektur des Gebäudes, das
selbst ein Quadrat ist und aus quadratischen Plat-
ten besteht. Das Wandbild des Malers Kenneth
Noland inspirierte zu den mehrfarbigen Streifen,
die auf allen Publikationen verwendet werden,
und diese Streifen erwiesen sich auch als perfekte
Lösung für das Logo des Gebäudes. Die Streifen
mit den endlosen Möglichkeiten der Farbkombination stehen für Forschung, Experimente und
alle anderen Aktivitäten des Labors. Die Box enthält verschiedene Broschüren über die Tätigkeit
des Media-Labors sowie zwei Hüllen mit einer
Compactdisc und einem Hologramm. Das Gebäude
wurde von den Architekten I.M. Pei & Partners
entworfen. Die Photos machte Steve Rosenthal.

*Jacqueline S. Casey, Massachusetts Institute of
Technology, Cambridge, MA/USA*
La MIT Media Lab Dedication Box et les publications connexes sont basées sur le plan carré du
bâtiment par ailleurs préfabriqué en dalles carrées.
Les bandes multicolores utilisées systématique-
ment dans toutes les publications sont inspirées
d'un mural du peintre Kenneth Noland et ont
semblé constituer la solution idéale pour le logo du
building. Ces bandes, avec leur combinatoire couleurs illimitée, identifient la recherche, l'expéri-
mentation et toutes les autres activités du labo. La
Media Lab Dedication Box renferme des brochures
diverses décrivant les activités du labo, deux four-
res avec un disque compact et un hologramme
créé spécialement pour cette occasion. Le Laboratoire a été conçu par I.M. Pei & Partners. Le mural
est de Kenneth Noland. Les photos ont été réalisées
par Steve Rosenthal.

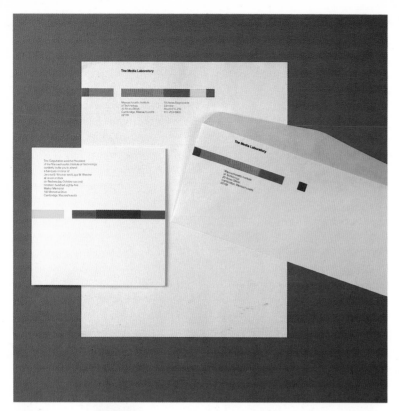

DESIGN FIRM:
MIT DESIGN SERVICES

ART DIRECTOR:
JACQUELINE S. CASEY

DESIGNER:
JACQUELINE S. CASEY

ARTIST:
KENNETH NOLAND

ARCHITECTS:
I.M. PEI & PARTNERS

PHOTOGRAPHER:
STEVE ROSENTHAL

CLIENT:
THE MEDIA LABORATORY

■The stripes inspired by Kenneth Noland's mural, in the most varied color combinations, and the design of the building, which is a square in itself, determine the image of the Media Laboratory, as seen here by the interior decor of the building and in the printed matter. The box contains informational literature designed to mark the occasion of the opening of the laboratory.

■Die von Kenneth Nolands Wandgemälde inspirierten Streifen in den verschiedensten Farbkombinationen und die quadratische Grundfläche des Gebäudes bestimmen das Erscheinungsbild des Media Laboratory, wie hier anhand der Drucksachen, einschliesslich der zur Eröffnung des Labors gestalteten Box mit Informationsmaterial, und der Innenausstattung des Gebäudes deutlich wird.

■Les muraux de Kenneth Noland sont la source d'inspiration des bandes de couleurs aux combinaisons multiples qui, associées au plan carré du bâtiment, composent l'image du Media Laboratory. On en voit ici l'application à des imprimés, au coffret de documentation créé pour la cérémonie d'inauguration du laboratoire, ainsi qu'à la décoration intérieure.

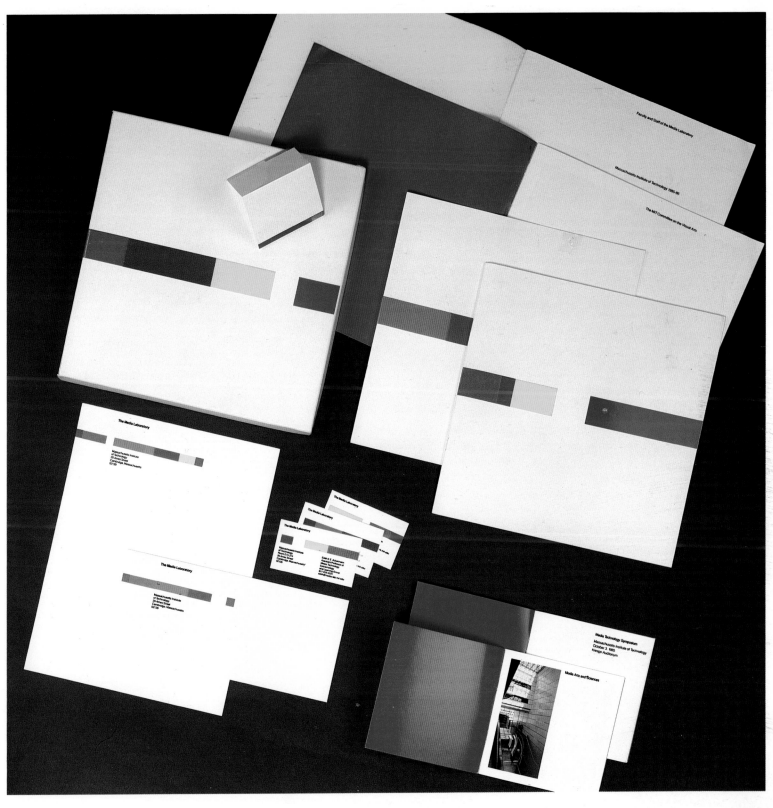

Anthony J. Farrell, Vice President Marketing, The Nature Company, Berkeley, CA/USA

The Nature Company, founded in 1973, started out as a small store – today it is a national chain of 28 stores selling a wide range of tasteful, well-made products inspired by nature or designed to encourage the joyous observation, understanding, and appreciation of the natural world: books, tools, instruments, limited edition art, photography, and sculpture etc. Much of the company's typography, colors, fixturing, and graphic elements echos the design sentiments of 19th Century England, the era of the great museums and the marvelous botanical and zoological prints. There is also a gentleness to the company, truly childlike in its mission to bring the sense of wonder to everyone, to enjoy nature without being hurtful to it. The wild hare ("the bunny") in the middle of the logo is evocative of this gentle, good-humored sentiment.

Anthony J. Farrell, Vice President Marketing, The Nature Company, Berkeley, CA/USA

The Nature Company, 1973 gegründet, begann als ein kleiner Laden – heute ist es eine Kette von 28 Geschäften in den USA, die eine ganze Reihe geschmackvoller, gut verarbeiteter Produkte herstellt, die mit der Natur zu tun haben und das Bewusstsein und Verständnis für ihre Schönheiten wecken sollen. Die Typographie, Farben, Ausstattungen und graphischen Elemente erinnern vielfach an englisches Design des 19. Jahrhunderts, jener Epoche der grossen Museen und wunderschönen botanischen und zoologischen Zeichnungen. Das Erscheinungsbild des Unternehmens hat auch etwas Sanftes, wahrhaft Kindliches in dem Bemühen, in jederman das Bewusstsein für die Natur zu wecken, Freude an ihr zu haben, ohne sie zu zerstören. Der Hase im Logo entspricht diesem Anliegen und der sanften, positiven Stimmung.

Anthony J. Farrell, Vice President Marketing, The Nature Company, Berkeley, CA/USA

La Nature Company fondée en 1983, à l'origine un petit magasin, s'est transformée en quelques années en une chaîne de 28 magasins répartis dans tout l'Amérique. On y vend une vaste gamme de produits de qualité de bon goût inspirés par la nature ou destinés à promouvoir l'observation, la compréhension et l'appréciation du monde naturel sur un mode de participation joyeuse. La typo, les couleurs, la présentation, les éléments graphiques évoquent sur nombre de points les grands courants du design du 19e siècle en Grande-Bretagne. L'image de l'entreprise comporte aussi un élément touchant d'idéalisme comme on le rencontre chez les enfants, une véritable ardeur missionnaire à rendre perceptibles les merveilles de la nature qui exigent le respect et un minimum d'interventions de la part de l'homme.

Kit Hinrichs, Pentagram Design Inc., San Francisco, CA/USA

The Nature Company has a clear concise mission statement which reads: "We are dedicated to providing products and experiences which encourage the joyous observation, understanding, and appreciation of the world of nature." With that statement as a point of reference, we felt that a friendly and approachable typography was needed and that the imagery required an authenticity that expressed the feeling of 19th Century museum prints and engravings. The final design for the logo incorporates Century Old Style type with an illustration of a European hare painted by Bruce Wolfe. The color palette is made up of rich greens and browns balanced by a neutral gray. In addition to the basic program we incorporated a secondary visual vocabulary including marblized paper, antique botanical prints, and recycled papers.

Kit Hinrichs, Pentagram Design Inc., San Francisco, CA/USA

Ausgangspunkt unserer Überlegungen war folgender Grundsatz der Nature Company: «Mit unseren Produkten und Anregungen wollen wir Freude, Interesse, Verständnis und Respekt für die Natur wecken und fördern.» Die Typographie musste deshalb freundlich und zugänglich wirken und die Illustrationen die gleiche Ausstrahlung wie die Museumsdrucke und Radierungen aus dem 19. Jahrhundert haben. Beim Logo entschieden wir uns für Century-Old-Style-Typographie und die Originalillustration eines europäischen Hasen von Bruce Wolfe. Die Farbpalette enthält satte Grün- und Brauntöne, ergänzt durch ein neutrales Grau. Als Ergänzung zu diesen Grundelementen benutzten wir ein sekundäres visuelles Vokabular, zu dem marmoriertes Papier, alte botanische Drucke und Umweltpapier gehören.

Kit Hinrichs, Pentagram Design Inc., San Francisco, CA/USA

La Nature Company a adopté la déclaration de principe suivante: «Nous nous vouons à la mise à disposition de produits et expériences encourageant l'observation joyeuse, la compréhension et l'appréciation du monde naturel.» En nous inspirant de ce programme, nous avons estimé qu'il nous fallait une typographie agréable et accessible et une image dont l'authenticité rappellerait celle des estampes et gravures diffusées par les musées du XIXe siècle. Le logo incorpore des caractères Century Old Style et l'illustration d'un lièvre du peintre Bruce Wolfe. La palette de coloris comprend des verts et bruns intenses équilibrés par un gris neutre. Outre ce programme de base, nous avons eu recours à un vocabulaire visuel secondaire comprenant du papier marbré, d'antiques estampes botaniques et des papiers recyclés.

DESIGN FIRM:
Pentagram Design

ART DIRECTOR:
Kit Hinrichs

DESIGNER:
Kit Hinrichs

ILLUSTRATOR:
Bruce Wolfe

CLIENT:
The Nature Company

■ Business stationery as well as the cover and pages from The Nature Company's mail catalog which offers a whole range of products inspired by nature or designed to help people appreciate nature. Included in the program are books, optics, fine-art prints, gifts, fossils and minerals, plus a line for children. The corporate design is deliberately oriented towards typography, colors, and graphic elements of the English 19th Century – the heyday of botanic and zoological prints.

■ Geschäftspapiere sowie Umschläge und Seiten aus den Katalogen der Nature Company, die Gegenstände anbietet, die mit der Natur zusammenhängen. Zum Programm gehören Bücher ebenso wie Ferngläser, Kunstdrucke, Geschenkartikel, Fossilien und Mineralien und ein ganzes Sortiment für Kinder. Das Corporate Design richtet sich in Typographie, Farben und graphischen Elementen bewusst nach dem englischen Stil des 19. Jahrhunderts, der Blütezeit botanischer und zoologischer Drucke.

■ En-têtes commerciaux, couvertures et pages des catalogues de VPC de la Nature Company, où sont offerts toutes sortes d'objets en relation avec la nature: des livres aussi bien que des jumelles, des gravures, des articles-cadeaux, des fossiles, des minéraux et tout un assortiment destiné aux enfants. Par la typo, les couleurs choisies et le graphisme, cette publicité d'entreprise s'inspire expressément du style anglais du XIXe siècle, où les estampes botanique et zoologiques eurent leur heure de gloire.

Judy Woodfin, Managing Director, Knoll International Holdings, Inc., New York, NY/USA

The '21' Club has been a mecca for dining in New York for sixty years and is located in landmark buildings on West 52nd Street. In 1984, '21' was purchased by Marshall S. Cogan and his partners in Knoll International Holdings Inc. A plan was laid out for the refurbishment of the interior of the Club and included a graphic image change which would achieve the same luster as the redesign. The goal was to marry the best of the past with a contemporary excellence so that current and future patrons would continue to be drawn to '21'. We did not want the kind of change that would upset the regular patrons' perceptions about the traditions within '21'. Pentagram worked with my office and with '21' to design a standard for the legendary name. Their success in all of the elements of the design program is more than subtle.

Deborah Duke Passik, Pentagram Design Services Inc., New York, NY/USA

The new identity program for the '21' Club was designed to include three identifying elements: a modification of the existing '21' logo, a new painting by Paul Davis that shows a jockey with racehorse and blanket displaying the number '21', and marble paper patterns because of their elegance and richness of color. The original symbols of the '21' Club had included the jockey, '21', the Club's iron entrance gate and a collection of paintings by Remington. The jockey and '2l' were retained but the iron gate and images of the wild west were rejected as inappropriate. For the logo, the typeface Torina was selected. It carries both modern and traditional connotations. After reviewing the color palette of the interiors a dark gray and dark red were selected as optional colors for the logo.

Judy Woodfin, Managing Director, Knoll International Holdings, Inc., New York, NY/USA

Der '21' Club ist seit 60 Jahren ein Mekka für Gourmets in New York. Er ist in historischen Gebäuden an der West 52nd Street untergebracht. 1984 kauften Marshall S. Cogan und seine Partner von Knoll International Holdings Inc. den Club. Man beschloss eine Renovierung der Räume und damit verbunden auch eine Überarbeitung des graphischen Erscheinungsbildes. Ziel war es, das Beste aus der Vergangenheit und der Gegenwart zu verbinden, so dass die jetzigen und auch zukünftige Gäste gerne in den '21' Club kommen. Wir wollten aber keine Änderung, die der mit dem '21' Club verbundenen Vorstellung von Tradition widersprechen würde. Pentagram arbeitete mit meinem Büro und dem '21' Club zusammen, um ein graphisches Erscheinungsbild für den legendären Club zu finden.

Deborah Duke Passik, Pentagram Design Services Inc., New York, NY/USA

Das neue Identitätsprogramm sollte drei prägnante Elemente enthalten: eine überarbeitete Version des '21' Logos, ein Bild von Paul Davis, das einen Jockey mit einem Rennpferd und einer Decke zeigt, auf der die Nummer '21' zu sehen ist, sowie Muster von marmoriertem Papier. Zu den ursprünglichen Symbolen des '21' Clubs gehörten der Jockey, '21', ein eisernes Tor als Club-Eingang und Bilder des Malers Remington. Der Jockey und die '21' blieben erhalten, doch das Eisentor und die Wildwestbilder erschienen ungeeignet. Für das Logo wurde die Schrifttype Torina ausgewählt, die Konnotationen von modern und traditionell zulässt. Auf der Basis der Farbpalette der Räume wurden ein dunkles Grau und Rot als Farbvarianten für das Logo ausgewählt.

Judy Woodfin, Managing Director, Knoll International Holdings, Inc., New York, NY/USA

Le Club '21' est depuis 60 ans la Mecque de la gastronomie à New York. Installé dans des locaux d'époque de la 52e Rue Ouest, il a été repris en 1984 par Marshall S. Cogan et ses associés de Knoll International Holdings, Inc. Le plan établi pour la restauration des locaux incluait l'élaboration d'une image graphique nouvelle à la hauteur du lifting du Club. Le but consistait à marier le meilleur du passé et l'excellence contemporaine de manière à continuer d'attirer les clients de marque. Nous entendions éviter une transformation qui serait de nature à choquer la perception que la clientèle habituelle avait du '21' et de ses traditions. Pentagram a collaboré avec mes bureaux et le Club afin de réaliser une identité nouvelle. La réussite de tous les éléments du programme de design adopté est digne de toutes les louanges.

Deborah Duke Passik, Pentagram Design Services Inc., New York, NY/USA

Le programme d'identité a été conçu de manière à inclure trois éléments: la transformation du logo '21' existant, une peinture de Paul Davis où l'on voit un jockey et un cheval de course avec une couverture au chiffre '21', et finalement des dessins de papier marbré. A l'origine, les symboles du Club '21' comprenaient le jockey, le chiffre '21', la grille de fer forgé à l'entrée du Club, ainsi qu'une collection de peintures de Remington. Le jockey et le '21' ont été gardés, tandis que la grille et les images du Far-Ouest ont été écartées comme ne convenant plus. Pour le logo, nous avons opté pour les caractères Torina chargés de connotations à la fois modernes et traditionnelles. Sur la foi des couleurs entrant dans la décoration intérieure, un gris foncé et un rouge foncé ont été choisis en alternance.

■The logo designed for this exclusive New York Club 21 was determined by the style of the interior decor and the emphasis on tradition. (Note the fireplace and wall decoration of the room shown here.) The exterior shot *(previous double spread)* shows the front of the building, with the logo on the lamps above the entrance.

■Das für den exklusiven New Yorker Club 21 entworfene Logo wurde vom Stil der Inneneinrichtung und dem Traditionsanspruch bestimmt. (Siehe Kamin- und Wandverzierung des hier gezeigten Raumes.) Die Aussenaufnahme *(vorangehende Doppelseite)* zeigt einen Teil des Gebäudes mit dem Logo auf den Laternen über dem Eingang.

■Le logo conçu pour le Club 21 exclusif à New York l'a été en fonction du style de la décoration intérieure et de la tradition du club. (Voir la décoration de la cheminée et des parois de la pièce visible ici.) La vue extérieure *(double page précédente)* montre une partie de l'immeuble avec le logo figurant sur les lanternes placées au-dessus de l'entrée.

DESIGN FIRM:
PENTAGRAM DESIGN

ART DIRECTORS:
PETER HARRISON/
SUSAN HOCHBAUM

DESIGNER:
SUSAN HOCHBAUM

ILLUSTRATOR:
PAUL DAVIS

CLIENT:
THE 21 CLUB

Hal Hilts, Vice President Advertising and Public Relations, TradeWell Group, Renton, WA/USA
The TradeWell Group, Inc., a full line retail grocery chain, has been in existence since the 1930's. Substantial change occurred within the company during 1986 and 1987. Store exteriors were renovated, interiors were remodeled, service departments were expanded and/or added, and a communication plan, which included the Corporate Identity program, was implemented. The Corporate Identity portion became a bigger factor than we first envisioned. In fact, it became a big part of our advertising program. Our objective was to establish the concept of several markets within a market. Therefore, to aid differentiation each department has its own icon. We chose to let the icons of each department be the focal point in both advertising and in-store presentation. Thus, when we feature products from the wine department, for example, we use the wine icon in a prominent fashion. The TradeWell Group was the first to implement icons for departments, and full color newspaper advertising for retail grocery chains in Seattle, Washington.

Hal Hilts, Vice President Advertising and Public Relations, TradeWell Group, Renton, WA/USA
Die Lebensmittelkette TradeWell existiert seit den 30er Jahren. In den Jahren 1986 und 1987 fanden grosse Veränderungen statt: Die Läden wurden aussen und innen renoviert bzw. neu gestaltet, Service-Abteilungen wurden ausgebaut oder eingerichtet und ein Kommunikationsplan, zu dem auch das C.I. Programm gehört, wurde eingeführt. Dabei wurde die Firmenidentität zu einem wichtigeren Faktor als ursprünglich geplant. Sie wurde zu einem Hauptaspekt unserer Werbung. Ziel war es, das Konzept von mehreren Spezialabteilungen innerhalb eines Ladens herauszustreichen. Deshalb erhielt jede Abteilung ihr eigenes Symbol, das jeweils auch zum wichtigsten Element in der Werbung und in der Ladengestaltung wurde. Wenn wir zum Beispiel besonders auf Produkte der Weinabteilung hinweisen wollen, wird das Zeichen dieser Abteilung an prominenter Stelle gezeigt. TradeWell war die erste Lebensmittelkette in Seattle, Washington, die Symbole für Abteilungen benutzte und in Zeitungen mit mehrfarbigen Anzeigen wirbt.

Hal Hilts, vice-président, publicité et relations publiques, TradeWell Group, Renton, WA/USA
La chaîne d'épiceries TradeWell Group, Inc. a vu le jour dans les années 30. Une refonte de l'organisation s'est imposée en 1986 et 1987. Les façades des magasins ont été rénovées, la décoration intérieure repensée, les départements de services agrandis ou ajoutés, et un plan de communications adopté. Un élément essentiel de ce dernier est le programme de publicité corporate, qui n'a cessé de prendre de l'importance. Il occupe aujourd'hui la place de choix dans notre action publicitaire. Notre objectif a tendu à formuler le concept d'un certain nombre de marchés à l'intérieur d'un même marché. C'est pourquoi une image code a été attribuée à chaque département pour les distinguer l'un de l'autre, image sur laquelle sont centrées la publicité aussi bien que la présentation en magasin. En mettant en avant des produits du département des vins, par exemple, nous avons mis en vedette l'image «vins». Le TradeWell Group a été le premier à doter ses départements de symboles imagés distincts et à adopter la couleur pour les annonces dans les quotidiens de Seattle.

Jeff Baker, Hornall Anderson Design Works, Inc., Seattle, WA/USA
TradeWell is a retail grocery chain that required a new logo/symbol to position the store visually as a quality "market" shopping experience. The typographic word mark for TradeWell created the foundation for the development of a system of individually specialized department symbols. The department symbols were created with illustration and enhanced clip art. This program was extended into an advertising campaign, direct mail, shopping bags, promotional material, and corporate communication newsletters.

Jeff Baker, Hornall Anderson Design Works, Inc., Seattle, WA/USA
TradeWell ist eine Lebensmittelkette und brauchte ein neues Logo/Symbol, um visuell auszudrücken, dass der Einkauf dort zu einem «Markt»-Erlebnis wird. Das typographisch gestaltete Logo bildete die Grundlage für die Entwicklung von speziellen Symbolen für die verschiedenen Abteilungen. Diese Abteilungssymbole entstanden aus Illustrationen, die mit Clip Art aufgelockert wurden. Auf diesem Programm wurden eine Werbekampagne, Direct-Mail-Aktionen, Tragtaschen, Promotionsmaterial und Firmenmitteilungen aufgebaut.

Jeff Baker, Hornall Anderson Design Works, Inc., Seattle, WA/USA
TradeWell est une chaîne d'épiceries qui devait se doter d'un nouveau logo faisant fonction d'emblème afin de faire comprendre visuellement le rôle du magasin lieu privilégié d'une expérience d'achat donnant accès à un marché de qualité. La typo du logo a fourni le point de départ de tout un système de symboles dérivés pour l'identification des différents départements. Ce programme a fourni une campagne publicitaire, des éléments de publicité directe, des sacs à commissions, du matériel promotionnel et des en-têtes.

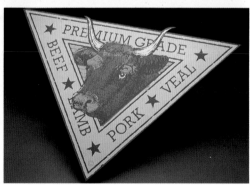

■ Application of the logotype on packaging, aprons, business stationery, wine-card, and signs in various forms, with different typography for the individual departments of the delicatessen business. *(Below)* Exterior and interior photograph of the shop, and examples taken from the newsletter for employees.

■ Anwendung des Namenszuges auf Verpackungen, Schürzen, Geschäftspapier, Weinkarte und Schildern in unterschiedlichen Formen und in verschiedener Typographie für die einzelnen Abteilungen des Delikatessengeschäfts. *(Unten)* Aussen- und Innenaufnahme des Geschäfts sowie Beispiele der Hauszeitschrift für Mitarbeiter.

■ Emploi du sigle sur les emballages, les tabliers, les en-têtes, la carte des vins et les enseignes, en compagnie des désignations des divers départements de ce traiteur. *(En bas)* Le magasin vu de l'extérieur et de l'intérieur et deux exemples de la revue qui est publiée par TradeWell pour ses employés.

SERVICE

NOBODY PROVIDES BETTER SERVICE

NOBODY

Service is taking a personal interest in each and the wishes of every customer. It's every taking that extra effort to anticipate the needs of the customer and providing them with whatever they need. It's being friendly, helpful and willing to assist. We want our customers to leave our Tradewell, PriceSetter or Prairie Markets convinced they got the most for their food dollar and that they were served by people who were happy to serve them and ready to serve them again. We'll do whatever it takes to ensure our customers have the finest shopping experience available. We want them to tell their friends and neighbors about the people of the Tradewell Group, our dedication to service, our friendliness and our desire to please. Nobody will provide better service then we do. Nobody!

Market Report
Volume 1, Number 1

Fall 1986
Tradewell Stores Group

Editor's Note

Welcome to the first issue of *Market Report*, the monthly newsletter for the employees of the Tradewell Group. *Market Report* will be coming to you each month filled with news of your company, its activities and people as well as corporate philosophies and practices. We think it will be a valuable asset in helping you understand the new direction we are taking in an effort to provide the very best service we can offer.

The next several months will be very exciting for all of us associated with the new Tradewell Group as we work to make our stores the very best in the Pacific Northwest. We're convinced we can accomplish this goal. Together we will lead the retail grocery industry through example and demonstrate we are indeed "On the Move Again."

This issue is devoted to a topic which will be the foundation of the new Tradewell Group-Service. The companies of Services Group of America have each succeeded by providing the very best service to their customers possible, no matter what industry they operate in. And, they make money doing it.

We're going to do the same. Each and every one of our customers will receive the best service available in the grocery business today!

We're here to serve you as much as you're here to serve the customer. We want to hear from you. Drop us a line and tell us what you think about *Market Report*. We want this publication to be useful to you and your input will help us accomplish that. So read on - we think you'll like what you see.

Bill Rozier
Editor

Store Directors to Meet Every Two Weeks. Common Language and Team Work is the Key.

All Tradewell Group Store Directors have began a bi-weekly meeting program in which everyone comes together for an evening to discuss operating priorities and problems similar to each store. The meetings are headed by President Tom Stewart and feature reports by the various operating divisions.

"We are completely restructuring and rethinking the way we approach the retail grocery business," explains Stewart. "If the Renton store is experiencing problems getting correct invoices from a supplier, it's a good bet someone else in the system is also having problems."

"These meetings are intended to establish a working communication between all stores in the system. If Renton has a problem, let's put 37 heads together and find the right answer."

The meetings are called to order by Stewart with a brief update on company performance and progress. Division vice presidents all

Continued on back page.

MARKET REPORT

December 1986
Volume 1, Number 3

MARKET REPORT is a monthly newsletter published for the employees of the Tradewell Group.

TOM STEWART

It's hard to believe the holiday season is already here. I think you will agree it's been quite a year for the Tradewell Group.

I'm so proud of this company I can't stay away from it. Rarely in today's business environment does a company achieve the level of teamwork and dedication we have as three separate entities — PriceSetter, Prairie Market and Tradewell stores.

As the Tradewell Group, we offer our customers two different approaches to serving their retail grocery needs. PriceSetter and Prairie Market stores provide their customers the best value and quality existing in a "box store" concept today. The dedicated individuals of PriceSetter and Prairie Market have been winning customers to their stores for some time. I can't overstate their importance enough.

On the other hand, Tradewell is like the caterpillar turning into the butterfly. Through hard work and dedication, the people at Tradewell are creating a network of stores that are second to none in quality

and service. And we're doing it as a team.

When we reference the Tradewell Group, we are really addressing each of our three individual teams under a single name. The strength of the Tradewell Group is each team executing their specialty better than their competition.

I have to tell you, I'm excited about the Tradewell Group. In the faces of each of you I see the spark that will put us on top.

1986 has been a demanding year for everyone. I congratulate you on the tremendous job you're doing. I respect the sacrifices you've made this year and you have my personal guarantee 1987 will belong to the Tradewell Group.

I wish you the very best this holiday season.

Thomas J. Stewart
President and
Chief Executive Officer
Tradewell Group

"Winning has a joy and discrete purity to it that cannot be replaced by anything else. Winning is important to any man's or woman's sense of satisfaction and well-being. Winning is not everything; but it is something powerful, indeed beautiful, in itself, something as necessary to the strong spirit as striving is necessary to the healthy character."

A. Bartlett Giamatti
Yale University President

TRADEWELL GROUP

MOSES LAKE PRAIRIE MARKET BECOMES PRICESETTER

Tradewell stores are not the only stores undergoing major remodeling projects. On October 29th, the Moses Lake Prairie Market was officially reopened as a PriceSetter store and a new era in Moses Lake grocery shopping began.

The remodeling project began in late September and was completed Wednesday morning, the 29th. The Grand Reopening that morning was very successful with local Moses Lake dignitaries, including the mayor, present. A local radio station reported live from the store and awarded prizes on the air. The local paper was also on hand to take pictures and interview Store Director Dan Wetter.

The old Prairie Market store was thoroughly remodeled, including new floor tiling, new paint, shelving, produce department, canopy, outdoor and indoor signage and decor package.

(Continued next page.)

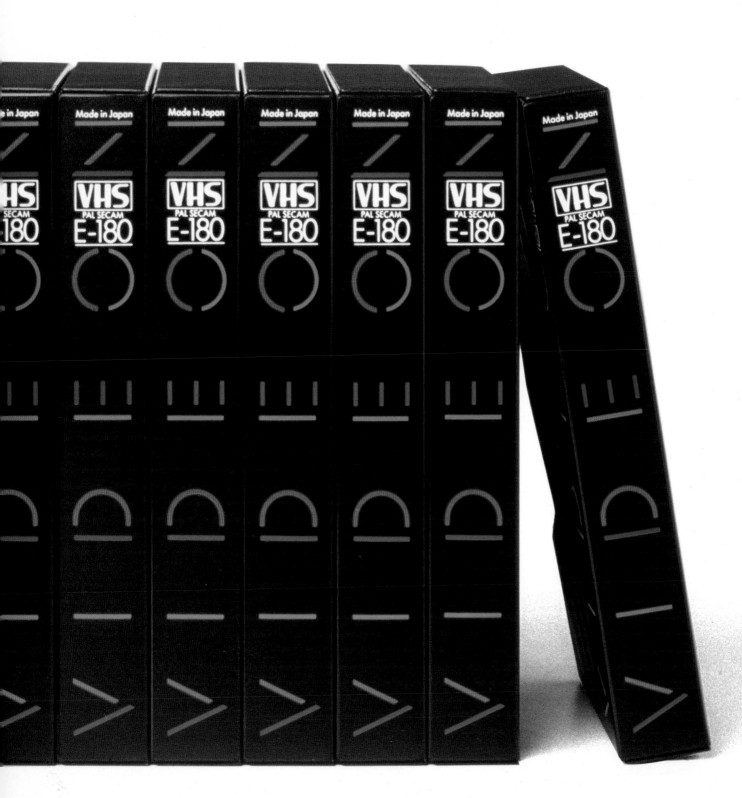

VIDEON

Rudolf Wiesmeier, former proprietor of Videon, Munich, Germany

At a time when so many visual impressions are all vying for attention in our streets, Videon needed a corporate image that would set it clearly apart from the maze. Mendell & Oberer were successful in developing a sign that, by its impressive color fascination, reduced sign language, and simplicity, entirely met this challenge. In addition to this its structuring, slant, color combination, and emphasis on the product name, create a total that is more that just the sum of its parts. It is a sign that fuses the three functions – denotation, connotation, and control. And it can be used for all three business activities (videotheques, sale of blank cartridges, and video-film productions). It represents a youthful, up-to-the-minute, dynamic medium.

Rudolf Wiesmeier, ehemaliger Inhaber der Videon, München, Deutschland

In einer Zeit der visuellen Überflutung im Strassenbild brauchte Videon ein Erscheinungsbild, das sich klar vom Umfeld absetzen würde. Mendell & Oberer gelang die Entwicklung eines Zeichens, das nicht nur durch den eindrucksvollen Farbreiz, die reduzierte Zeichensprache und seine Einfachheit dieser Voraussetzung gerecht wird. Darüber hinaus lässt die Strukturierung, Schräglage, Farbkombination und Herausbildung des Produktnamens ein Ganzes entstehen, das mehr als die Summe seiner Teile ist, ein Zeichen, das drei Funktionen wahrnimmt: Denotation, Konnotation und Kontrolle. Es lässt sich für alle drei Unternehmensbereiche anwenden und entspricht einem jungen und dynamischen Medium.

Rudolf Wiesmeier, ancien propriétaire de Videon, Munich, Allemagne

A une époque où le déferlement d'images s'amplifie dans nos rues, il fallait impérativement à Videon une image d'entreprise qui sorte de l'ordinaire. Mendell & Oberer ont réussi à créer un symbole qui ne satisfait pas seulement par ses qualités chromatiques impressionnantes, par la sobriété des lignes et sa simplicité: sa structure, son obliquité, sa combinaison de couleurs et l'émergence du nom du produit composent un tout supérieur à la somme de ses constituants, un symbole remplissant trois fonctions: la dénotation, la connotation et le contrôle. La nouvelle image s'applique avec un bonheur égal aux trois secteurs d'activité et est tout à fait conforme à un média encore jeune, brûlant d'actualité et empreint de dynamisme.

Pierre Mendell, Mendell & Oberer, Munich, Germany

Videon is engaged in videotheques, the sale of blank video-cassettes, and the production of its own video films. These three activities had to be integrated in the corporate design. In order to project an unmistakable identity, it was paramount to develop a very simple and easy-to-grasp design that would always be recognized. It had to radiate energy and life, and not only be immediately associated with video but also contain the connotative aspects of the medium. Apart from this it also had to convey some idea of the diversity of applications. It had to be equally suitable for interior decors and the lettering of the videotheques, as well as for the product design and external advertising. Besides all these viewpoints, the target group – a relatively young and prestige-conscious public - had to be taken into consideration.

Pierre Mendell, Mendell & Oberer, München, Deutschland

Bei der Firmengruppe Videon handelt es sich um Videotheken, den Vertrieb von Leer-Kassetten und die Produktion eigener Video-Filme. Diese drei Bereiche sollten in das Corporate Design integriert werden. Um eine unverwechselbare Identität zu projizieren, war es wichtig, ein möglichst einfaches, wiedererkennbares und leicht zu erfassendes Design zu entwickeln. Es sollte Energie und Leben ausstrahlen und nicht nur sofort mit Video assoziiert werden, sondern auch die konnotativen Aspekte des Mediums ins Bild setzen. Ausserdem musste es für die Innenausstattung und Beschriftung der Videotheken ebenso geeignet sein wie für die Produktgestaltung und Aussenwerbung. Neben all diesen Gesichtspunkten musste auch die Zielgruppe, ein relativ junges, statusbewusstes Publikum berücksichtigt werden.

Pierre Mendell, Mendell & Oberer, Munich, Allemagne

Le groupe Videon exerce ses activités dans trois directions: les vidéothèques, la vente de cassettes vierges et la production de films vidéo. Ces trois secteurs devaient être intégrés dans l'image institutionnelle. Afin de projeter une identité à nulle autre pareille, il importait de mettre au point un design très simple, facile à assimiler et à mémoriser. Il devait frémir de vie et d'énergie et ne pas seulement évoquer la vidéo, mais aussi les divers aspects connotatifs de ce média. Il fallait aussi qu'il tienne compte de la multiplicité des applications possibles: décoration intérieure, signalisation des vidéothèques, conception de produits, publicité extérieure, etc. Outre ces divers points de vue, il fallait aussi considérer le public ciblé, un public relativement jeune, conscient de son statut socio-professionel.

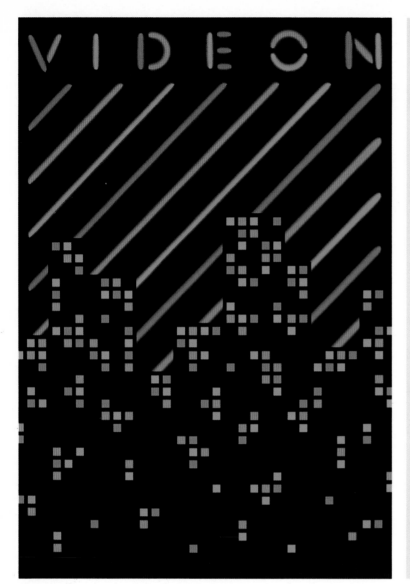

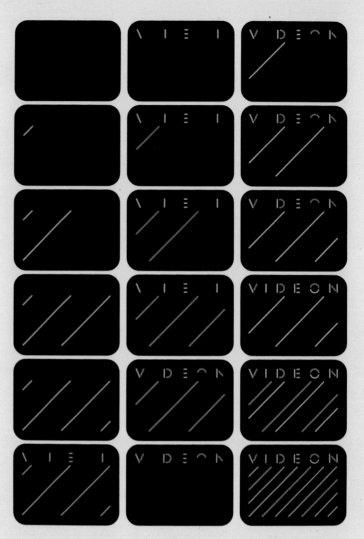

DESIGN FIRM:
MENDELL & OBERER

ART DIRECTOR:
PIERRE MENDELL

DESIGNER:
PIERRE MENDELL

CLIENT:
VIDEON

■Examples of the different uses for the corporate image developed and interpreted for Videon: a poster created for inside use and as a customer gift, sequences of a film trailer for their own video production, packaging design for video cartridges, and a shop-front and signage, with a view to the interior lighting (by Danilo Silvestrin) as part of the total design concept.

■Beispiele aus den Anwendungsbereichen, für die sich das für Videon entwickelte Erscheinungsbild umsetzen lassen musste: ein für den Innenaushang und als Kundengeschenk bestimmtes Plakat, Sequenzen eines Filmvorspanns, Packungsgestaltung und eine Ladenfront mit Neonschrift, mit Blick auf die nach dem Design-Konzept ausgeführte Innenbeleuchtung von Danilo Silvestrin.

■Exemples choisis dans divers domaines d'application auxquels l'image mise au point par Videon a dû s'adapter: affiche destinée à la P.L.V., séquence d'un générique pour une production vidéo de l'entreprise, étude d'emballage pour cassettes vidéo, façade de magasin avec inscription en façade, vue de l'éclairage intérieur exécuté en fonction du design d'ensemble par Danilo Silvestrin.

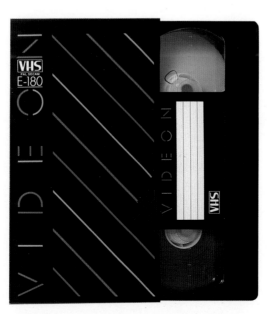

Bob Hall, President of Allegra, Inc. (formerly Vuarnet-France), El Segundo, CA/USA

Allegra, Inc., importer and distributor of sunglasses, was founded in 1981 and operated until November 1988 as Vuarnet-France. Originally, the sunglasses bore the name Vuarnet-France and the logo of their Parisian manufacturer, Sporoptic Pouilloux, but no Vuarnet-France logo. This was created to give graphic strength to the product name. It quickly became a status symbol, a symbol of high-quality style and performance. According to market research results it is one of the most highly recognized logos in its product category in the U.S. As it provides name recognition, the Vuarnet-France logo is an integral part of our Corporate Identity program and marketing strategy. The instant success of the recently launched Vuarnet-France brand sportswear is a direct result of the strength and popularity of the logo.

Bob Hall, Präsident der Allegra, Inc. (ehemals Vuarnet-France), El Segundo, CA/USA

Allegra, Inc., Importeur und Verteiler von Sonnenbrillen, 1981 gegründet, operierte bis November 1988 als Vuarnet-France. Ursprünglich trugen die Sonnenbrillen zwar den Namen Vuarnet-France und das Logo ihres Pariser Herstellers, Sporoptic Pouilloux, aber kein Vuarnet-France-Logo. Dies wurde geschaffen, um den Produktnamen graphisch zu unterstützen. Es wurde schnell zum Statussymbol, zum Symbol für Qualität und erstklassiges Design. Marktforschungsergebnisse besagen, dass es zu den bekanntesten Logos dieser Produktkategorie in den USA gehört. Angesichts des vom Logo unterstützten Markenbewusstseins wurde es fester Bestandteil des C.I.-Programms und der Marketing-Strategie. Der Erfolg der kürzlich lancierten Sportartikel ist direkt auf die Stärke und Popularität des Logos zurückzuführen.

Bob Hall, président d'Allegra, Inc. (ex Vuarnet-France), El Segundo, CA/USA

Allegra, Inc., société importatrice et distributrice de lunettes de soleil, a été fondée en 1981. Jusqu'en novembre 1988, elle a opéré sous la raison sociale de Vuarnet-France. A l'origine, ces lunettes de soleil étaient commercialisées sous l'appellation Vuarnet-France et avec le logo du fabricant parisien, Sporoptic Pouilloux, mais sans un logo spécifique Vuarnet-France qui fut conçu pour donner un appui graphique au nom du produit. Celui-ci est rapidement devenu synonyme d'un statut social certain, un symbole de qualité supérieure et de design exceptionnel. Les études de marché montrent que ce logo est l'un de ceux de la branche qui sont le plus aisément identifiés aux Etats-Unis. Le logo Vuarnet-France fait partie intégrante de notre programme d'identité institutionnelle et de notre stratégie en matière de marketing.

Robert Miles Runyan, Robert Miles Runyan & Associates, Playa Del Rey, CA/USA

The objective was to develop a symbol that would work well in different environments - on packaging, on apparel of all shapes and sizes, and on eyewear. The identity required it be "fashionable" and appealing to a relatively young, active sports market. We wanted to position the company as European, and we achieved this by using the name of the product's origin - France - and its national colors - red, blue, and white - encased in a round, symmetrical shape. We selected the letter "V" as the major design focus, which dominates the entire design system. The symbol has been successfully used by the company in a variety of symbol iterations on its many different apparel lines. The symbol has become a benchmark for eyewear quality for the active sports market.

Robert Miles Runyan, Robert Miles Runyan & Associates, Playa del Rey, CA/USA

Ziel war es, ein Symbol zu finden, das in verschiedenen Bereichen gut funktionieren würde - auf Packungen, auf Kleidungen aller Art sowie auch auf Brillen. Das Image sollte modisch sein und ein relativ junges, sportliches Publikum ansprechen. Wir wollten den Hersteller als europäische Firma positionieren und erreichten dies durch Nennung des Herkunftslandes der Produkte - Frankreich - und unter Verwendung der Nationalfarben - Blau, Rot, Weiss. Wir entschieden uns für den Buchstaben «V» als hervorragendes Design-Element, das sich durch das ganze Design-Programm zieht. Die Firma hat das Symbol mit Erfolg für viele verschiedene Bekleidungslinien eingesetzt. Im Bereich der Brillen für den Sportmarkt wurde das Symbol zu einem Begriff für Qualität.

Robert Miles Runyan, Robert Miles Runyan & Associates, Playa del Rey, CA/USA

Il s'agissait de mettre au point un symbole qui s'imposerait dans n'importe quel environnement - sur un emballage aussi bien que sur des habits de tout genre ou sur des lunettes. L'image institutionnelle devait être résolument moderne et s'adresser à un public relativement jeune et sportif. Nous voulions souligner l'origine européenne de l'entreprise, d'où la mention du pays - la France - et l'utilisation des couleurs nationales du drapeau - bleu, blanc, rouge - le tout inscrit dans un cercle. La lettre «V» nous a servi d'élément central de l'image et du programme d'identité tout entier. Ce symbole a déjà été utilisé avec succès pour diverses lignes d'habillement. Sur le marché du sport, il s'est imposé comme marque distinctive de qualité pour des lunettes haut de gamme.

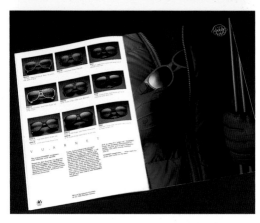

■The Vuarnet symbol in a simple execution and as a rubber stamp or as a company signboard in neon tubes, as T-shirt print or eyeglass label, it stands for sports articles and accessories that were originally developed for professionals – i.e. those who make the highest demands. For amateur sportsmen and other discerning customers too, the quality and design is upheld. The brochure design – shown for sunglasses – is in line with this image, as is a beach outfit or a skicap. The man behind this brand is Jean Vuarnet – 1960 Olympic downhill ski champion. *(Following page)* Cardboard packaging for Vuarnet sunglasses. The illustration allows a particularly effective presentation on the sales stand.

■Das Vuarnet-Signet in einfacher Ausführung und als Stempel oder als Firmenhinweisschild in Leuchtröhren, als T-Shirt-Aufdruck und Brillenetikett steht für Sportartikel und Accessoires, die ursprünglich für Profis entwickelt wurden und somit den höchsten Ansprüchen – auch der Amateursportler und anderer Kunden – in Bezug auf Qualität und Design gerecht werden. Die Prospektgestaltung – hier für Sonnenbrillen – entspricht diesem Image ebenso wie eine Strandausrüstung oder eine Skimütze. Hinter der Marke steht der Olympiasieger in der Ski-Abfahrt 1960 Jean Vuarnet. *(Nächste Seite)* Für *Vuarnet*-Skibrillen gestaltete Verpackung, deren Illustration eine besonders wirkungsvolle Präsentation im Verkaufsgestell erlaubt.

■L'emblème de Vuarnet dans une exécution simple et comme timbre, enseigne néon, sur un tee-shirt et une étiquette de lunettes. Il caractérise des articles et accessoires de sport destinés primitivement aux professionnels et satisfaisant donc aux exigences les plus poussées en matière de qualité et de design. La conception des prospectus s'inspire de cette image au même titre qu'une tenue de plage ou une casquette de ski. La marque a été créée par Jean Vuarnet, champion olympique de la descente en 1960. *(Page suivante)* Emballage carton conçu pour les lunettes de ski *Vuarnet*. L'illustration choisie autorise une présentation particulièrement efficace sur les présentoirs.

DESIGN FIRM:
ROBERT MILES RUNYAN & ASSOCIATES
ART DIRECTOR:
ROBERT MILES RUNYAN
DESIGNER:
ROBERT MILES RUNYAN & ASSOCIATES
CLIENT:
VUARNET FRANCE

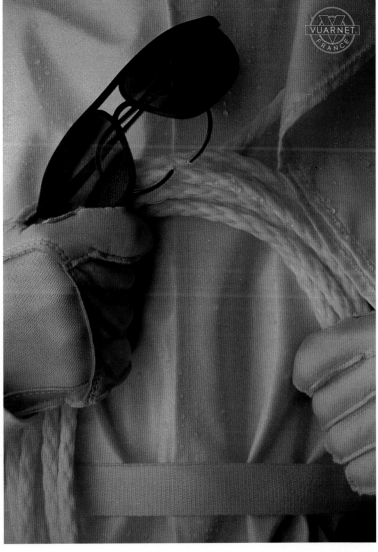

THE IMPORTANCE OF CORPORATE IDENTIFICATION STANDARDS

Corporations invest huge sums of money to establish and maintain images that accurately reflect their reality. It is desirable, in fact, that image lead reality in order to heighten positive perception of the corporation. Enhanced images allow corporations to be seen as distinctive, well-managed, profitable, growing and innovative leaders in their respective industries. At the same time, the corporation gains visibility.

It is no easy task to break through the barrage of communications that bombard the public: television, radio, newspapers, magazines, point of sale, packaging, product merchandising, etc. To do so requires communications that are unique, memorable and well-managed. Too often, however, corporations that spend extraordinary amounts of money on their identities are communicating more inefficiently than those who spend considerably less.

The answer is efficient communications; the planned method of structuring corporate communications to maximize the use of communications dollars to project a credible, functional corporate presentation directed to specific audiences. A consistent and carefully structured communications plan should avoid redundancy, dilution or clouding of public's perception. If well conceived, it will provide the framework for a visual identification system that is flexible and encourages creativity, while still achieving continuity of purpose. Since corporations vary considerably in size and organizational structure, it is essential that their identification system and its mode of implementation be carefully considered.

A global, multidivisional corporation will have a totally different set of application requirements than one that is monolithic and regional in nature. The corporation with a strong retail marketing capability will apply its program in still another manner; there will be greater emphasis between the corporation and its association with its brands.

DIE BEDEUTUNG VON FIRMEN-IDENTIFIKATIONS-STANDARDS

Unternehmen investieren riesige Summen, um ein ihrem Selbstverständnis genau entsprechendes Image aufzubauen und zu erhalten. Es ist sogar wünschenswert, dass das Image zu einem Leitbild wird und die positive Einschätzung des Unternehmens steigert. Die Förderung des guten Images hilft einem Unternehmen, sich von den Mitbewerbern abzuheben und gute Führung, Rentabilität, Wachstum und Weitsicht zu signalisieren. Gleichzeitig verschafft es sich einen verstärkten, sichtbaren Auftritt.

Angesichts der über die Öffentlichkeit hereinbrechenden Flut von Kommunikationen ist es keine leichte Aufgabe, sich durchzusetzen. Man braucht Kommunikationsmittel, die einzigartig und leicht erfassbar sind und sinnvoll eingesetzt werden. Notwendig ist eine durchdachte Methode für den Aufbau der Firmenkommunikation, die den wirkungsvollen Einsatz der Geldmittel für eine glaubwürdige, sinnvolle Darstellung des Unternehmens gegenüber einem spezifischen Zielpublikum gewährleistet. Ein konsequent und sorgfältig strukturierter Kommunikationsplan sollte Überflüssiges vermeiden. Wenn gut durchdacht, wird er zum Gerüst für ein visuelles Identifikationssystem, das flexibel ist und neue Ideen zulässt, ohne die generelle Zielrichtung zu verlieren.

Da sich Unternehmen in Grösse und Struktur erheblich unterscheiden, ist die sorgfältige Planung des Identifikationssystems und seiner Anwendung von entscheidender Bedeutung.

Ein globales, weitverzweigtes Unternehmen benötigt ein ganz anderes Instrumentarium als ein monolithisches, regional gebundenes Unternehmen. Eine Gesellschaft, deren Stärke im Einzelhandels-Marketing liegt, wird ihr Programm wiederum noch anders gestalten, indem grösseres Gewicht auf die mit der Firma verbundenen Markennamen gelegt wird.

Es gibt noch andere Aspekte, die bei der Festlegung der Anwendungsmassnahmen von Bedeutung

L'IMPORTANCE DES NORMES GRAPHIQUES D'IDENTIFICATION

Les entreprises consentent à des investissements énormes pour établir et maintenir des images reflétant avec précision la réalité de leurs activités. En fait, il est souhaitable que cette image précède la réalité de sorte qu'elle contribue à renforcer la perception positive que le public peut avoir de l'entreprise en question. Une image valorisée fait interpréter une société donnée comme un leader de sa branche distinct de ses concurrents. En même temps, cette entreprise renforce sa visibilité.

Il n'est guère facile de forcer le barrage des communications bombardant le public. Il y faut des communications exceptionnelles, mémorables et bien mises en œuvre.

Il faut une méthode réfléchie pour structurer les communications d'entreprise de manière à optimiser chaque dollar employé dans une présentation crédible et fonctionnelle de la société en question à l'intention d'un public spécifique. A raison d'être bien conçu, un tel plan tracera le cadre d'un système d'identification visuelle qui soit flexible et laisse le champ libre à la créativité tout en préservant la cohérence de l'intention de base.

Les entreprises diffèrent fortement par leur taille et leur organisation interne. Il faut donc apporter le plus grand soin à l'élaboration d'un système d'identification approprié et à la mise en œuvre de celui-ci. Un groupe planétaire aux divisions multiples aura besoin d'un ensemble de spécifications d'applications tout différent de celui qui régira une entreprise régionale monolithique. Une société développant une forte capacité de marketing détaillants appliquera son programme de publicité institutionnelle encore autrement en mettant probablement davantage l'accent sur les marques appartenant à l'entreprise. Il existe d'autres aspects de l'entité appelée entreprise qui concourent à déterminer les paramètres de la mise en œuvre d'un système d'identification donné, qu'il s'agisse de la structure générale, du style de direction, de la culture de l'entreprise ou de son fonc-

There are other aspects of the corporate makeup that help establish the parameters and implementation of the identification system such as corporate structure, management style, corporate culture as well as a centralized or decentralized mode of management. It all boils down to the fact that corporations are so different from each other that they must conceive tailor-made identification programs which must be applied in a prescribed manner; there are no "cookie-cutter" solutions.

The carefully developed corporate identification program designed precisely to accommodate a corporation's communications needs is only as effective as its implementation. The optimum program is doomed to fail without a well thought out implementation plan.

Answers to such questions as "Who is in charge of the program?"; "Will it be monitored by an individual, group or department?"; and "What degree of management support will help to insure the program's success?" are critical. Purchasing policy, and the quality of creative sources employed to apply the program become crucial to its continual maintenance and effectiveness.

After all, a corporate identification program is not merely the creation of a new symbol or logotype with instructions as to how and where it is to be used. It is a strategically designed system of verbal and visual components, structured to communicate consistent appropriate characteristics about a constantly changing corporate entity directed to a host of varied audiences. These components comprise the basic ingredients of an identification system; to achieve a consistently high quality level of program implementation corporations must establish methods to control their use.

THE NEED FOR CONTROL

Often, standards manuals are viewed as an expression of corporate management's commitment to administer a planned and efficient approach to communications. More importantly, they are the necessary "tool" used to accomplish appropriate control over the program.

sind, so z.B. die Unternehmensstruktur, Stil des Managements, Unternehmenskultur sowie eine zentrale oder dezentrale Geschäftsführung. All dies besagt, dass Unternehmen so unterschiedlich sind, dass sie massgeschneiderte Identifikationsprogramme brauchen, die nach bestimmten Richtlinien angewendet werden; es gibt keine Patentrezepte.

Das sorgfältig entwickelte und genau auf die Kommunikationsbedürfnisse des Unternehmens abgestimmte Identifikationsprogramm ist nur so erfolgreich wie seine Durchsetzung. Von grösster Bedeutung sind Antworten auf Fragen wie «Wer ist für das Programm verantwortlich?» und «Wird es von einem Einzelnen, einer Gruppe oder einer Abteilung überwacht?» oder «Was muss die Geschäftsleitung tun, um den Erfolg des Programms zu gewährleisten?». Für die konsequente Durchführung und Wirksamkeit des Programms ist die Wahl der für die Anwendung verantwortlichen Leute ausschlaggebend.

Ein Identifikationsprogramm erschöpft sich schliesslich nicht in der Erstellung eines neuen Symbols oder Logos und der entsprechenden Anwendungsinstruktionen. Es ist ein strategisch aufgebautes System, das aus verbalen und visuellen Komponenten besteht und so aufgebaut ist, dass es zahlreichen verschiedenen Zielgruppen die grundlegenden, gleichbleibenden charakteristischen Eigenschaften der Gesamtheit eines Unternehmens, das ja ständigen Änderungen ausgesetzt ist, vermittelt. Diese Komponenten umfassen die Grundbestandteile des Identifikationssystems; um eine gleichbleibend hohe Qualität zu erreichen, müssen die Unternehmen Kontrollmethoden entwickeln.

KONTROLLE MUSS SEIN

Das Standards Manual gilt oft als Zeichen der Bereitschaft der Geschäftsleitung, einen konsequenten und wirksamen Einsatz der Kommunikationsmittel zu gewährleisten. Darüber hinaus ist es ein unentbehrliches «Werkzeug».

Die Notwendigkeit, sich bei der Anwendung des

tionnement centralisé ou décentralisé. Tout cela implique en définitive que les entreprises sont tellement différentes l'une de l'autre qu'il leur faut envisager des programmes d'identification faits sur mesure à appliquer de la manière appropriée; il n'existe pas de solutions passe-partout.

Un programme d'identification élaboré avec soin pour répondre aux besoins d'une entreprise en matière de communications n'est efficace que pour autant que sa mise en œuvre l'est.

Les questions du genre «Qui est le responsable du programme?», «L'exécution du programme sera-t-elle contrôlée par une seule personne, par un groupe ou par un département?» et «Quel soutien peut-on attendre de la part de la direction pour que le programme puisse être un succès?» sont décisives en la matière. La politique d'achats et la qualité des sources créatives utilisées pour l'application du programme s'avèrent déterminantes pour le suivi et l'efficacité de l'action entreprise.

Après tout, un programme d'identification d'entreprise ne consiste pas simplement à créer un nouveau symbole ou logo, ainsi que les instructions afférentes à leur emploi. Il s'agit en fait d'un système de composants verbaux et visuels dont la conception répond à des considérations stratégiques et qui est structuré de manière à communiquer les caractéristiques appropriées et cohérentes d'une entité institutionnelle en constante transformation à une foule de publics très variés. Les composants en question comprennent les ingrédients de base d'un système d'identification; afin d'assurer à la mise en œuvre du programme un constant niveau de qualité élevé, les entreprises doivent nécessairement mettre au point des méthodes propres à en contrôler l'application.

IL FAUT DU CONTROLE

Les répertoires de normes sont fréquemment considérés comme l'expression même de l'engagement des dirigeants d'entreprise en faveur d'une gestion planifiée et efficace des communications. Ce qui compte davantage, c'est leur rôle d'outils indispensables si l'on veut assurer le contrôle qui

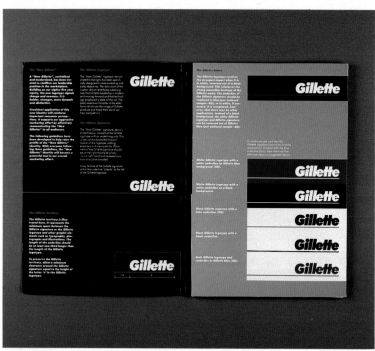

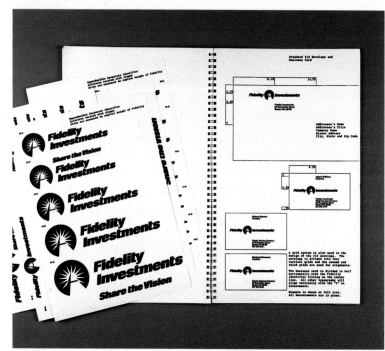

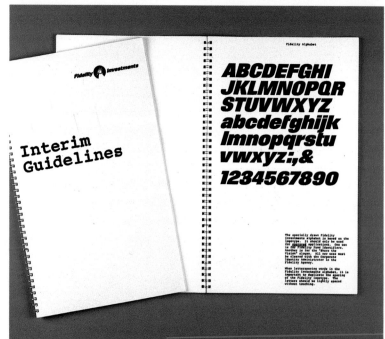

With the need of corporations to rely upon many different sources for program implementation, control becomes essential. Consultants, agencies, printers, writers, fabricators, designers, and individuals inside and outside the corporation have responsibility for program implementation. Therefore, guidelines, specifications, and program controls must be written to be clear and appropriate to various levels of individual talent and expertise; being neither primer-like nor overly technical.

There are many types of manuals that may be created to accommodate specific corporate communications requirements, and they will vary considerably in their composition.

It is important, however, that manuals not be seen merely as symbols of a corporation's identity, but as a working document to guide the user toward achieving excellence in the implementation of the program.

INTERIM MANUALS

Interim manuals, or guidelines as they are frequently called, are written to guide program implementation during early developmental stages. They are intended to be general and merely touch on program basics. Being of a temporary nature, they will be replaced with complete documents when the program design is completed. Interim guidelines will not be supplemented, and therefore may be spiral-bound or saddle-stitched to keep production costs at a minimum. Frequently they are reproduced in two or three colors on moderately priced stock with typewritten rather than typeset text and specifications.

The three interim guidelines shown here vary in their physical form, content, amount of text, and style of presentation.

In reviewing them individually, the Star Market guidelines (p. 238), developed for Texaco's retail convenience store operations, is a promotional, poster-like presentation. The design approach is appealing and appropriate, yet it provides sufficient information to deliver an overall impression

Programms auf viele verschiedene Stellen verlassen zu müssen, macht die Kontrolle unerlässlich. Berater, Agenturen, Drucker, Autoren, Hersteller, Designer und einzelne Personen innerhalb oder ausserhalb des Betriebes tragen die Verantwortung. Deshalb müssen Richtlinien, Spezifikationen und Programmkontrollen klar umschrieben werden, und auch die unterschiedlichen Begabungen und Erfahrungen der Einzelnen sollten berücksichtigt werden – die Richtlinien dürfen weder zu elementar noch zu technisch sein.

Es gibt viele Arten von Manuals, die unter Berücksichtigung spezifischer Kommunikationsbedürfnisse der Unternehmen aufgebaut und entsprechend unterschiedlich sind.

Es ist jedoch wichtig, Manuals nicht nur als Symbol für die Identität einer Firma zu betrachten, sondern auch als Arbeitsdokument, das dem Benutzer den Weg zu einer optimalen Durchsetzung des Programms zeigen soll.

INTERIM MANUALS

Interim Manuals werden erstellt, um den Einsatz des Programms in den frühen Entwicklungsphasen zu gewährleisten. Sie sind als allgemeine Richtlinien gedacht und berühren nur das Grundsätzliche des Programms. Da sie für den Übergang bestimmt sind, werden sie durch eine vollständige Dokumentation ersetzt, sobald das Design-Programm abgeschlossen ist.

Übergangsrichtlinien werden nicht ergänzt und sind darum aus Kostengründen häufig spiralgebunden oder geheftet. Oft sind sie in zwei oder drei Farben auf günstigem Papier gedruckt, wobei der Text und die technischen Daten nicht gesetzt, sondern maschinengeschrieben sind.

Die hier gezeigten drei Interim Manuals unterscheiden sich in der äusseren Form, im Inhalt, in der Textmenge und im Stil der Darstellung.

Eines davon, die Star-Market-Richtlinien (S. 238), die für Texacos Verkaufsstellen entwickelt wurden, präsentiert sich als plakatartige Promotion. Die Gestaltung ist ansprechend und angemessen, wobei dem Zielpublikum trotzdem genügend Infor-

s'impose quant à la mise en application.

Dans la mesure où les entreprises éprouvent le besoin de s'adresser à plusieurs sources pour la mise en œuvre de leur programme d'identification, le contrôle devient essentiel. L'exécution d'un tel programme incombe aux consultants, aux agences, aux imprimeurs, aux rédacteurs, aux concepteurs, aux designers et à toutes sortes d'individus au sein de l'entreprise et à l'extérieur. C'est pourquoi il faut des directives, un cahier des charges et des contrôles énoncés en des termes clairs adaptés aux différents niveaux de talent et de compétence des individus concernés.

Il existe une grande variété de répertoires de normes envisageables pour satisfaire aux exigences spécifiques des communications d'entreprise.

Il est toutefois important que ces répertoires ne soient pas simplement interprétés comme symbolisant l'identité d'une société, mais qu'ils soient utilisés comme un document de travail.

NORMES PRELIMINAIRES

Ces normes sont conçues de manière à accompagner les premiers stades de la mise en œuvre d'un programme. Ils ont donc un caractère plus général et sont remplacés par des documents complets dès que le design du programme est achevé.

Les catalogues d'instructions préliminaires font l'objet d'un seul tirage à reliure spirale ou piqûre à cheval pour réduire autant que possible les coûts de production. Très souvent ils sont reproduits en deux ou trois couleurs sur du papier de prix modique, le texte et les spécifications apparaissant en dactylographie plutôt qu'en typo.

Les trois catalogues d'instructions préliminaires que nous vous présentons ici diffèrent l'un de l'autre par leur forme physique, leur contenu, le volume de texte et le style de présentation.

Dans le détail, le répertoire préliminaire de Star Market (p. 238), mis au point pour les magasins minute de Texaco, adopte une présentation d'affiche promotionnelle. La conception en est aguichante et adéquate tout en condensant assez d'informations pour obtenir une vue d'ensemble.

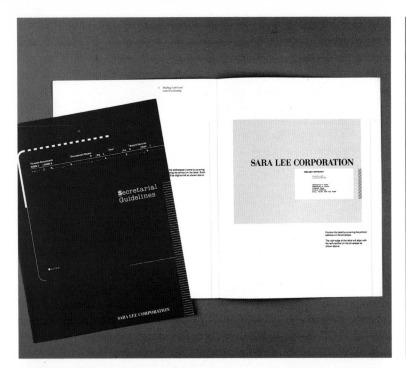

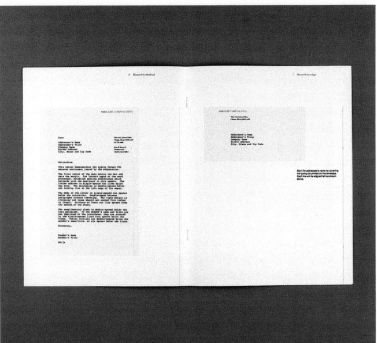

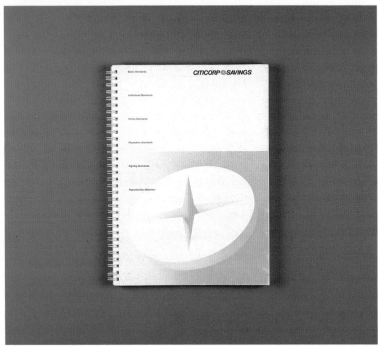

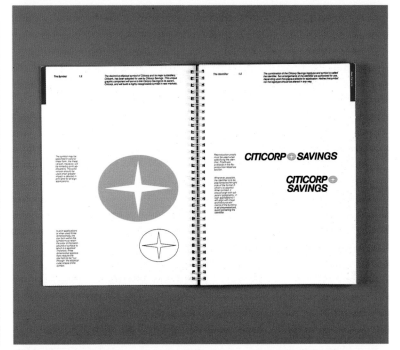

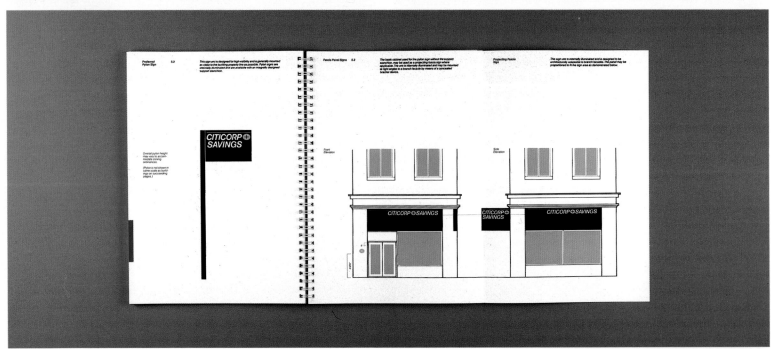

of the program to its audience, generating excitement and anticipation prior to the program's implementation.

Gillette's interim guidelines (p. 238), designed as an information kit, are also highly promotional in nature. Basically international, these guidelines describe the application of Gillette's new brand logotype and its relationship to well-established marketing names. The instructions are simple, and do not attempt to specify information in detail. Essentially, the manual's purpose is to introduce the logotype and supply enough information to avoid its incorrect use. Logotype reproduction sheets are supplied, along with color control chips to preserve design integrity of the program during early implementation stages.

Still considered as interim, the Fidelity Investments guidelines (p. 238) are somewhat more detailed. Spiral-bound with typewritten texts, the manual was inexpensive to produce. Illustrations keyed to general specifications are designed to provide enough information to develop particular communications materials. These illustrations also demonstrate the visual style of the forthcoming program and serve to familiarize the audience with the identification system.

CLERICAL GUIDELINES

Because typewritten correspondence, and how it appears on corporate stationery, is an important visual communication, clerical guidelines are developed to ensure typing consistency. These manuals, such as the one designed for Sara Lee Corporation (p. 240), are directed to clerical personnel in an attempt to apprise them of the newly developed typing formats for stationery items. In many instances these are considerably different from previously used styles. Word processor guidelines, for typing stationery and related business forms, are specified and illustrated.

Since there is a particular tendency among clerical personnel to resist change, these manuals serve to functionally and psychologically muster their valuable support.

mationen gegeben werden, um einen Gesamteindruck des Programms zu bekommen.

Die Interim-Richtlinien für Gillette (S. 238), als Informationspaket gestaltet, haben ebenfalls einen sehr promotionellen Charakter. Grundsätzlich als Instruktionen konzipiert, beschreiben diese Richtlinien die Anwendung des neuen Markenzeichens und den Zusammenhang mit den gut etablierten Marketing-Namen. Die Instruktionen sind einfach, und es wird nicht versucht auf Details einzugehen. Zweck dieses Manuals ist vor allem, das Logo vorzustellen und genügend Informationen zu liefern. Reproduktionsvorlagen des Logos mit Farbkontrollkarten sind vorhanden, um die Integrität des Designs in der Einführungsphase zu bewahren.

Die Richtlinien für Fidelity Investments (S. 238) sind etwas detaillierter. Mit der Spiralbindung und dem maschinengeschriebenen Text war die Herstellung des Manuals nicht aufwendig. Die mit allgemeinen technischen Daten verbundenen Illustrationen bieten genügend Information für die Entwicklung bestimmter Kommunikationsmittel. Diese Illustrationen zeigen ausserdem den visuellen Stil des Programms und machen das Zielpublikum mit dem Identifikationssystem vertraut.

BÜRO-RICHTLINIEN

Da die Darstellung der Geschäftskorrespondenz ein wichtiger Teil der visuellen Kommunikation ist, werden Richtlinien für eine einheitliche optische Gestaltung festgelegt. Diese Manuals, so wie das für die Sara Lee Corporation (S. 240), wenden sich an das Büropersonal, um es mit der Gestaltung geschriebener Mitteilungen vertraut zu machen, die in vielen Fällen von den bis anhin benutzten Darstellungsmethoden erheblich abweicht. Die Richtlinien für Textverarbeitung, Maschinenschreiben und verschiedene Geschäftsformulare sind spezifiziert und illustriert.

Da gerade Büropersonal dazu neigt, Änderungen abzulehnen, sind diese Manuals als funktionelle und psychologische Mittel gedacht, um die notwendige Unterstützung zu bekommen.

Le catalogue d'instructions préliminaires de Gillette (p. 238) conçu comme kit d'information a également un aspect hautement professionnel. Il contient des directives pour l'application du nouveau logo de la marque Gillette en relation avec des noms de marketing déjà bien établis. Ces instructions sont simples et ne cherchent pas à accumuler des détails superflus. Le répertoire a pour but essentiel d'introduire le logo et de donner assez d'informations pour éviter qu'il soit employé à tort et à travers. Les feuilles de reproduction du logo et les pastilles du contrôle couleur servent à préserver l'intégrité du programme durant les premiers stades de sa mise en œuvre.

Rentrant encore dans cette catégorie de documents provisoires, le répertoire de Fidelity Investments (p. 238) est un peu plus détaillé. Le texte dactylographié et la reliure spirale font de cette brochure un imprimé bon marché. Les illustrations qui se rapportent aux spécifications générales sont conçues de manière à fournir suffisamment d'informations pour élaborer des matériels de communication spécifiques. Ces illustrations manifestent également le style visuel du programme à venir et servent à familiariser le public avec les systèmes d'identification.

LE SECRETARIAT

Puisque la correspondance tapée à la machine et sa présentation sur l'en-tête constituent un élément de communication visuel important pour l'entreprise, des catalogues d'instructions destinées au secrétariat tendent à y mettre bon ordre. Ces catalogues, par exemple celui mis au point pour la Sara Lee Corporation (p. 240), tendent à informer le personnel de bureau des nouveaux formats. Les instructions de traitement de texte et de dactylographie, pour la préparation d'imprimés, etc., sont expliquées et illustrées.

Le personnel de bureau a des habitudes fortement enracinées, ce qui explique sa résistance au changement. Ces catalogues préparent par conséquent le terrain fonctionnellement et psychologiquement afin de s'assurer son précieux soutien.

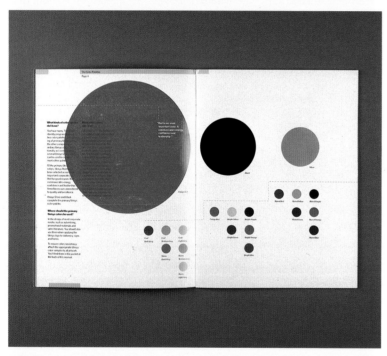

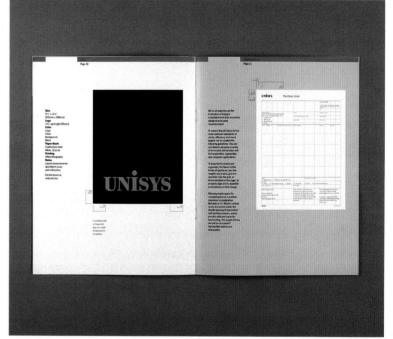

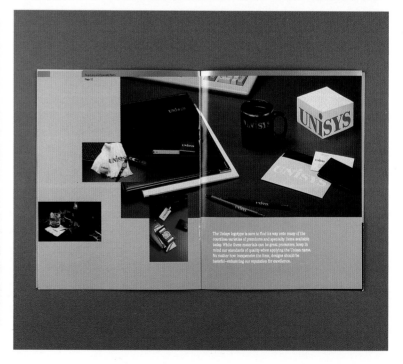

PERMANENT IDENTIFICA-TION STANDARDS MANUALS

Permanent standards manuals may be structured in a variety of ways. The amount of detail, number of pages and writing style are largely dictated by the complexity of the program and the audiences it must reach.

The degree of internal management control for monitoring a corporate program will establish the depth of information and specification detail within a standards manual. Generally, more centrally monitored identification programs will be better served by briefer standards manuals; for programs where less communications management control is exercised, a more comprehensive set of guidelines would be more appropriate.

The familiar adage, "a picture is a thousand words," is particularly applicable to the development of identifications standards. Manuals are for the most part visually oriented. Clear and simple specifications for prototype materials are important. Their physical size, typographic details, stock selection, color, and use of graphic components applied within the grid are directly related to color illustrations. This presentation of prototype materials is the most effective approach toward insuring a quality interpretation of program standards. Whenever possible the presentation of designed examples, treated in full size, is particularly desirable. Full scale treatments of stationery items, business forms, publications and advertising are easier to understand and tend to produce a higher level of program implementation.

The manual developed for Citicorp Savings (p. 240) is a good example of this. Because the degree of program control at Citicorp Savings was moderate, the manual was developed to provide more specific design guidelines. The Citicorp Savings manual is illustrative, user-friendly, and treated informally with physical characteristics such as a soft cover, wire binding, and a page-integrated indexing system, which creates a "work book"-like quality for the document.

STANDARDS MANUALS FÜR DEN PERMANENTEN GEBRAUCH

Diese endgültigen Standards Manuals lassen sich auf verschiedene Arten aufbauen. Die Zahl der Details, Umfang und Stil des Textes werden weitgehend von der Vielfältigkeit des Programms und des Zielpublikums bestimmt.

Das Ausmass, in welchem das interne Management das C.I. Programm überwacht, ist ausschlaggebend für Art und Umfang der Informationen und technischen Angaben. Allgemein gesehen, sind relativ kurz gefasste Manuals für zentral überwachte C.I. Programme am geeignetsten, während in Fällen einer weniger starken und konzentrierten Überwachung umfangreichere Richtlinien zu empfehlen sind.

Der bekannte Ausspruch «Ein Bild sagt mehr als tausend Worte» stimmt besonders im Zusammenhang mit der Erstellung von Identifikationsstandards. Die Manuals sind zum grössten Teil visuell ausgerichtet. Es ist wichtig, dass die technischen Angaben für Prototypmaterial klar und einfach sind. Ihr Umfang, typographische Einzelheiten, Papierauswahl, Farbe und der Einsatz graphischer Elemente innerhalb des Rasters stehen in direktem Zusammenhang mit den Farbillustrationen. Diese Präsentation von Prototypmaterial ist der beste Weg zu einer erstklassigen Verwirklichung der Programmstandards. Wo immer möglich, sind illustrierte Beispiele in grosszügigem Format wünschenswert. Gerade bei Briefpapier, Formularen, Publikationen und Werbematerial sind solche Darstellungen leichter verständlich.

Das Manual für Citicorp Savings (S. 240) ist ein gutes Beispiel dafür. Weil die Kontrollmöglichkeiten bei Citicorp Savings beschränkt sind, enthält das Manual ganz spezifische Design-Richtlinien. Es wirkt dank der Illustrationen freundlich und informell; der weiche Einband, die Spiralbindung und ein Seitenindex geben dem Dokument den Charakter eines Nachschlagwerkes.

Standards Manuals, die den Benutzer nicht einschüchtern, werden sicher häufiger benutzt als

REPERTOIRES DE NOR-MES D'IDENTIFICATION PERMANENTS

Ces normes se structurent de manière très variée. L'abondance des détails, le nombre de pages et le style rédactionnel sont dictés dans une large mesure par la complexité du programme et le genre de public auxquels ils sont destinés.

L'information sera plus ou moins élaborée, le cahier des charges plus ou moins détaillé en fonction du degré de contrôle déterminé par la direction de l'entreprise. En règle générale, les programmes soumis à un contrôle centralisé s'accomoderont mieux d'un répertoire de normes succinct. Dans le cas de programmes dont l'exécution est moins soumise à contrôle, un ensemble d'instructions plus complet est préférable.

L'adage familier qui veut qu' «une image vaut mille mots» prouve toute son utilité lors de l'élaboration de normes d'identification. Les répertoires sont pour l'essentiels visuels. La clarté et la simplicité des spécifications de matériels prototypes sont donc déterminantes. Les dimensions, les détails typographiques, le choix du papier, la couleur et l'emploi d'éléments graphiques à l'interieur de la grille relèvent directement de l'agencement des illustrations couleur. Là où c'est possible, les exemples illustrés grandeur nature s'avèrent particulièrement avantageux. La présentation au format original des en-têtes, des formules commerciales, des publications et des annonces facilite la compréhension et aide à garantir un niveau d'exécution satisfaisant.

Le répertoire élaboré pour Citicorp Savings (p. 240) en est un parfait exemple. Le contrôle du programme étant modéré, ce répertoire renferme des instructions très complètes et se présente sous un jour agréable, avec force illustrations et renseignements utiles pour le lecteur, avec une couverture souple brochée au fil métallique et un système d'indexage intégré qui fait de ce document un manuel pratique à l'utilité indiscutable.

Et puis, il y a les répertoires illustrés au texte concis tels que celui de l'Unisys Corporation (p. 242);

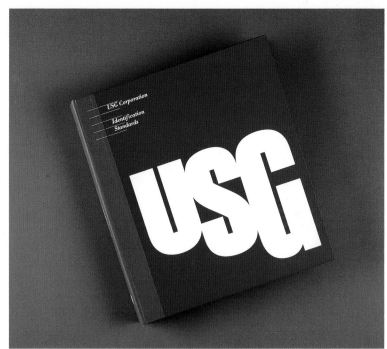

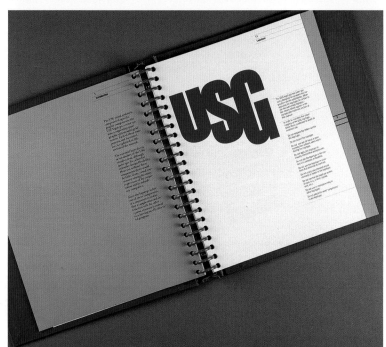

Identification standards manuals that do not appear intimidating to the user are likely to be referred to more frequently. While these manuals are somewhat less detailed, they can provide ample information with effective results.

Briefer, more illustrative manuals, such as the one designed for Unisys Corporation (p. 242), provide sufficient specifications to inform the user of the program essentials, but in an inviting manner. Text written in a friendly and informal style coupled with a more elaborate use of color help to avoid a "text-book" presentation.

The unique physical structure of the manual, a series of individually saddle-stitched volumes in a sleeve-like holder, provides ease of storage and use at a generally lower cost than the more frequently used loose-leaf binders. Each Unisys volume is specific to particular areas of the implementation process: basic standards, stationery systems, signing, etc.

Because Unisys' communications management wanted a greater degree of personalized guidance and implementation control for its program, this briefer manual format is both appropriate and functional.

Manuals designed in a more traditional style, using loose-leaf binders, are possibly the most practical means for specifying corporate identification guidelines. As communications needs change, the standards for control must be flexible enough to accommodate these changes. The addition or deletion of pages or sections allow for revision at the lowest possible cost.

Manuals such as those developed for USG Corporation (pp. 244, 246) and Raytheon Company (pp. 244, 246) are designed for maximum flexibility. These manuals have been designed to transmit a great deal of information about their respective programs, since less internal implementation control will be exercised by the corporation.

Specifically, the Raytheon manual provides detailed information about the structure of its communications system by describing and illustrating how its operating subsidiaries associate graphically with the parent company's identity. An

andere. Obwohl diese Manuals weniger detailliert sind, können sie doch genügend Informationen enthalten und effektiv sein.

Mit anderen Worten, Manuals mit vielen Illustrationen wie das für Unisys Corporation (S. 242) enthalten genügend Information, um dem Benutzer das Wesentliche des Programms zu verdeutlichen und dies auf einladende Art. Ein freundlich, informell geschriebener Text, verbunden mit dem gelungenen Einsatz von Farbe, hilft einen zu starken Lehrbuchcharakter zu vermeiden.

Die einzigartige äussere Form des Manuals, eine Reihe einzeln gehefteter Broschüren in einem umschlagartigen Einband, erlaubt einfache Aufbewahrung und Handhabung bei allgemein niedrigeren Kosten als bei den häufiger verwendeten Ringbüchern. Jede Broschüre bezieht sich auf ein bestimmtes Gebiet: grundsätzliche Vorschriften, Geschäftspapiere, Beschilderungen etc.

Weil die Geschäftsführung von Unisys mehr persönliche Anleitung und Kontrolle bei der Anwendung des Programms wünschte, ist dieses kurz gefasste Manual angemessen und funktionell.

Die in herkömmlicher Weise als Ringbücher gestalteten Manuals sind vielleicht die geeignetste Form für die Identifikationsrichtlinien. Da Änderungen im Kommunikationskonzept der Firmen notwendig sind, müssen die Richtlinien für die Kontrolle flexibel genug sein, um dies zuzulassen. Die Möglichkeit, Seiten oder Teile hinzuzufügen oder herauszunehmen, halten die Kosten für eine Überarbeitung niedrig.

Manuals wie jene für die USG Corporation (S. 244, 246) und die Raytheon Company (S. 244, 246) erlauben ein optimales Mass an Flexibilität. Diese Manuals enthalten eine grosse Anzahl von Informationen über das jeweilige Programm, da von beiden Firmen relativ wenig interne Kontrolle bei der Anwendung ausgeübt wird.

Besonders das Raytheon-Manual enthält detaillierte Informationen über das Konzept des Kommunikationssystems, wobei beschrieben und illustriert wird, wie die Filialen der Identität der Muttergesellschaft graphisch gerecht werden. Ein wichtiger Aspekt des Raytheon-Manuals ist der

l'essentiel y est présenté sous une forme attrayante, sans pousser plus loin. Le texte adopte un ton amical, sans façon, et l'emploi prolifique de la couleur vient à la rescousse pour écarter toute impression pédagogique austère.

La structure physique exceptionnelle de ce répertoire, une collection de volumes pîqués à cheval sous emboîtage, en facilite le rangement et l'utilisation pour un coût modique par rapport aux classeurs habituels à feuillets mobiles. Chaque volume Unisys traite en particulier d'un secteur déterminé de la mise en œuvre du programme, soit les principes de base, les systèmes de papier à lettres, la signalisation, etc.

La direction des communications souhaitait personnaliser la surveillance et le contrôle de l'exécution; aussi le format réduit adopté semble-t-il à la fois répondre aux exigences fonctionnelles et être approprié au but recherché.

Les répertoires à feuillets mobiles, d'inspiration plus classique, sont probablement le moyen le plus pratique de mettre en évidence les instructions relatives à l'identité institutionnelle. Les besoins inhérents aux communications d'entreprise viennent à changer: il faut donc que les normes d'exécution soient assez flexibles pour s'accommoder de ce changement. L'addition ou le retrait de pages ou de sections entières du répertoire permettent la révision au moindre coût.

Les répertoires tels que ceux qui ont été préparés pour l'USG Corporation (p. 244, 246) et la Raytheon Company (p. 244, 246) ont été étudiés spécialement en vue d'une flexibilité maximale en fournissant une foule de détails, ces sociétés n'entendant pas exercer un contrôle tâtillon de la mise en œuvre de la nouvelle image institutionnelle.

Le répertoire Raytheon en particulier contient des informations détaillées quant à la structure de son système de communications. On y décrit par le texte et l'image la manière dont les filiales du groupe s'associent au plan graphique à l'image de la société-mère. Un aspect important de ce répertoire, c'est le caractère exhaustif de la section consacrée aux matériels reproductibles. Le groupe désirant contrôler la présentation des signatures

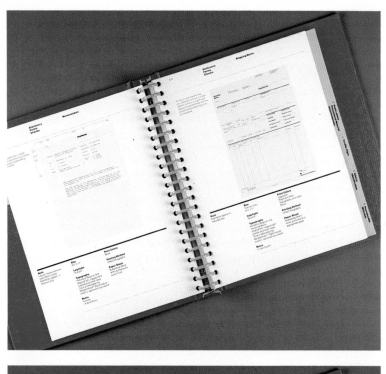

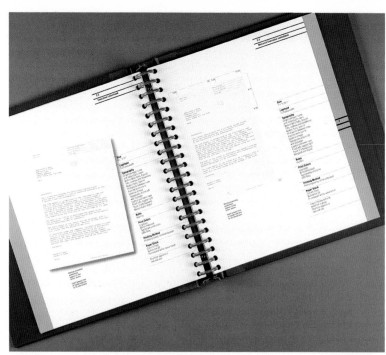

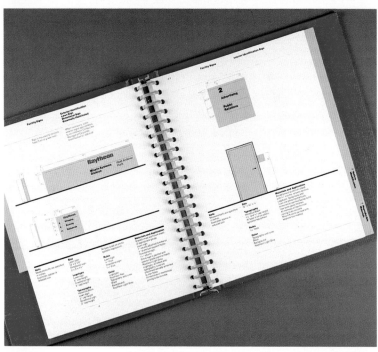

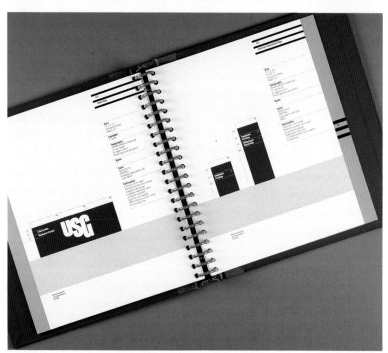

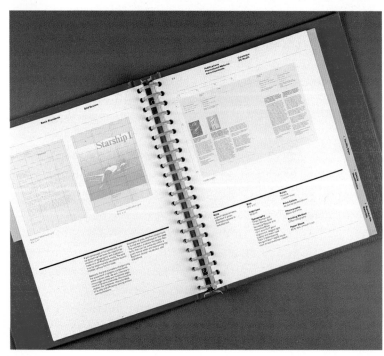

important feature of the Raytheon manual is the comprehensiveness of its reproducible materials section. Raytheon, in its desire to exercise control over the presentation of its operating unit signatures, created reproducible signature sheets for each. Although somewhat expensive initially, this method of control can be valuable over the long term. As a result, Raytheon has managed to maintain a significant degree of program integrity.

Standards manuals such as USG and Raytheon are sectioned and structured in a typical manner. A message from corporate management articulating management's commitment to the program is followed by an introduction stating the rationale for adopting a planned approach to corporate identification along with a description of the program's scope.

The basic standards section essentially introduces the corporate identifier, symbol or logotype, and controls for its application. Also contained in this section is the introduction of the program's visual design vocabulary and the essential design elements that contribute to the corporation's distinctive presentation.

Corporate color and its supporting color system, use of typography and its specification, and the introduction of a grid system designed to provide the structure upon which the visual system is built are also discussed and illustrated within the basic standards section.

The subsequent sections deal with how visual components are applied to such corporate materials as stationery, business forms, promotional materials, advertising, signing, vehicles, etc. Specific applications are illustrated and explained in detail to achieve the optimum level of program implementation. Finally, the reproducible materials section provides signature artwork and color control chips to guarantee reproduction accuracy. Unfortunately, a manual cannot guarantee quality implementation. But if properly followed, the implementor of a corporate identification system can apply program specifications to literally any piece of corporate material in a consistent and creative manner.

grosse Umfang des Sektors mit Reproduktionsvorlagen. Raytheon wünschte, die Schriftzüge aller Filialen kontrollieren zu können und erstellte deshalb Reproduktionsvorlagen für jeden einzelnen Schriftzug. Obwohl dies anfänglich einen gewissen Kostenaufwand bedeutet, kann diese Kontrollmethode auf lange Sicht sehr wertvoll sein. Raytheon gelang es dank dieser Methode, eine bemerkenswerte Übereinstimmung und Einhaltung des Programms zu erzielen.

Standards Manuals wie die von USG und Raytheon sind nach einem typischen Muster aufgebaut. Eine Botschaft, in der sich die Firmenleitung ausdrücklich zu dem Programm bekennt, wird gefolgt von einer Einführung, die auf die Hintergründe und den Umfang eingeht.

Das Kapitel über die grundlegenden Standards stellt das für die Identifikation der Firma verwendete Zeichen, Symbol oder Logo sowie die Anwendungsvorschriften vor. Ausserdem enthält es eine Einführung in das visuelle Design-Vokabular und die wichtigsten Design-Elemente, die zum unverwechselbaren Auftritt gehören.

Die Firmenfarben und das dazugehörige Farbsystem, die Anwendung der Typographie und die genauen Angaben für die Anwendung eines Rastersystems, das als Grundgerüst für den Aufbau des visuellen Systems dient, werden ebenfalls in dem Kapitel über die grundlegenden Standards besprochen und illustriert.

Die folgenden Kapitel zeigen, wie visuelle Elemente für Firmenmaterial wie Geschäftspapier und -formulare, Promotionsartikel, Werbung, Beschilderung, Fahrzeuge etc. angewendet werden. Spezifische Anwendungen sind illustriert und im Detail erklärt, um eine optimale Durchsetzung des Programms zu gewährleisten. Der Sektor mit den Reproduktionsvorlagen enthält Vorgaben für Schriftzüge und Farbkontrollkarten, um originalgetreue Reproduktionen zu ermöglichen.

Leider kann ein Manual nicht für die Qualität der Anwendung garantieren. Wenn jedoch die Vorgaben richtig befolgt werden, kann der Anwender das Programm für jegliches Firmenmaterial konsequent und kreativ einsetzen.

de ses unités opérationnelles, des feuillets de signatures reproductibles ont été réalisés pour chacune d'entre elles. Ce faisant, Raytheon a réussi à maintenir l'intégrité du programme.

Les répertoires de normes du genre USG et Raytheon ont une division en chapitres et une structure typées. Un message de la direction des communications affirmant son engagement délibéré en faveur du programme est suivi d'une introduction justifiant l'approche planifiée adoptée pour le programme d'identification et énumérant les objectifs dudit programme.

La section consacrée aux normes fondamentales présente essentiellement le symbole ou logo d'identification et les méthodes de contrôle mises au point pour son application. La même section contient l'introduction du vocabulaire de design visuel du programme, ainsi que les principaux éléments de design contribuant à former une image distinctive de l'entreprise.

La couleur type de l'entreprise et le système de couleurs associé, la typographie et ses caractéristiques, l'introduction d'une grille de référence définissant la structure sur laquelle appliquer le système visuel, tout cela est également discuté et illustré dans la section des normes permanents.

Les sections suivantes traitent de l'application des composants visuels à des matériels divers tels que les imprimés de l'entreprise, les formules commerciales, la signalisation, les véhicules, etc. Les applications particulières sont illustrées et expliquées en détail afin d'assurer que la mise en œuvre du programme se fera de manière optimale. Pour finir, le chapitre consacré aux matériels reproductibles fait le point des compositions pour la signature et des pastilles de contrôle pour la couleur, ce qui doit garantir la fidélité de la reproduction.

Malheureusement le répertoire ne saurait garantir à lui seul l'exécution de haut niveau du programme d'identité qu'il définit. Pourtant, à condition de suivre ces instructions à la lettre, le responsable de la mise en œuvre du système est en mesure d'en appliquer les spécifications à n'importe quel élément de publicité institutionnelle de manière cohérente et créative.

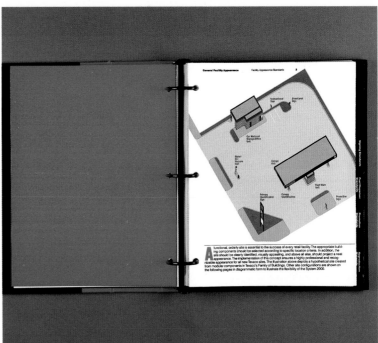

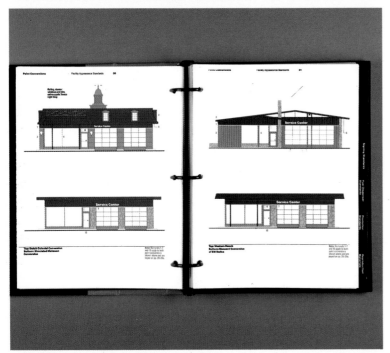

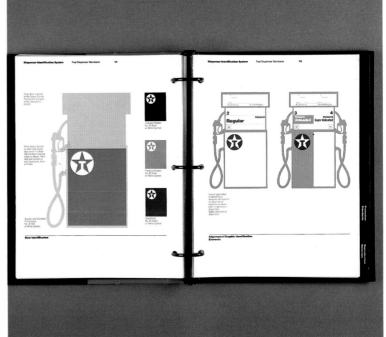

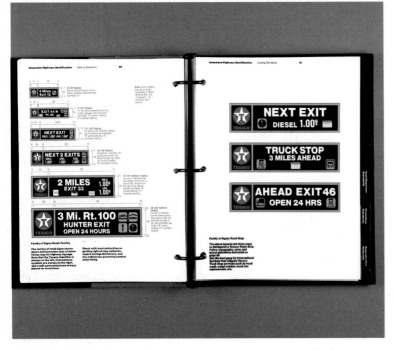

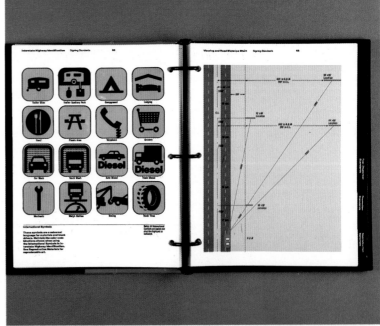

RETAIL IDENTIFICATION STANDARDS

While identification standards manuals are relevant to corporations, there is also a need to develop standards for retail identification purposes. The Texaco retail identification standards manual (p. 248) specifically addresses how an international graphic and environmental program can be controlled and used to maintain standards for virtually all of Texaco's marketing outlets, packaging, vehicle design, and signing applications.

Descriptions, illustrations, and specifications for graphics, architectural components, and space planning aspects are also presented.

Because Texaco installations are either corporate owned and operated, franchised or independently owned, the requirement for program control becomes critical. The global reach of the program reinforces this need. The scope of the manual is substantial, covering new retail installations as well as those existing units requiring rehabilitation or adaptation of the retail system.

Upgrading and revising the Texaco manual within a six-year period is evidenced by the development of a second edition of retail standards to reflect the rapid changes in the petroleum industry. Integrating the original retail standards with those recently developed demonstrates once again the flexibility of the loose-leaf binder system.

THE CITIBANK MANUAL

Probably one of the most thorough and comprehensive corporate standards manuals is the one developed for Citibank (p. 250). As the bank had branches located in 108 countries, management preferred not to create an international communications management group to monitor the widespread program. Instead it was decided to create a set of standards so complete that the manual became the ultimate international authority.

The manual covers standards for the usual printed materials but incorporates an extremely thorough section on the bank's facility signing system. The

ABSATZGERICHTETE STANDARDS

Während sich die Identifikations-Standards-Manuals auf die Unternehmen selbst beziehen, müssen auch Richtlinien für die Identifikation im Verkaufsbereich entwickelt werden. Das Texaco Standards Manual (S. 248) für diesen Bereich zeigt, wie ein internationales Programm für Graphik und Umfeldgestaltung kontrolliert werden kann und wie sich die Einhaltung der Richtlinien für praktisch alle Texaco-Verkaufsstellen, Verpackungen, Fahrzeugbeschriftungen und Beschilderungen erreichen lässt.

Beschreibungen, Illustrationen und genaue Angaben für die Graphik, architektonische Komponenten und Aspekte der Raumplanung im Rahmen des Systems sind ebenfalls enthalten.

Da Texacos Tankstellen in Firmenbesitz oder Privatbesitz sind, von Texaco oder von Konzessionären betrieben werden, ist die Kontrolle des Programms von äusserster Wichtigkeit. Hinzu kommt seine weltweite Anwendung.

Eine zweite Ausgabe der absatzbezogenen Standards nach einer Zeit von sechs Jahren, in denen die Richtlinien verbessert und revidiert wurden, trägt den rapiden Veränderungen in der Erdölbranche Rechnung. Die Integration der ursprünglichen und der neuen Richtlinien demonstriert einmal mehr die Flexibilität eines Ringordners.

DAS CITIBANK MANUAL

Wahrscheinlich eines der umfassendsten Standards Manuals ist das für die Citibank (S. 250). Angesichts der Bankfilialen in 108 Ländern entschied sich die Geschäftsführung für die Erstellung von Richtlinien, die so vollständig sind, dass dieses Manual - und nicht eine Kontrollgruppe - weltweit zur letzten Instanz wurde.

Das Manual enthält Standards über das übliche gedruckte Material sowie auch ein sehr ausführliches Kapitel über die Bankenbeschilderung. Die Tatsache, dass die Aussenkennzeichnung in den jeweiligen Ländern hergestellt werden muss,

NORMES RELATIVES AUX POINTS DE VENTE

Si les répertoires de normes relèvent de la politique d'image de l'entreprise dans son ensemble, des normes séparées doivent couvrir les besoins des points de vente au détail. C'est ainsi que le répertoire de normes de Texaco (p. 248) destiné à ces derniers traite des problèmes spécifiques qui concernent l'application d'un programme graphique et environnemental international à la totalité des points de vente Texaco, y compris les emballages, le design des véhicules et la signalétique.

Des descriptions, illustrations et spécifications des éléments graphiques, architecturaux et environnementaux du système y figurent également.

Les installations de Texaco sont soit propriété du groupe et gérées par lui, soit franchisées ou encore propriété indépendante, ce qui pose de réels problèmes à qui veut exercer un contrôle sur la mise en œuvre du programme. Qui plus est, la portée globale du programme réclame impérativement un contrôle efficace.

La parution d'une deuxième édition des normes régissant l'image des points de vente était nécessitée par les transformations rapides qui ont affecté l'industrie pétrolière. La souplesse de la formule de classeur à feuillets mobiles est amplement démontrée par le mariage harmonieux des normes originales et des nouvelles normes.

LES NORMES CITIBANK

L'un des répertoires les mieux conçus et les plus complets qui aient vu le jour est certes celui qui interprète l'image de marque de Citibank (p. 250). Cette banque compte des filiales dans 108 pays, ce qui a amené les dirigeants à ne pas mettre en place une équipe chargée des communications au plan international. A la place, on décida de mettre au point un ensemble d'instructions si complètes que le répertoire des normes assumerait la fonction d'autorité suprême au plan international.

Ce répertoire comprend outre les normes indispensables pour les matériels imprimés tradition-

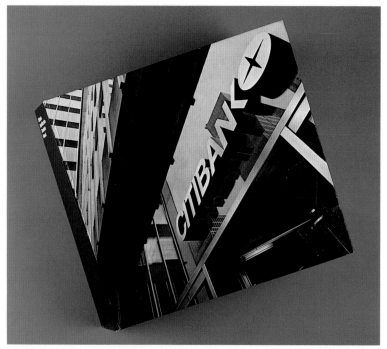

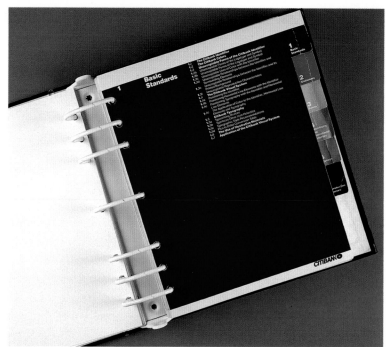

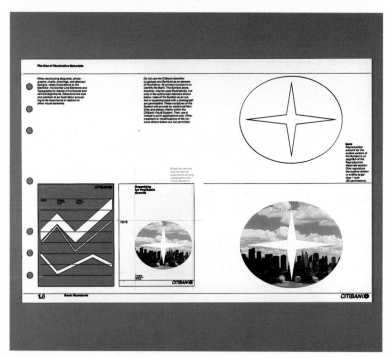

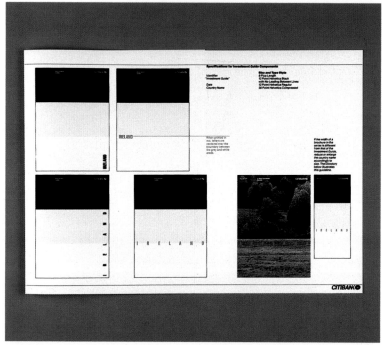

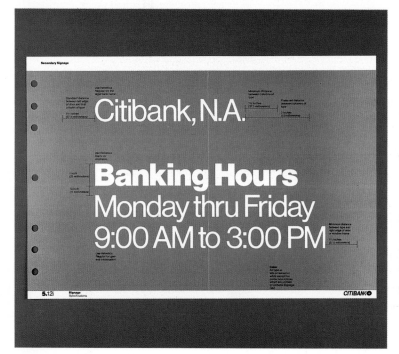

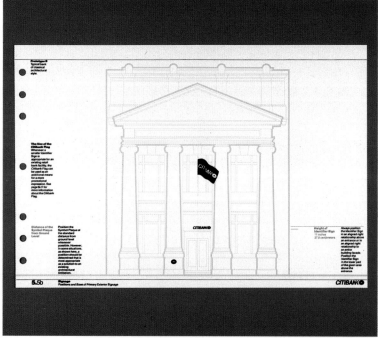

fact that exterior signs would be manufactured in local countries was of concern since Citibank's facilities department was unable to control their construction and application. As a result, the manual incorporates elaborate engineering details for sign construction in order to maintain the design integrity of the system.

Another interesting aspect of the Citibank manual is its detailed explanation of the conversion of the design program to the metric system for purposes of adaptation to the bank's international affiliates. As well, physical samples of paper stock, specified for use in the United States, were incorporated in the manual's reproducible materials section so that an approved equivalent grade of stock could be selected in local countries.

In retrospect, the desire for the manual to become a total controlling force for the Citibank program was not realistic. Many who were involved in its implementation found the manual too far-reaching and perhaps too technical in its content.

METHODS OF CONTROLLING THE PROGRAM

It takes more than a well-conceived, written control document to effectively control an identification program. The added value of a functioning communications team or department with enough authority to keep the program on track will certainly reinforce written standards. A manual really cannot answer all of the questions that surface during the application process.

The liaison between those responsible for program implementation and the corporate identification management team is often a desirable combination; it has been successful in practice in many instances.

The optimum solution for maintaining a corporate identification program is the establishment of an internal corporate design center (often considered to be a corporate luxury). This select group can implement the program based upon the authorized manual and work closely with local constituencies in order to solve everyday commu-

bedeutete, dass eine zentrale Kontrolle der Konstruktion und Anwendung nicht möglich ist. Folglich enthält das Manual ausführliche technische Details für die Herstellung der Schilder, um die Design-Integrität des Systems zu erhalten.

Ein weiterer interessanter Aspekt des Citibank Manuals ist die ausführliche Erläuterung der Anpassung des Design-Programms an das metrische System mit Rücksicht auf die internationalen Zweigstellen der Bank. Ausserdem enthält das Kapitel mit den Reproduktionsvorlagen auch Papiermuster, die für den Gebrauch in den USA bestimmt sind, aber gleichzeitig als Richtlinien für das in anderen Ländern zu verwendende Papier gelten.

Im Rückblick sei gesagt, dass der Wunsch, mit dem Manual eine totale Kontrolle über das Citibank-Programm zu erreichen, nicht realistisch war. Viele der für die Durchsetzung zuständigen Leute fanden, dass es zu weit gehe und dass der Inhalt zu technisch sei.

DIE KONTROLLE DES PROGRAMMS

Man braucht mehr als ein gut aufgebautes, schriftliches Kontrolldokument, um ein Identifikationsprogramm wirkungsvoll zu kontrollieren. Ein gut funktionierendes Kommunikations-Team oder eine entsprechende Abteilung mit genügend Autorität ist sicherlich eine sinnvolle Ergänzung der schriftlichen Vorschriften. Ein Manual kann nicht alle Fragen beantworten, die in der Praxis auftauchen. Eine direkte Verbindung zwischen den für die Anwendung des Programms Verantwortlichen und dem Management Team, das sich mit der Firmenidentität befasst, ist eine in vielen Fällen vorteilhafte Kombination, die sich in der Praxis oft bewährt hat.

Eine optimale Lösung für die Einhaltung eines Identifikationsprogramms ist die Einrichtung einer internen Design-Abteilung (für viele ein Luxus). Diese Gruppe kann das Programm auf der Basis des Manuals durchsetzen und mit lokalen Stellen zusammenarbeiten, um die alltäglichen

nels une section très étudiée consacrée au système signalétique applicable aux bâtiments. Le fait que les symboles visibles à l'extérieur sont fabriqués localement a préoccupé les responsables de Citibank. Par conséquent, le répertoire contient des détails techniques pour la construction de tels signes, afin d'assurer l'intégrité du design.

Le répertoire Citibank comporte encore un autre aspect intéressant en ce qu'il expose de manière détaillée les modalités de conversion du programme de design au système métrique en usage à l'étranger. Des échantillons réels des papiers utilisés aux Etats-Unis ont été incorporés dans la section des matériels reproductibles, ce qui doit permettre de déterminer une qualité équivalente dans les différents pays d'implantation.

Avec le recul, la volonté d'obtenir le contrôle total du programme Citibank via ce répertoire n'apparaît pas très réaliste. Un grand nombre des personnes appelées à le mettre à exécution l'ont trouvé trop ambitieux et probablement trop technique.

METHODES DE CONTROLE DU PROGRAMME

Un document de contrôle aussi élaboré soit-il ne saurait suffire à garantir l'efficacité du contrôle d'un programme d'identification. Les normes écrites doivent encore bénéficier de l'autorité d'une équipe ou d'un département de communications. Aucun répertoire de normes ne saurait répondre d'avance à toutes les questions qui se posent au fur et à mesure que l'application du programme progresse. Souvent il paraît utile de prévoir une liaison efficace entre le personnel chargé de l'exécution du programme et l'équipe dirigeante responsable du programme d'identité institutionnelle.

Évidemment, il existe une solution idéale quoique coûteuse: c'est la création d'un centre de design rattaché à l'entreprise. Ce groupe peut mener à bien le programme en s'inspirant du répertoire officiel et collaborer étroitement avec les responsables locaux: On cible ainsi mieux les solutions nécessaires tout en les faisant entrer dans le cadre opérationnel défini par le programme.

nications/design problems, thereby achieving on target, appropriate design solutions.

Unquestionably, computer software technology for developing identification standards and maintaining them is available today. Accessing or modifying information by computer is undoubtedly the most efficient and flexible means of maintaining corporate implementation standards. As an information storage and accessing mechanism for corporate standards, the computer is excellent. Its ability to print out precise color examples is still relatively crude compared to those from offset printed manuals, however, the quality gap is closing at a very rapid rate.

It is apparent that the documentation and maintenance of the standards for complex corporate identification programs may be accomplished in a variety of ways. There is no question, however, that once a corporate identification program is completed, a series of control factors need be put into place, regardless of the physical form they take. Standards manuals provide the specifications necessary for the program's success; without them there is no benchmark for quality.

Kommunikations- und Design-Probleme zu lösen, und zwar entsprechend den besonderen Bedürfnissen und doch im Rahmen des Programms. Natürlich gibt es heute Computer Software für die Entwicklung und Einhaltung von Identifikationsstandards. Im Hinblick auf Zugänglichkeit, Speicherung und Modifizierung der Information ist der Computer zweifellos das effizienteste und flexibelste Mittel für die Einhaltung der Anwendungsvorschriften. Die Möglichkeiten für den Ausdruck exakter Farbmuster von Prototyp-Illustrationen sind verglichen mit dem Offsetdruck der Manuals allerdings immer noch relativ rudimentär, doch schliesst sich diese Lücke sehr schnell.

Es ist offensichtlich, dass die Dokumentierung und Einhaltung von Richtlinien für komplexe Firmen-Identifikationsprogramme auf verschiedene Weise möglich ist. Es steht jedoch ausser Frage, dass nach Erstellung eines Programms eine Reihe von Kontrollmassnahmen erforderlich sind, in welcher Form auch immer. Standards Manuals enthalten Angaben, die für den Erfolg des Programms notwendig sind. Ohne sie gibt es keinen Massstab für Qualität.

Sans aucun doute, nous disposons aujourd'hui de logiciels d'ordinateur qui nous permettent d'élaborer des normes d'identification et d'en assurer le maintien. L'accès à l'information, sa modification et l'enregistrement à l'aide de la technologie informatique est très certainement le moyen le plus fiable et le plus souple pour gérer la mise en application des normes en question. Sa capacité à imprimer des exemples précis d'illustrations prototypes en couleur est encore assez limitée comparée à l'impression offset. Cet écart de qualité se comble toutefois rapidement.

Il est évident que la documentation relative aux normes inhérentes à des programmes complexes d'identité institutionnelle et leur exploitation peuvent se concevoir de manière fort variée. Ce qui est indiscutable, par contre, c'est qu'une fois un programme d'identité d'entreprise établi, une série de facteurs de contrôle doivent nécessairement être mis en place, quelle que soit par ailleurs la forme physique qu'ils puissent adopter. Le répertoire de normes fournit les spécifications nécessaires pour la réussite du programme. Sans les contrôles afférents, il ne peut y avoir de repères de qualité.

EUGENE J. GROSSMAN is a founder and principal of Anspach Grossman Portugal, New York. He has designed identity programs for American Electric Power, Avco, Citibank, Emhart, Grace, GTE, Mitsubishi Bank, New York Stock Exchange, Quaker Oats, Raytheon, J. Walter Thompson, and USG Corporation. His work has been cited for design excellence by the American Institute of Graphic Arts, the Art Directors Club, Clio, Graphis Magazine, Industrial Design's annual Design Reviews, the Mead Library of Ideas, the One Show, the Packaging Institute, Print Magazine, the Type Directors Club, and the Society of Typographic Arts. Gene Grossman, who holds degrees in Psychology from Rutgers University and Industrial Design from Pratt Institute, is a member of the Board of Directors of the American Institute of Graphic Arts.

EUGENE J. GROSSMAN ist Direktor und einer der Gründer von Anspach Grossman Portugal, New York. Er hat für folgende Firmen Identitäts-Programme gestalterisch umgesetzt: American Electric Power, Avco, Citibank, Emhart, Grace, GTE, Mitsubishi Bank, die New Yorker Börse, Quaker Oats, Raytheon, J. Walter Thompson und USG. Das American Institute of Graphic Arts, der Art Directors Club, Clio, Graphis, die jährlichen Design Reviews von Industrial Design, Mead Library of Ideas, The One Show, das Packaging-Institute, die Zeitschrift Print, der Type Directors Club und die Society of Typographic Arts haben ihn für seine Design-Arbeit ausgezeichnet. Gene Grossman, der an der Rutgers Universität Psychologie und am Pratt Institute Industrie-Design studierte, ist Vorstandsmitglied des American Institute of Graphic Arts.

EUGENE J. GROSSMAN est le président-fondateur d'Anspach Grossman Portugal, New York. On lui doit des programmes d'identité pour American Electric Power, Avco, Citibank, Emhart, Grace, GTE, Mitsubishi Bank, la Bourse de New York, Quaker Oats, Raytheon, J. Walter Thompson et USG Corporation. Ses travaux ont été cité pour leur design hors pair par l'American Institute of Graphic Art, l'Art Directors Club, Clio, le magazine Graphis, les bilans de l'année en matière de design publiés par Industrial Design, la Mead Library of Ideas, le One Show, le Packaging Institute, le magazine Print, le Type Directors Club et la Society of Typographic Art. M. Grossman, diplômé en psychologie de Rutgers University, diplômé en esthétique industrielle du Pratt Institute, est membre du conseil d'administration de l'American Institute of Graphic Art.

INDEX/VERZEICHNIS/INDEX

CALL FOR ENTRIES/EINLADUNG/APPEL D'ENVOIS

CALL FOR ENTRIES/EINLADUNG/APPEL D'ENVOIS

CALL FOR ENTRIES

FOR GRAPHIS' INTERNATIONAL YEARBOOKS

GRAPHIS DESIGN

ALL ENTRIES MUST ARRIVE ON OR BEFORE NOVEMBER 30

Advertising: Newspaper and magazine
Design: Promotion brochures, catalogs, invitations, record covers, announcements, logotypes and/or entire corporate image campaigns, calendars, books, book covers, packages (single or series, labels and/or complete packages)
Editorial Design: company magazines, newspapers, consumer magazines, house organs
Illustration: All categories may be black and white or color

GRAPHIS ANNUAL REPORTS

ALL ENTRIES MUST ARRIVE ON OR BEFORE JANUARY 31

All material printed and published in connection with the annual report of a company or other organization.
Design, illustration, photography, typography, as well as the overall conception of the annual report are the criteria to be judged.
In order to do justice to this complex medium, we will present double-page spreads from the annual reports selected which are exemplary in their design and/or illustration.

GRAPHIS PHOTO

ALL ENTRIES MUST ARRIVE ON OR BEFORE JUNE 30

Advertising Photography: Advertisements, promotional brochures, catalogs, invitations, announcements, record covers, calendars.
Editorial Photography for press media – journalism and features – for books, corporate publications, etc. on the following subjects: fashion, cosmetics, architecture, arts, nature, science, technology, daily life, sports, current affairs, portraits, still life, etc.
Fine Art Photography: Personal studies
Unpublished Photography: Experimental and student work

GRAPHIS POSTER

ALL ENTRIES MUST ARRIVE ON OR BEFORE APRIL 30

Culture: Posters announcing exhibitions and events of all kind, film, theater, and ballet performances, concerts etc.
Advertising: Posters for fashion, cosmetics, foods, beverages, industrial goods; image and self-promotional campaigns of companies and individuals
Society: Posters which serve primarily a social and/or political purpose; from the field of education; for conferences and meetings; as well as for political and charitable appeals.

GENERAL RULES

THESE ARE APPLICABLE TO ALL BOOKS MENTIONED.

By submitting work to GRAPHIS, the sender expressly grants permission for his publication in any GRAPHIS book, as well as in any article in GRAPHIS magazine, or any advertising brochure, etc. whose purpose is specifically to promote the sales of these publications.

Eligibility: All work produced in the 12 month period previous to the submission deadlines, as well as rejected or unpublished work from this period, by professionals and students.

A confirmation of receipt will be sent to each entrant, and all entrants will be notified at a later date whether or not their work has been accepted for publication. All the winning entries will be reproduced in a generous format and in four colors throughout.
By submitting work you qualify for a 25% discount on the purchase of the respective book.

What to send:
Please send the actual printed piece (unmounted but well protected). Do not send original art. For large, bulky or valuable pieces, please submit color photos or (duplicate) transparencies.
Please note that entries cannot be returned. Only in exceptional cases and by contacting us in advance will material be sent back.

Entry Fees:
For each single entry: North America: US$ 10.00 West Germany: DM 10,00 All other countries: SFr. 10.00
For each campaign entry of 3 or more pieces: North America: US$ 25.00 West Germany: DM 25,00 All other countries: SFr. 25.00
Please make checks payable to GRAPHIS PRESS CORP. Zurich, and include in parcel. These fees do not apply to students, if copy of student identification is included. (For entries from countries with exchange controls, please contact us.)

How and where to send:
Please tape (do not glue) the entry label provided (or photocopy) – with full information – on the back of each piece. Entries can be sent by airmail, air parcel post or surface mail. **Please do not send anything by air freight.** Declare "No Commercial Value" on packages, and label "Art for Contest". The number of transparencies and photos should be indicated on the parcel. (If sent by air courier, please mark "Documents, Commercial Value 00.00").

Thank you for your contribution. Please send all entries to the following address:

GRAPHIS PRESS CORP., DUFOURSTRASSE 107, CH-8008 ZURICH, SWITZERLAND

FÜR DIE GRAPHIS JAHRBÜCHER

GRAPHIS DESIGN

EINSENDESCHLUSS: 30. NOVEMBER

Werbung: In Zeitungen und Zeitschriften
Design: Werbeprospekte, Kataloge, Einladungen, Schallplattenhüllen, Anzeigen, Signete und/oder Imagekampagnen, Kalender, Bücher, Buchumschläge, Packungen (einzelne oder Serien, Etiketten und/oder vollständige Packungen)
Redaktionelles Design: Firmenpublikationen, Zeitungen, Zeitschriften, Jahresberichte
Illustration: Alle Kategorien, schwarzweiss oder farbig

GRAPHIS ANNUAL REPORTS

EINSENDESCHLUSS: 31. JANUAR

Alle gedruckten und veröffentlichten Arbeiten, die im Zusammenhang mit dem Jahresbericht einer Firma oder Organisation stehen.
Design, Illustration, Photographie, Typographie und die Gesamtkonzeption eines Jahresberichtes sind die beurteilten Kriterien.
Um diesem komplexen Medium gerecht zu werden, werden aus den ausgewählten Jahresberichten verschiedene typische Doppelseiten gezeigt, die beispielhaft für die Gestaltung und/oder Illustration sind.

GRAPHIS PHOTO

EINSENDESCHLUSS: 30. JUNI

Werbephotographie: Anzeigen, Prospekte, Kataloge, Einladungen, Bekanntmachungen, Schallplattenhüllen, Kalender.
Redaktionelle Photographie für Presse (Reportagen und Artikel), Bücher, Firmenpublikationen usw. in den Bereichen Mode, Kosmetik, Architektur, Kunst, Natur, Wissenschaft und Technik, Alltag, Sport, Aktuelles, Porträts, Stilleben usw.
Künstlerische Photographie: Persönliche Studien
Unveröffentlichte Aufnahmen: Experimentelle Photographie und Arbeiten von Studenten und Schülern.

GRAPHIS POSTER

EINSENDESCHLUSS: 30. APRIL

Kultur: Plakate für die Ankündigung von Ausstellungen und Veranstaltungen aller Art, Film-, Theater- und Ballettaufführungen, Musikveranstaltungen.
Werbung: Plakate für Mode, Kosmetik, Lebensmittel, Genussmittel, Industriegüter; Image- und Eigenwerbung von Firmen und Einzelpersonen
Gesellschaft: Plakate, die in erster Linie einem sozialen oder politischen Zweck dienen, auf dem Gebiet der Ausbildung und Erziehung oder für die Ankündigung von Konferenzen und Tagungen sowie für politische und soziale Appelle

TEILNAHMEBEDINGUNGEN

DIESE GELTEN FÜR ALLE AUFGEFÜHRTEN BÜCHER.

Durch Ihre Einsendung geben Sie GRAPHIS ausdrücklich die Erlaubnis zur Veröffentlichung der eingesandten Arbeiten sowohl im entsprechenden Jahrbuch als auch in der Zeitschrift GRAPHIS oder für die Wiedergabe im Zusammenhang mit Besprechungen und Werbematerial für die GRAPHIS-Publikationen.

In Frage kommen alle Arbeiten von Fachleuten und Studenten – auch nicht publizierte Arbeiten – welche in den zwölf Monaten vor Einsendeschluss entstanden sind.

Jeder Einsender erhält eine Empfangsbestätigung und wird über Erscheinen oder Nichterscheinen seiner Arbeiten zu einem späteren Zeitpunkt informiert.
Alle im Buch aufgenommenen Arbeiten werden vierfarbig, in grosszügigem Format reproduziert.
Durch Ihre Einsendung erhalten Sie 25% Rabatt auf das jeweilige Jahrbuch.

Was einsenden:
Bitte senden Sie uns das gedruckte Beispiel (unmontiert, aber gut geschützt).
Senden Sie keine Originale. Bei unhandlichen, umfangreichen oder wertvollen Sendungen bitten wir um Farbphotos oder Duplikat-Dias.
Bitte beachten Sie, dass Einsendungen nicht zurückgeschickt werden können. Ausnahmen sind nur nach vorheriger Absprache mit GRAPHIS möglich.

Gebühren:
SFr. 10.00/DM 10,00 für einzelne Arbeiten
SFr. 25.00/DM 25,00 für Kampagnen oder Serien von mehr als drei Stück
Bitte senden Sie uns einen Scheck (SFr.-Schecks bitte auf eine Schweizer Bank ziehen) oder überweisen Sie den Betrag auf PC Zürich 80-23071-9 oder PSchK Frankfurt 3000 57-602.
Diese Gebühren gelten nicht für Studenten. Bitte schicken Sie uns eine Kopie des Studentenausweises.
(Für Einsendungen aus Ländern mit Devisenbeschränkungen bitten wir Sie, uns zu kontaktieren.)

Wie und wohin schicken:
Bitte befestigen Sie das vorgesehene Etikett (oder eine Kopie) – vollständig ausgefüllt – mit Klebstreifen (nicht mit Klebstoff) auf der Rückseite jeder Arbeit. Bitte per Luftpost oder auf normalem Postweg einsenden. **Keine Luftfrachtsendungen.** Deklarieren Sie «Ohne jeden Handelswert» und «Arbeitsproben für Wettbewerb». Die Anzahl der Dias und Photos sollte auf dem Paket angegeben werden. (Bei Air Courier Sendungen vermerken Sie «Dokumente, ohne jeden Handelswert».)

Herzlichen Dank für Ihre Mitarbeit. Bitte senden Sie Ihre Arbeiten an folgende Adresse:

GRAPHIS VERLAG AG, DUFOURSTRASSE 107, CH-8008 ZURICH, SCHWEIZ

GRAPHIS DESIGN

DATE LIMITE D'ENVOI: 30 NOVEMBRE

Publicité: journaux et magazines
Design: brochures de promotion, catalogues, invitations, pochettes de disques, annonces, emblèmes, en-têtes, campagnes de prestige, calendriers, livres, jaquettes, emballages (spécimen ou série, étiquettes ou emballages complets)
Editorial Design: magazines de sociétés, journaux, revues, rapports annuels
Illustration: toutes catégories en noir et blanc ou en couleurs

GRAPHIS ANNUAL REPORTS

DATE LIMITE D'ENVOI: 31 JANVIER

Tous travaux imprimés et publiés en relation avec le rapport annuel d'une entreprise ou d'une organisation.
Les critères retenus pour l'appréciation sont le design, l'illustration, la photo, la typo et la conception d'ensemble des rapports annuels.
Afin de rendre justice à ce média complexe, nous présentons diverses doubles pages types des rapports annuels sélectionnés en veillant à ce qu'elles soient représentatives de la conception et/ou de l'illustration.

GRAPHIS PHOTO

DATE LIMITE D'ENVOI: 30 JUIN

Photographie publicitaire: annonces, brochures de promotion, catalogues, invitations, pochettes de disques, calendriers
Photographie rédactionnelle pour la presse (reportages et articles), livres, publications d'entreprises, etc. dans les domaines suivants: Mode, arts, architecture, nature, sciences et techniques, vie quotidienne, sports, l'actualité, portraits, nature morte, etc.
Photographie artistique: études personnelles
Photographie non publiée: travaux expérimentaux et projets d'étudiants

GRAPHIS POSTER

DATE LIMITE D'ENVOI: 30 AVRIL

Affiches culturelles: annonçant des expositions et manifestations de tout genre, des projections de films, des représentations de théâtre et de ballet, des concerts et festivals.
Affiches publicitaires: pour la mode, les cosmétiques, l'alimentation, les produits de consommation de luxe, les biens industriels; publicité institutionnelle et auto-promotion d'entreprises.
Affiches sociales: essentiellement au service d'une cause sociale ou politique dans les domaines de l'éducation et de la formation, ainsi que pour l'annonce de conférences et réunions et pour les appels à caractère social et politique.

MODALITÉS D'ENVOI

VALABLES POUR TOUS LES LIVRES CITÉS.

Par votre envoi, vous donnez expressément à GRAPHIS l'autorisation de reproduire les travaux reçus aussi bien dans le livre en question que dans le magazine GRAPHIS ou dans tout imprimé relatif aux comptes rendus et au matériel publicitaire concernant les publications GRAPHIS.

Sont acceptés tous les travaux de professionnels et d'étudiants - même inédits - réalisés pendant les douze mois précédant le délai limite d'envoi.

Pour tout envoi de travaux, nous vous faisons parvenir un accusé de réception. Vous serez informé par la suite de la parution ou non-parution de vos travaux. Tous les travaux figurant dans l'ouvrage en question sont reproduits en quadrichromie dans un format généreux.
Votre envoi vous vaut une réduction de 25% sur l'annuel en question.

Que nous envoyer:
Veuillez nous envoyer un exemplaire imprimé (non monté, mais bien protégé). N'envoyez pas d'originaux. Pour les travaux de grand format, volumineux ou de valeur, veuillez nous envoyer des photos ou des diapositives (duplicata). **Veuillez noter que les travaux ne peuvent pas être retournés,** sauf dans des cas exceptionnels et si vous nous en avisez à l'avance.

Droits d'admission:
SFr. 10.00 pour les envois concernant un seul travail
SFr. 25.00 pour chaque série de 3 travaux ou davantage
Veuillez joindre à votre envoi un chèque tiré sur une banque suisse ou en verser le montant au compte chèque postal Zürich 80-23071-9.
Les étudiants sont exemptés de cette taxe. Prière de joindre une photocopie de la carte d'étudiant.
(Si vous résidez dans un pays qui connaît le contrôle des changes, veuillez nous contacter préalablement.)

Comment et où envoyer:
Veuillez scotcher (ne pas coller) au dos de chaque spécimen les étiquettes ci-jointes (ou photocopies) - dûment remplies. Envoyez les travaux de préférence par avion, ou par voie de surface. **Ne nous envoyez rien en fret aérien.** Indiquez «Sans aucune valeur commerciale» et «Echantillons de spécimens pour concours». Le nombre de diapositives et de photos doit être indiqué sur le paquet. (Pour les envois par courrier, inscrire «Documents, sans aucune valeur commercial».)

Nous vous remercions chaleureusement de votre collaboration. Veuillez faire parvenir vos travaux à l'adresse suivante:

EDITIONS GRAPHIS SA, DUFOURSTRASSE 107, CH-8008 ZURICH, SUISSE

261

SUBSCRIBE TO GRAPHIS: FOR USA AND CANADA

MAGAZINE	USA	CANADA
☐ GRAPHIS (One year/6 issues)	US$ 79.00	CDN$ 99.00
☐ 1988 Portfolio (Case holds six issues)	US$ 11.00	CDN$ 15.00

☐ Check enclosed
☐ Please bill me (My subscription will begin upon payment)
☐ Students may request a 25% discount by sending student ID.
IMPORTANT! PLEASE CHECK THE LANGUAGE VERSION DESIRED:
☐ ENGLISH   ☐ GERMAN   ☐ FRENCH
Subscription fees include postage to any part of the world.
Surcharges: US$ 57.00 (CDN$ 75.00) for Airmail,
US$ 22.50 (CDN$ 30.00) for Registered Mail.

NAME

TITLE

COMPANY

ADDRESS

CITY

STATE/PROV.   POSTAL CODE

COUNTRY

PROFESSION

SIGNATURE   DATE

Please send coupon and make check payable to:
GRAPHIS US, INC., 141 LEXINGTON AVENUE, NEW YORK, NY 10016, USA.
Guarantee: You may cancel your subscription at any time and receive a full refund on all
unmailed copies. Please allow 6–8 weeks for delivery of first issue.

REQUEST FOR CALL FOR ENTRIES
Please put me on your "Call for Entries" list for the following title(s).
Please check the appropriate box(es).
☐ GRAPHIS PHOTO   ☐ GRAPHIS POSTER   ☐ GRAPHIS DESIGN
☐ GRAPHIS PACKAGING   ☐ GRAPHIS DIAGRAM   ☐ GRAPHIS ANNUAL REPORTS
By submitting material to any of the titles listed above, I will automatically qualify for a
25% discount toward the purchase of the title.   CI 89

BOOK ORDER FORM: FOR USA AND CANADA

ORDER YOUR GRAPHIS ANNUALS NOW!

BOOKS	USA	CANADA
☐ Graphis Corporate Identity	US$ 75.00	CDN$ 105.00
☐ Graphis Photo 89	US$ 65.00	CDN$ 98.00
☐ Graphis Poster 89	US$ 65.00	CDN$ 98.00
☐ Graphis Packaging 5	US$ 75.00	CDN$ 105.00
☐ Graphis Design 89	US$ 65.00	CDN$ 98.00
☐ Graphis Photo 88	US$ 65.00	CDN$ 98.00
☐ Graphis Diagram 1	US$ 65.00	CDN$ 98.00
☐ Graphis Annual Reports 1	US$ 65.00	CDN$ 98.00
☐ 42 Years of Graphis Covers (1944-1986)	US$ 49.50	CDN$ 60.00

☐ Check enclosed
☐ Please bill me (Mailing costs in addition to above book price will be charged)

NAME

TITLE

COMPANY

ADDRESS

CITY/STATE/PROV.

POSTAL CODE   COUNTRY

PROFESSION

SIGNATURE   DATE

Please send coupon and make check payable to:
GRAPHIS US, INC., 141 LEXINGTON AVENUE, NEW YORK, NY 10016, USA.

REQUEST FOR CALL FOR ENTRIES
Please put me on your "Call for Entries" list for the following title(s).
Please check the appropriate box(es).
☐ GRAPHIS PHOTO   ☐ GRAPHIS POSTER   ☐ GRAPHIS DESIGN
☐ GRAPHIS PACKAGING   ☐ GRAPHIS DIAGRAM   ☐ GRAPHIS ANNUAL REPORTS
By submitting material to any of the titles listed above, I will automatically qualify for a
25% discount toward the purchase of the title.   CI 89

SUBSCRIBE TO GRAPHIS: FOR EUROPE AND THE WORLD

MAGAZINE	BRD	WORLD	U.K.
☐ GRAPHIS (One year/6 issues)	DM 156,-	SFr. 126.-	£ 48.00
☐ 1988 Portfolio (Case holds six issues)	DM 24.-	SFr. 19.-	£ 8.00

☐ Check enclosed (for Europe, please make SFr.-checks payable to a Swiss bank)
☐ Please bill me (My subscription will begin upon payment)
☐ Students may request a 25% discount by sending student ID.
IMPORTANT! PLEASE CHECK THE LANGUAGE VERSION DESIRED:
☐ ENGLISH   ☐ GERMAN   ☐ FRENCH
Subscription fees include postage to any part of the world.
Surcharges: SFr. 84.00/DM 102,00/£ 34.50 for Airmail,
SFr. 30.00/DM 36,00/£ 12.00 for Registered Mail.

NAME

TITLE

COMPANY

ADDRESS

CITY   POSTAL CODE

COUNTRY

PROFESSION

SIGNATURE   DATE

Please send coupon and make check payable to:
GRAPHIS PRESS CORP., DUFOURSTRASSE 107, CH-8008 ZÜRICH, SWITZERLAND
Guarantee: You may cancel your subscription at any time and receive a full refund on all
unmailed copies. Please allow 6–8 weeks for delivery of first issue.

REQUEST FOR CALL FOR ENTRIES
Please put me on your "Call for Entries" list for the following title(s).
Please check the appropriate box(es).
☐ GRAPHIS PHOTO   ☐ GRAPHIS POSTER   ☐ GRAPHIS DESIGN
☐ GRAPHIS PACKAGING   ☐ GRAPHIS DIAGRAM   ☐ GRAPHIS ANNUAL REPORTS
By submitting material to any of the titles listed above, I will automatically qualify for a
25% discount toward the purchase of the title.   CI 89

BOOK ORDER FORM: FOR EUROPE AND THE WORLD

BOOKS	BRD	WORLD	U.K.
☐ Graphis Corporate Identity	DM 160,-	SFr. 132	£ 48.00
☐ Graphis Photo 89	DM 148,-	SFr. 118.-	£ 46.50
☐ Graphis Poster 89	DM 148,-	SFr. 118.-	£ 46.50
☐ Graphis Packaging 5	DM 160,-	SFr. 132.-	£ 48.00
☐ Graphis Design 89	DM 138,-	SFr. 112.-	£ 45.00
☐ Graphis Photo 88	DM 138,-	SFr. 112.-	£ 45.00
☐ Graphis Diagram 1	DM 138,-	SFr. 112.-	£ 45.00
☐ Graphis Annual Reports 1	DM 138,-	SFr. 112.-	£ 45.00
☐ 42 Years of Graphis Covers (1944-1986)	DM 98,-	SFr. 85.-	£ 35.00

☐ Check enclosed (For Europe, please make SFr. checks payable to a Swiss Bank)
☐ Amount paid into Graphis account at the Union Bank of Switzerland, Acct No 3620063
in Zürich.
☐ Amount paid to Postal Cheque Account Zürich 80-23071-9 (Through your local post office)
☐ Please bill me (Mailing costs in addition to above book price will be charged)

NAME

TITLE

COMPANY

ADDRESS

CITY   POSTAL CODE

COUNTRY

PROFESSION

SIGNATURE   DATE

Please send coupon and make check payable to:
GRAPHIS PRESS CORP., DUFOURSTRASSE 107, CH-8008 ZÜRICH, SWITZERLAND

REQUEST FOR CALL FOR ENTRIES
Please put me on your "Call for Entries" list for the following title(s).
☐ GRAPHIS PHOTO   ☐ GRAPHIS POSTER   ☐ GRAPHIS DESIGN
☐ GRAPHIS PACKAGING   ☐ GRAPHIS DIAGRAM   ☐ GRAPHIS ANNUAL REPORTS
By submitting material to any of the titles listed above, I will automatically qualify for a
25% discount toward the purchase of the title.   CI 89

GRAPHIS PRESS CORP.
DUFOURSTRASSE 107
CH-8008 ZÜRICH
SWITZERLAND

GRAPHIS U.S., INC.
141 LEXINGTON AVENUE
NEW YORK, NEW YORK 10016
U.S.A.

GRAPHIS PRESS CORP.
DUFOURSTRASSE 107
CH-8008 ZÜRICH
SWITZERLAND

GRAPHIS U.S., INC.
141 LEXINGTON AVENUE
NEW YORK, NEW YORK 10016
U.S.A.